English Postcoloniality

Recent Titles in
Contributions to the Study of World Literature

Storied Cities: Literary Imagining of Florence, Venice and Rome
Michael L. Ross

Women Writers in Russian Literature
Toby W. Clyman and Diana Greene, editors

Writing the Good Fight: Political Commitment in the International Literature of the Spanish Civil War
Peter Monteath

Money: Lure, Lore, and Literature
John Louis DiGaetani, editor

Smollett's Women: A Study in an Eighteenth-Century Masculine Sensibility
Robert D. Spector

English Country Life in the Barsetshire Novels of Angela Thirkell
Laura Roberts Collins

Bakhtin, Stalin, and Modern Russian Fiction: Carnival, Dialogism, and History
M. Keith Booker and Dubravka Juraga

Aspects and Issues in the History of Children's Literature
Maria Nikolajeva, editor

Reluctant Expatriate: The Life of Harold Frederic
Robert M. Myers

The Decline of the Goddess: Nature, Culture, and Women in Thomas Hardy's Fiction
Shirley A. Stave

Postcolonial Discourse and Changing Cultural Contexts
Gita Rajan and Radhika Mohanram, editors

Prometheus and Faust: The Promethean Revolt in Drama from Classical Antiquity to Goethe
Timothy Richard Wutrich

ENGLISH POSTCOLONIALITY

Literatures from Around the World

Edited by
Radhika Mohanram
and Gita Rajan

Contributions to the Study of World Literature, Number 66
Emmanuel S. Nelson, Series Adviser

GREENWOOD PRESS
Westport, Connecticut • London

Library of Congress Cataloging-in-Publication Data

English postcoloniality : literatures from around the world / edited by Radhika Mohanram and Gita Rajan.
p. cm. — (Contributions to the study of world literature, ISSN 0738-9345 ; no. 66)
Includes bibliographical references and index.
ISBN 0-313-28854-2 (alk. paper)
1. Commonwealth literature (English)—History and criticism. 2. Commonwealth countries—In literature. 3. Developing countries—In literature. 4. Indigenous peoples in literature. 5. Decolonization in literature. I. Mohanram, Radhika. II. Rajan, Gita. III. Series.
PR9080.E55 1996
820.9'9171241—dc20 95-33071

British Library Cataloguing in Publication Data is available.

Library of Congress Catalog Card Number: 95-33071
ISBN: 0-313-28854-2
ISSN: 0738-9345

First published in 1996

Greenwood Press, 88 Post Road West, Westport, CT 06881
An imprint of Greenwood Publishing Group, Inc.

The paper used in this book complies with the Permanent Paper Standard issued by the National Information Standards Organization (Z39.48-1984).

10 9 8 7 6 5 4 3 2

Copyright Acknowledgments

The editors and publisher are grateful for permission to reprint excerpts from the following copyrighted materials:

Margaret Atwood. "Backdrop Addresses Cowboy." In *Poets of Contemporary Canada 1960–1970.* Ed. Eli Mandel. Toronto: McClelland and Stewart, 1972.

Cathie Dunsford. *Überlebende—Survivors.* O.B.E.M.A. (Osnabrücker Bilinguale Editionen von Minoritäten AutorInnen). Münster: Wurf Verlag, 1990.

Bill Neidjie. *Story about Feeling.* Ed. K. Taylor. Broome: Magabala Books, 1989.

Roma Potiki. *Stones in Her Mouth.* Auckland: Iwa, 1992.

Powhiri Rika-Heke. "Neighbours." *Spiral* 7. Ed. Spiral Collective. Wellington: Spiral, 1993.

Powhiri Rika-Heke. "Human Rights, a la Carte, With Salt." *Gulliver* 33. Berlin/Bremen, 1993.

Amos Tutuola. *The Palm-Wine Drinkard.* New York: Grove Press, 1953. Copyright © 1953. By permission of Grove/Atlantic, Inc.

Every reasonable effort has been made to trace the owners of copyright materials in this book, but in some instances this has proven impossible. The editors and publisher will be glad to receive information leading to more complete acknowledgments in subsequent printings of the book and in the meantime extend their apologies for any omissions.

Contents

Acknowledgments

The editors would like to thank the University of Waikato, Fairfield University, and the University of New Orleans for their support in preparing this manuscript. We would particularly like to thank Barry Parsonson, the Dean of the School of Social Sciences at the University of Waikato, who gave Radhika a generous grant to come to the United States to finish the project, and the staff at the Communications Center at the University of New Orleans for their prompt and cheerful transmittal of editorial queries between the United States and New Zealand.

We are particularly grateful to Joy Harjo, who contributed a poem for this collection. We want to express our gratitude to Emmanuel Nelson, who encouraged us to put this volume together, challenged us continually to be rigorous in our scrutiny of the essays, and helped us to make difficult decisions. We thank Rohin Rajan for his good-humored encouragement. Also innumerable thanks to Susan Sayer and Helen Baird at the University of Waikato, who went above and beyond the call of friendship and pitched in with secretarial work to help us meet the deadline. We would like to thank Mary Beth Brown, Gita's student at Fairfield University, for her careful reading of the manuscript. We would like to thank Vijay Lakshmi Chauhan for her insightful comments and the members of the Cultural Studies Group at the University of Pennsylvania. We wish to thank Maureen Melino at Greenwood Publishing for her continued and unflagging assistance in preparing this volume.

And, finally, we thank our families for their continued encouragement and support.

English Postcoloniality

I

GENERAL INTRODUCTION

Introduction: The Concept of English Postcoloniality

Radhika Mohanram and Gita Rajan

The title *English Postcoloniality: Literatures from Around the World* is based upon our intent to raise questions surrounding the role of language in power relations between Britain and its colonies. Essays in this collection focus upon historical surveys of colonial literatures, the problematics in explicating the dynamic relationship between indigenous and mediated literatures/cultures of the neocolonial phase, and some basic interpretations of postcolonial theory in the analyses of literary texts. The essays collected here range beyond the disciplinary parameters of geography, or history, or politics in the oppressor/oppressed sequence; they focus upon the *imprint of language* in constructing subjectivites and the nuances of synchronous tensions among the colonizer, colonized, native, foreign, male, female subjects, which exceed clear dichotomies of "us" and "them." Postcoloniality in this frame is treated as a process, a methodology, and not as a genre category. The most commonly used tropes in postcolonial analyses are meant to reveal tracks of aggressions through the deconstruction of such polar terms as nation/location, identity/subjectivity, rootedness/diaspora, and, in some cases, writing and literature.[1] In this volume, we have focused upon language as a master trope and circumscribed the space where *English* has been deployed as a colonizing agent. As Ngugi wa Thiong'o maintains from his contextual perspective, in effecting an "epistemological break with the past," the logic of postcoloniality uses language as a tool to re-think and re-write the history of colonized nations. Such a move simultaneously functions as a theoretic for postcoloniality as well as an activist gesture in the theater of decolonization. His novel *Petals of Blood* is important in this aspect. He states in a recent interview with Sara Suleri:

> Every language has two aspects. One aspect is its role as an agent that enables us to communicate with one another in our struggle to find the means for survival. The other is its role as the carrier of the history and the culture built into the process of that communication over time. In my book, *Decolonizing the Mind,* I have described language as

the collective memory bank of the people. The two aspects are inseparable; they form a dialectic unity.[2] (283)

But the use of language is a recent critical tool. Tropes of nationhood, identity, and stereotypes of modernity in decolonized nations have provided fertile ground for debates and analyses for the last four decades or so for postcolonial scholars. With the end of the Second World War, and as more and more countries became gradually decolonized, nations and peoples saw a renaissance in art, literatures, and cultures of their own land. Colonial power and cultural patterns of older regimes collided and colluded with indigenous traditions, myths, and mores to produce a new kind of work, loosely called the postcolonial text. Often structured with a re-shaped identity that was born out of a nationalistic creative energy, the postcolonial text underscored a mass of diverse discourses ranging from simple notations of aggression, to a romanticized nationalism, to a sense of displacement from the homeland in exilic subjects, and so on, but always revealing the tense relationship to the imperial language. In appropriating the dominator's language, that is, English, most often texts managed to encode subversive and problematic meanings. Such tensions and the subsequent subversiveness have clearly provided material for two kinds of postcolonial readings: one where the new texts have been forcefully hierarchized in British/American canons as inferior, and one where the nuances of the indigenous use (and abuse) of English have been valorized as a uniquely Commonwealth/multicultural tradition. Sneja Gunew raises the specter of language in relation to identity formation or the decolonized self from a slightly different angle when she asks, "What is very much a question for me at the moment is that if you are constructed in one particular kind of language, what kinds of violence does it do to your subjectivity if one then has to move into another language, and suppress whatever selves or subjectivities were constructed by the first?" (*The Postcolonial Critic* 66). In the past, "identity talk" based upon essentialism (formed out of biological essences as belonging to a particular race) or constructionism (social theories of identity formed by cultural and psychological interaction) formed competing grounds of analyses of postcolonial works. More recently, the structural opposition between *intellectual constructionism* (giving one the opportunity to examine colonial history at a remove from engaging the physical body) and *essential corporeality* (which allows one to situate oneself inside the physical body and speak from specific sociocultural locations) has been deconstructed by theorists such as Gayatri Chakravorty Spivak. The first option, a legacy of poststructuralism and deconstruction, is deemed by critics as being the more objective (and theoretical) one. But in *Outside in the Teaching Machine*, Spivak points to the value of a reasoned essentialism:

In a personalist culture, even among people within the humanities, who are generally wordsmiths, it's the idea of a *strategy* that has been forgotten. The strategic has been taken as a point of self-differentiation from the poor essentialists. So long as the critique of essentialism is understood not as an exposure of error, our own or others', but as an ac-

> knowledgement of the dangerousness of something one cannot not use. I would stand by it as one stand among many. The critique of essentialism should not be seen as being critical in the colloquial, Anglo-American sense of being adversely inclined, but as a critique in the robust European, philosophical sense. (5)

However, prior to sophisticated technologies of postcolonial theorizing, Ashcroft et al. in *The Empire Writes Back: Theory and Practice in Post-Colonial Literatures* helped define the parameters of inquiry in this emerging discipline. Their work also helped shift the focus and nomenclature from Commonwealth literatures to postcolonial literatures, which, in turn, indicated the shift in vocabulary and sensibility of postcoloniality. As Jacques Lacan and Michel Foucault have argued from differing perspectives, the very act of naming is an attempt to exert power, and consequently, the term "Commonwealth" signals the primacy of Empire even after the historico-political process of decolonization became a reality. This is an instance where language has the power to create and maintain a reality. Ashcroft et al. were among the first few scholars to suggest that postcoloniality is not so much a genre category as a mode of thinking and writing. However, they fail to qualify the fact that "writing" is fundamentally a cultural activity; every kind of writing therefore bears the marks of a culture, and in this case, a colonial culture. Consequently, Ashcroft et al. look at different forms of power than we do in this volume. We want to emphasize the *negotiatory* capacity of language in the colonial-postcolonial equation. Ashcroft et al. discuss the field from within their locus; they see the point of debate in postcoloniality as emanating from the center itself:

> Imperial expansion has had a radically destabilizing effect on its own preoccupations and power. In pushing the colonial world to the margins of experience the center pushed consciousness beyond the point at which monocentrism in all spheres of thought could be accepted without question. In other words, the alienating process which initially served to relegate the postcolonial world to the margin turned upon itself and acted to push that world through a kind of mental barrier to a position from which all experience could be viewed as uncentered, pluralistic, and multifarious. Marginality thus became an unprecedented source of creative energy. (12)

While postcoloniality has been largely examined through its *effect* by using literary (and political) texts as evidence of domination and as revealing a potential for insurgence of the colonized, the *cause* of such a phenomenon as being rooted in the cultural fabric of the colonized nations has been largely bypassed. The relevance of cultural formations in postcoloniality is only recently gaining critical attention. Contemporary scholars find the impulse to textualize colonialism limiting in its examination of postcoloniality from a cultural perspective. Edward Said, who argued that history is central to debates on colonial/postcolonial consciousness in *Orientalism*, continues that line of thought in his recent book, *Culture and Imperialism*:

For the first time the history of imperialism and its culture can now be studied as neither monolithic nor reductively compartmentalized, separate, distinct. True, there has been a disturbing eruption of separatist and chauvinist discourse whether in India, Lebanon, or Yugoslavia, or in Afrocentric, Islamocentric, or Eurocentric proclamations; far from invalidating the struggle to be free from empire, these reductions of cultural discourse actually prove the validity of a fundamental liberationist energy that animates the wish to be independent, to speak freely, and without the burden of unfair domination. The only way to understand this energy, however, is historically.[3] (xxi)

While Said's comments on transnational identities vis-à-vis his attempts to sketch the figure of the postcolonial become blurred by his broad brush strokes and generalized landscapes, Henry Louis Gates, Jr., and Kwame Anthony Appiah discuss the specific cross-overs of race and gender in positioning one's identity inside any given culture. They see the potential for inter-disciplinary and cross-disciplinary inquiries into the arena of postcoloniality as having a certain "anti-essentialist" premise based upon "critiques of ethnic, sexual, national, and racial identities [so that] . . . multiple intersections of race, class, and gender in feminist, lesbian, and gay studies" can be examined. Similar to Spivak's argument regarding a coalesced essentialism and constructionism mentioned previously, Appiah and Gates note that:

Racial identities, like those along the dimensions of gender and sexuality, are defined in a peculiarly corporeal way: one's identity as an African-American is rooted in one's embodiment as a black body. And it is not surprising that important events occur in the landscape of identity when race and gender compete for and combine in a single body.[4] (625)

Such a focus on integrating race and sexuality in the identity of a colonized subject elaborates upon Frantz Fanon's brilliant theory of the damaged psyche in *Black Skin, White Masks*, and corrects Fanon's blind spot of gender.[5] To some degree this quotation explains both the shared premises and the divergent agendas of situating people inside geographies, histories and politicosocial regimes which are clouded over with issues of colonialism/imperialism and collude with debates on the role of the metropolitan citizen polarized between modernity and postcoloniality.[6] James Clifford and Vivek Dhareshwar summarize this problem succinctly in their introduction to *Traveling Theories and Traveling Theorists*[7]:

If theories no longer totalize, they do travel. Indeed, in their diverse rootings, uprootings, theories are constantly translated, appropriated, contested, grafted. Theory travels; so do theorists. In the late twentieth century the producers and audiences of theory can no longer be situated in a more-or-less stable map of "First World" and "Third World" places. (v)

The university, then, by providing a ground for theorizing and an itinerary of such theories, has played a prominent role in both generating *and* controlling postcolonial discourse or dialogue. First at the intellectual level, or in *theoria*, the academy (and intellectual) draws a boundary around this obviously volatile and political discourse, in effect, challenging and re-focusing theories of oppression, and regulating its flow into the world (or culture) at large. Next at the pedagogic level, or in *praxis*, the intellectual engaged in this endeavor expands a Eurocentric canon with an aim to ratify the experience of a changing student body in the classroom, which too is no longer purely Eurocentric. Or, more importantly, postcolonial discourse and consciousness ultimately hope to problematize the place of non-Eurocentric students and intellectuals in productive ways. And the rapidly changing political and demographic climate of the contemporary world has helped to create (even unwittingly) a space to situate this emergent geopolitical reality. Debates, ranging from the material body to the textual body, include recent fights over canon and culture re-formation of Europe's "other" in academia and its shrill double—the media.

The Western academy has used "modernity" as the defining trope for the third-world, which means that not cartography but rather technological progress and powerful economic and political bases in capitalistic modes of cultural and material production mark the boundaries of the first-world. (Ironically, this leaves Ireland out of the circuit, and puts countries of the East European bloc on par with previously colonized nations.) Claude Levi-Strauss, in his pamphlet called "Race and History" delivered in 1952 to the officials of UNESCO, attempted to explicate cultural relativism in the language of modernity. He writes:

> Cultural relativism, one of the foundations of anthropological thought, at least in my generation and the one before it (some are contesting it today), states that there is no criterion that enables one to make an absolute judgement as to how one culture is superior to another. If, at certain times and certain places, some cultures "move" while others "stand still," it is not, as I said, because of the superiority of the first, but from the fact that historic or geographical circumstances have brought about a collaboration among cultures, which are not unequal (nothing makes it possible to decree them as such), but different. (148)

This powerful insight into the pejorative concept of "modernity" is still one of the main areas of debate among postcolonial scholars almost half a century later.

Another way of categorizing the postcolonial nation-space is borrowed from post-Fordist and post-war language of political economy. Previously colonized nations are now called the "Third World" (again, this makes Ireland an anomaly). A problem implicit in the conflation of the terms postcolonial and third-world is analyzed by Ella Shohat in "Notes on the 'Post-Colonial' " within a temporal frame. She indicates that the notion of the third world with all its implicit complexity, differences in history, culture and modes of production gets subsumed under a pseudo-linguistic umbrella like *post*. She remarks that post immediately signals the time-bound progression of a philosophical model rather than the ongoing process and struggle for negating imperial hegemony. The specific locations that she uses to make her point are post-feminism, post-marxism, post-deconstructionism, post-structuralism, etc. Shohat's rhetoric and logic are very astute indeed, because, as she herself points out, postcolonial is not merely the theory of resistance and its implications for studying colonial hegemonies as an academic exercise, but rather, the term also carries with it the historical truth of a nation under domination. Shohat's idea of focusing our scrutiny on that "ambiguous spatio-temporality" (102) of the phenomenon of postcoloniality implicitly carries with it the developmental ideology wherein the first world has reached a sophisticated level of maturation which the third world is constantly striving towards. She asks "how does one negotiate sameness and difference within the framework of a 'postcolonial' whose 'post' emphasizes rupture and de-emphasizes sameness?" (106). In effect, this leaves the "Third World" out of any meaningful discussion of power except in a differential mode of self/other, us/them. The advantage of this approach is that it takes postcoloniality into a new level of self-conscious examination of subjectivity(ies), but a simultaneous drawback is that it grants that very subjectivity through Lacanian, western psychoanalytical models which leaves out an anthropological, cultural model of subject formation.

Further, the notion of modernity or progress as locked into a one part of the globe has been challenged by postcolonial theorists such as Homi K. Bhabha, whose theory of hybridity undermines any notion of an epistemologically pure first world. In "Signs Taken for Wonders," Bhabha describes hybridity as "a partial and double force that is more than the mimetic but less than the symbolic, that disturbs the visibility of the colonial presence and makes the recognition of its authority problematic" (173). An extension of the trope of the hybrid to include the colonial in the mother country complicates any singular notion of the first and the third world. In his essay "Narrating the Nation" Bhabha reinterprets the geographically and hierarchically connected first and third world via the metaphor of a hybrid stage. He states:

> The locality of national culture is neither unified nor unitary in relation to itself, nor must it be seen simply as "other" in relation to what is outside or beyond it. The boundary is Janus-faced and the problem of outside/inside must always be a process of hybridity, incorporating new "people" in relation to the body politic, generating other sites of meaning and, inevitably, in the political process, producing unmanned sites of political antagonism and unpredictable forces for political representation. (4)

In such a formulation, any carefully delineated borders of periphery and metropole, colony (India is his example) and empire (again, he uses England) become blurred, de-territorialized, and unbounded.

Within the context of *British* colonization, contemporary theorists such as Gayatri Chakravory Spivak, Edward Said, Bill Ashcroft, Helen Tiffin, Paul Gilroy, Homi Bhabha, Angela McRobie, Henry Louis Gates, Jr. and others have argued that postcolonial consciousness is born out of a dislocated sensibility that takes as its model English culture and English myths and values (with of course, English language as the unstated guarantor). This, in turn, suggests that such postcolonial bodies (material/textual) are only a shadow or mimicry of an English*ness*. Another important aspect of postcolonial scholarship thus far has been to treat all domination or colonization as being limited to nonwhite peoples. By deliberately using language as a marker of colonialism we wish this anthology to politicize postcoloniality by re-examining the limits of imperialism with an over-arching premise of *English* and *England* as the dominating impulse. Consequently, reading the literatures and cultures of colonized terrains through this wide angle lens demarcates settler colonies (i.e., peoples who moved and emigrated with the goodwill of the British) from forcefully occupied countries (i.e., people who were politically and economically disenfranchised by the British). This distinction is invaluable in distilling metaphors of resistance as it includes African-American literatures and cultures as categories of postcolonial study. And following such a logic of marginalization allows the exclusion of American literature from this group. Certain American Studies scholars would argue that American literature is indeed postcolonial because it offers a classic chronicle of a culture that began as a colony. But it is evident that American literature quickly changed to an imperial/dominant one.

Our volume consciously imitates the process of colonization itself; it is based on an *evolutionary* model and provides some of the *historical* context. In addition to tracing particular histories of writing in English, this section oscillates around the following questions: What is postcoloniality in the larger frame? Is it a discipline named by the Western academy? That is, is it created, used, and exchanged within the logic of that economy? Or is it a political space created by history and capital? In other words, locked into the logic of evolution is the status of postcolonial literatures and consciousness, and that is one focus of our anthology. Next, this volume moves on to an analysis of *indigenous* literatures. The authors of the essays in this section are preoccupied with questions such as, Who constructs our knowledge? If one needs authority to speak in oppositional terms such as the native and the foreigner, what is the substance of indigenous identity and subjectivity? If a subject is constructed in/by language, what does this category mean for indigenous (as well as all postcolonial) peoples since they/we speak the language of the masters? We felt the need to separate postcolonial from indigenous literatures so that this volume could function as a reference and source book for both sets of literatures. Such an organization of essays is also relevant when we consider the role of literature and narration in the construction and the maintenance of subjectivity and agency in any nation. Hence our foregrounding of the historical and indigenous models of writing. However, along with Bhabha we are cognizant that the "locality of national culture is neither unified nor unitary in relation to itself" (*Nation and Narration* 4).

ESSAYS IN THE VOLUME

Historical Surveys

The relevance of writing in English forms the basis for including the following essays in the historical survey section. If postcolonial literature has been primarily an insistence of historical and cultural specificities in opposition to the homogenization of the other, a common literary practice of the metropolis, Ralph Crane's "Out of the Center: Thoughts on the Postcolonial Literatures of Australia and New Zealand" appears to go against this prime directive. He conflates Australian/New Zealand literature into Australasian writing. His arguments for such a move are persuasive, because he points out their common settler culture, their use of language and the similarity of their reactions to literary movements such as Romanticism and Modernism which permit such a conflation. Crane, however, differentiates *Australasian* literature from other postcolonial writing from parts of Africa or South America in that these two countries define themselves as Western. This alignment with the west has resulted in the proliferation of fiction which resembles that of the contemporary United States, in that human relationships and aspects of contemporary society are the emphasis of a lot of Australian/New Zealand writers too. However, the Australian/New Zealand difference can be perceived in the reconstitution of the center/periphery model which is the cornerstone of postcolonial writing. The center/periphery model gets reproduced in the settler colonies as if in a hall of mirrors with settler writing occupying the center and the indigenous writers pushed to the periphery. They reclaim their histories and "educate non-indigenous readers about Aboriginal and Maori cultures" occupying the periphery. The cultural heterogeneity implicit in such a model becomes a signifier of non-monocultural national identity of these settler colonies.

Ian Crump's essay, "A Terrible Beauty Is Born," borrows from the paradigm suggested by the authors of *The Empire Writes Back* who outline four major models for postcolonial texts: regional, race, comparative and syncretic (15). In fact, several other essays in this collection also deal with the various models of postcolonial texts which either reinforce or break out of the mold. Crump argues that Irish literature reveals itself as the oldest sibling of postcolonial writing. He provides a blueprint of the various stages (five in number) that postcolonial writing inevitably goes through. In the first stage, Irish writers revel in their sense of Otherness. This first stage came about in the aftermath of the Act of Union in 1800 and is strategic in reinscribing the cultural difference of Ireland and uniting it against England. This embracing of otherness, however, led to feelings of inferiority and dependency and resulted in the second stage, spearheaded primarily by James Joyce, who extended the parameters of the previously Gaelic Ireland to a European Ireland. In the third stage, vigorous demythologizing of Gaelic identity took place by the counter-revivalists. The fourth and fifth stages of postcoloniality are simultaneous and ongoing and seem to address in particular neocolonialism and the double colonization of women. If Irish literature is the oldest sibling, then Caribbean literature must be a newer, younger, and equally exciting one.

P. S. Chauhan's essay deals with the twin thematics of the "schizophrenic split between the love for the soil but hatred for its history" present in the works of the Caribbean fiction writers in English. Chauhan points out that of the two generations of writers in this developing region of writing, the first one consisted mostly of males who attempted to come to terms with the brutal history of the islands, and the second of females whose predominant theme has been their flight from their mothers. Ultimately, Chauhan draws links between the first generation of American fiction writers—Irving, Cooper, Hawthorne and Melville—and the Caribbean writers, who, too, are faced with the task of re/creating new myths about their newly independent countries, to *caribbeanize* what was considered purely European. Such a move is reminiscent of the strategy of mimicry described by Homi K. Bhabha.

John Hawley's survey essay on South African writing in English traces the literatures produced by both white and black South Africans simultaneously. He records its transformation from a frontier literature about the African veld where the Boers are the Other and Xhosa and Zulus the noble savages in need of British governance, to an urban literature of townships dominated by apartheid. Hawley points out that black South African writing has become primarily a literature of anger and resistance, while that of white South Africans has become a literature of dread. Most importantly, from the 1960s onward South African writing in English claims to be primarily a literature of exile.

Jeannine DeLombard's essay on East African writing focuses on the language debate, nuances of high and low literature and their reception by urban audiences, and the impact of "political repression on a nation's literature." DeLombard threads all these concerns through her narrative of Ngugi wa Thiong'o's status in East African writing to deal with the issue of the role of the East African intellectual.

Anthonia Kalu's essay on West African writing makes a very convincing plea for the re-interpretation of the debate over the validity of postcolonial writing in English to represent the indigenous culture because West African writing in English is fraught with questions of the (in)significance of the African intellectual who writes in English. She points out that the structure and vocabulary of the master discourse (English) precludes the categories by which postcolonial articulation in Africa could be made. Kalu argues that writing in English enabled the West African writer not only to explore the disabling features of English but "also to evoke a postcolonial future within the colonial present." Such a reading of West African writing allows for postcoloniality to be seen as a process rather than a specific temporal, historical event.

Aparna and Vinay Dharwadker's essay on Indian postcolonial writing is a generic-historic survey that traces the debate over the relevance of writing in English in a decolonized nation and the construction of Indianness in narration. They argue that global mobility—a true postcolonial condition—has rendered the question of authenticity and relevance of English in India difficult. As editors, we wish to point out to our readers that posing such a question is itself problematic. The very call to authenticity is an imperial gesture of hierachizing colonial/postcolonial voices, an Arnoldian/Leavisite legacy that seals culture securely into a patriarchal, heterosexual economy. And secondly, it makes noticeable the absence of writers such as Suniti Namjoshi with her sexual/textual politics and her specifically interruptive discourse, in the construction and re-construction of Indianness in narration.

Alamgir Hashmi articulates the anxiety of Pakistan's colonial relationship to English writing. Hashmi challenges the relevance of Pakistani writing in English and asks what happens to the production of Pakistani writing in English when only 3 percent of the population—the urban elite—speak it. Hashmi's essay traces not the hegemony of English in Pakistan, but the *urduization* and appropriation of English in this country and fits seamlessly with the essays in this group.

Expanding the boundaries of postcoloniality allows the inclusion of Christopher Wise and Cora Agatucci's essay on African-American writing within the context of postcoloniality. They argue that it is a response to the global process of colonization, specifically that of neocolonialism. Wise and Agatucci point out that since literary genres arise specifically from within social and political contexts, and since the enslaved African was constructed primarily within an oral tradition, s/he was excluded from American literature for over two hundred years. Wise and Agatucci point out that the postcolonial status of African-American writing is brought about more dramatically not by the male writer who used a separatist logic but by African-American women writers who braid the various theories of oppression based upon race, class, and gender, and who have carved out a subject position for themselves through their antiseparatist identity politics. Similarly, Litvack's essay on Canadian writing deals with the politics of multiculturalism in Canada. He argues that Canadian writing in English must also be considered as truly postcolonial in that its emerging national identity not only is overshadowed by the mother country England, but also contains the tension of being situated next door to its aggressive and imperialist neighbor, the United States. Since 1982, Canada's national identity is located in multiculturalism, adopted as state policy. However, such a move is intended as much to break the gridlock between francophone and anglophone Canada as it is to include its multiethnic immigrant population. Litvack's essay traces the impact of this state policy on Canadian writing in English—particularly on native Canadian writers.

Due to the various and varying models of situating the colonized-colonizer paradigm, some of our authors have used a hyphen in the term post-colonial, and as all our writings are meant to tease out the problematics of this term, we have not edited out the hyphen.

Indigenous Models

Postcolonial as an oppositional construct to indigeneity has interesting implications. Tracing the various strategies by which the native writer in English manages to inscribe her difference, the writers of *The Empire Writes Back* point out that the

> link with the land and its effects on Indigenous notions of textuality may well serve as an interesting generator of change in all indigenous communities as writers from these societies seize the post-colonial means of communication in a different way from its appropriation in settler cultures . . . [for l]ocked into the process of appropriation through which

Indigenous groups write is an alternate metaphysic, as well as a political rage, which has proved a powerful creative stimulant. (144–45)

The central question raised by the group of writers in this section focuses on the possibility of locating and recording indigenity in the postcolonial/neocolonial world. The term "indigenous" is itself problematic because, like its counterpart term "third world," it functions as a binary opposite to define "western." The *Oxford English Dictionary* defines "indigenous" as "born naturally in a land or region," then adds without pause that this particular term is reserved for aboriginality. The implication of this definition is, of course, that the western subject is *not* rooted to her/his land of origin. Colonizing new territories is inevitable to such a subject, who in transcending her relationship with her land of origin, is rendered indefinable and, therefore, complex. It is within this context that Arjun Appadurai points out in "Putting Hierarchy In Its Place," that the native/indigene is tied to ideologies of authenticities. He says "[p]roper natives are somehow assumed to represent their selves and their history, without distortion or residue" (37). In contrast, the western subject is exempt from any claims of authenticity because of the complexities and diversities of her histories and societies. Appadurai adds that the term native/indigene is particularly problematic in that it has implications of "incarceration" attached to it (37). The indigene/native has value to the western subject as long as s/he remains confined to the place of origin.

Such foregrounding statements inevitably require that we question the very validity of our postcolonial project because it is predicated not only on the critique of imperialism but also on the legitimacy and sovereignty of the native/indigene. Notions such as indigenous textuality are suspect to a theorist such as Romila Thapar, who within the context of Indian colonialism has pointed out that much of our understanding of the entire Indian past is derived from interpretations of Indian history made within the last 200 years, the years of British colonialism (3). Our comprehension and construction of oppositional indigenous discourse can, therefore, be seen as a structural requirement and structural construction of the dominant colonial voice in its will to represent itself. Gayatri Chakravorti Spivak alludes to this pitfall when she states in "Who Claims Alterity," that "the new culturalist alibi, working within a basically elitist culture industry, insisting on the continuity of a native tradition untouched by a Westernization whose failures it can help to cover, legitimizes the very thing it claims to combat" (281).

However, a postcolonial, indigenous project which must encode the existence and self-definition of the native is necessary since, as we have argued, indigenous writing like all postcolonial writing is directly implicated in the construction of a decolonized nation. All four essays on indigenous writing included in this collection carry these tensions of the legitimacy of indigenous epistemology, oppositional consciousness, and difference. Powhiri Rika-Heke's powerful piece on Maori writing is a history of indigenous literature in Aotearoa/New Zealand "from the perspective of the indigene." Rika-Heke traces the decline of traditional oral literature of Maori with the onset of their Christianization. She points out that early settler writing which dealt with the trials faced by the pioneer in an exotic, savage land covered over the traces of a "history of invasion and oppression" of the Maori. Given the decline of traditional oral literature, Rika-Heke turns to the writing which has emerged in the Maori Renaissance (1960s to present) which records the self-expression of the indigenous writing in New Zealand. In a continuation of the thematic in Rika-Heke's essay, Sigrid Markmann's "Woman's Writing in Aotearoa/New Zealand" deals precisely with the tension of writing within the Maori tradition and the reality of Maori lives in Aotearoa/New Zealand. While the essay overtly attempts to deal with the strategies of Maori writers, her analysis of novelists Patricia Grace and Keri Hulme in particular is preoccupied with the constitution of indigenity. She asks: can the indigene exist prior to or without the western subject? She ultimately concludes that the works of the three writers, Hulme, Grace, and Cathie Dunsford, reveal that "the intersections of race, class and sex are neither presented in a hierarchy nor completely neglected. Differences and conflicts are not explored from their antagonistic content but as integral parts of an entity."

Norma C. Wilson overtly begins her essay "Nesting in the Ruins" with a seeming moment of white liberal guilt by asking whether there is an implicit recolonization when an anglo woman writes about Native American art. She quickly dispels this notion by dealing with the thematic of American history via the Native American perspective. What Wilson's essay exposes is the way in which totalizing history appropriates the other as a form of knowledge. Existent American history, then, is a product of the imperialistic enterprise of the European which re-encodes the racism and sexism of that enterprise. Wilson's essay deals with Native American artists—painters, poets, and fiction writers—who expose the dialectic of the same and the other in the central events of the Americas. However, in their exposé and revisionary history, these artists do not reinscribe the polar existences of dominant Americans and minorities. Instead, poets such as Joy Harjo constantly move between culturally specific backgrounds to other oppressed groups. As Wilson points out "[t]his broad vision far from being contradictory to the world view of Native Americans is fully consistent with a philosophical understanding of reciprocity and interrelatedness of the universe." Working within such a philosophy and interrogating the construction of history, Norma Wilson's original question—Can a white person ever be innocent of the colonialism when she writes about things Native American?—becomes rhetorical. In her essay on "Notes on the 'Post-colonial,' " Ella Shohat too argues that the term "postcolonial" when used in settler colonies glosses over inaccuracies in that it effaces differences between the indigenous people and settler groups in these colonies. This particular problem can be traced to the fact that lodged at the core of the meaning of the term "postcolonial" is the mother-country.

Hugh Webb's essay continues this line of argument when he wonders whether indigenous writing is not conflated with postcolonial writing in Australia. Webb asks, "If [t]he 'colonial' in Australia has ended [for the aboriginal], . . . whose social and political needs are fulfilled by the claim that [that which] was the 'colonial' is of the past? And whose temporal scheme of past-present-future (pre-present-post) informs the category?" Webb warns that the effacement of specificities and emphasis on a certain neutralized similarity render the postcolonial a "purely textual phenomenon."

We have tried to depict various viewpoints, and have been unable to discuss those that address the multicultural, multi-ethnic view from the United States, or the Native American view from Canada. Another area that has not been covered by this volume is the literatures and cultures of the natives of Alaska and Greenland. And, notwithstanding the debate between indigenous rights, postcolonialism, and multiculturalism, all of which are predicated on the prioritizing of difference, we want to underscore that this collection is about the *shared heritage of colonizing*, which the indigene, the postcolonial, and the diasporic individual share in today's global culture. Accordingly we want to conclude the introduction with the words of the Native American poet, Joy Harjo, who specially wrote this poem for this collection:

A POSTCOLONIAL TALE
Joy Harjo

Everyday is a reenactment of the creation story. We emerge from dense unspeakable material, through the shimmering power of dreaming stuff.

This is the first world, and the last.

Once we abandoned ourselves to television, the box that separates the dreamer from the dreaming. It was as if we were stolen, put into a bag carried on the back of a whiteman who pretends to own the earth and the sky. In the sack were all the people of the world. We fought until there was a hole in the bag.

When we fell we were not aware of falling. We were driving to work, or to the mall. The children were in school learning how to travel with guns, although they appeared to be in classes.

We found ourselves somewhere near the diminishing point of civilization, not far from the trickster's bag of tricks.

Everything was as we imagined it. The earth and stars, every creature and leaf imagined with us.

The imagining needs praise as does any living thing. Stories and songs are evidence of this praise.

The imagination conversely illumines us.

Stories and songs are like humans who when they laugh are indestructible.

No story or song will translate the full impact of falling, or the inverse power of rising up.

Yet each act of creation must try.

NOTES

1. For a full range of explications on various literatures in the postcolonial frame, see *The Empire Writes Back: Theory and Practice in Post-Colonial Literatures. The Empire Writes Back*, which was one of the foundational texts in the emerging field of postcoloniality. It was nonetheless critiqued not only for coalescing different geographical, therefore cultural terrains (like Asia, Africa, and America under one category), but also for not distinguishing between forcefully occupied territories and settler colonies (like Australia and New Zealand). It was also seen as not sufficiently differentiating among literatures, cultures, and peoples who have been colonized under very different historical circumstances. This is in response to the criticism against *The Empire Writes Back*. Thus, Tiffin et al. suggest that "Commonwealth" be replaced by a more appropriate term, and in their later works elaborate upon the idea of not discussing the non-Western world under the old category of "Commonwealth" because it resonates with overtones of imperial rule. Ella Shohat furthers the discussion in this debate in "Notes on the 'Post-colonial' " by outlining the problems of offering a generic term like postcolonial.

2. For a fuller description, see the interview between Ngugi wa Thiong'o and Sara Suleri in the *Yale Journal of Criticism*.

3. See Edward Said's *Culture and Imperialism*. Edward Said is one of the first literary critics to document the fact that the west has fashioned the east in its own image. In *Orientalism*, Said argues that the west generates a series of representations of the east so that the eastern hemisphere is constructed as its alterity, emphasizing the power and authority of the west not only to create, define, and derive meaning from the east, but to perpetuate that meaning as universally true. Consequently, in western discourse the east is revealed as a world which is incompetent to represent itself. As Said says, "for if it is true that historians like Michelet, Ranke, Tocqueville, and Burckhardt *emplot* their narratives 'as a story of a particular kind,' the same is also true of Orientalists who plotted Oriental history, character, and destiny for hundreds of years. During the nineteenth and twentieth centuries the Orientalists became a more serious quantity, because by then the reaches of imaginative and actual geography had shrunk, because the Oriental-European relationship was determined by an unstoppable European expansion in search of markets, resources, and colonies, and finally, because Orientalism had accomplished its self-metamorphosis from a scholarly discourse to an imperial institution" (*Orientalism*, 95).

4. See the special issue of *Critical Inquiry* (1992), edited by Kwame Anthony Appiah and Henry Louis Gates, Jr. See the editors' introduction, "Multiplying Identities."

5. In the chapters on "The Woman of Color and the White Man" and "The Man of Color and the White Woman," in *Black Skin, White Masks*, Frantz Fanon appears first to subordinate gender to race. Eventually he completely deletes any consideration of gender and class in his analysis of race within the context of colonialism.

6. In *The Colonizer and the Colonized*, Albert Memmi, speaking from a specifically African context, insists that the very construct of colonialism forcefully situates both the aggressor and the victim within an extremely limited space. According to Memmi, the behaviors of the colonizer and colonized are predictable in that the colonizer can only function in two ways—either as repressive or as liberal within the limits of white privilege. And the colonized can only function either as victims or as elite resistors, who then usually emerge as nativists. Both of the latter positions are completely damaging to the subjectivity of the colonized, while the colonizer assumes an uncritical position of superiority or an

ineffectual posture of guilt. Levi-Strauss wrote in 1971 (much like critics of political correctness today) that he felt a "growing irritation with periodic displays of fine feelings [among westerners] as if that could suffice" (Eribon, 1992 see the chapter "Politics and Race" 148). What Levi-Strauss enunciates as the empty gestures of liberalism, Memmi speaks about with greater force from within the African area, where the ravages of material production make it easier to trace the lines of imperial power. Antonio Gramsci, perhaps one of the most insightful critics of the period, examines hegemony and insurgence from his place in Fascist Italy and proposes the idea of an "organic intellectual" who will serve as the revolutionary figure. For more on Gramsci, see *The Antonio Gramsci Reader: Selected Writings, 1916–1935.* Scholars from the Subaltern Studies Group also attempt to theorize and write another, alternate account of imperial domination and its recordings of Indian history. Dominant Indian history had systematically excluded the disenfranchised masses, which was going to be retold by the Subaltern Studies Group as their historiography. Their methodology is primarily Marxist and Foucauldian and their data base consists of using "unconventional or neglected sources in popular memory, oral discourse, [and] previously unexamined colonial administrative documents" (vi). Admirable though the initiative taken by this group in deliberately decolonizing the discourses of Indian history is, it nonetheless reinscribes the west through the primacy of western intellectual platforms/apparati by privileging Marx, Foucault, etc. over other possible Indian theorists. In the pioneering issue of *Subaltern Studies,* Gayatri Chakravorty Spivak points to lack of "women's voices" as another blind spot in this Marxist re-writing of historiography. For more on this see the volumes of *Selected Subaltern Studies* where this ongoing debate is conducted. More recently, Aijaz Ahmed remarks ironically in "The Politics of Literary Postcoloniality" that even the distinctions that we have attempted here do not go far enough. He writes that "postcolonial writing," "postcolonial criticism," "minority literatures," and "emergent literatures" are now being lumped together by scholars and critics in the United States, Canada, Europe, Australia, and New Zealand in convenient and uncritical ways vis-à-vis colonialism.

7. James Clifford and Vivek Dhareshwar, eds., *Traveling Theories and Traveling Theorists,* special issue, *Inscriptions.* The volume is useful in formulating questions regarding (a) location/diaspora, (b) speaking subject positions, (c) metropolitan or margin versus colonized or marginalized power relations, and (d) language and history intersections in notations of empire in the general arena of postcolonial discourses.

WORKS CITED

Ahmad, Aijaz. "The Politics of Postcoloniality." *Race and Class,* 36:3, 1–20.

Anzaldua, Gloria, ed. *Making Face Making Soul/Hacienda Caras.* San Francisco: An Aunt Lute Foundation, 1990.

Appadurai, Arjun. "Putting Hierarchy in Its Place." *Cultural Anthropology* 3 (1988): 36–49.

Appiah, Kwame, and Henry Louis Gates, Jr., eds. "Multiplying Identities." *Critical Inquiry* 18 (1992): 625–28.

Ashcroft, Bill, Gareth Griffiths, and Helen Tiffin. *The Empire Writes Back: Theory and Practice in Post-Colonial Literatures.* New York and London: Routledge, 1989.

Bhabha, Homi K. "Dissemi Nation: Time, Narrative, and the Margins of the Modern Nation." In *Nation and Narration.* Ed. Homi K. Bhabha. New York and London: Routledge, 1990. 291–322.

———. "Introduction: Narrating the Nation." *Nation and Narration*, ed. Homi K. Bhabha. New York and London: Routledge, 1990. 1–7.

———. "Signs Taken for Wonders: Questions of Ambivalence and Authority under a Tree outside Delhi, May 1817. In *"Race," Writing and Difference*. Ed. Henry Louis Gates, Jr. Chicago: University of Chicago Press, 1986. 163–84.

———. "World and the Home." *Social Text* 10 (1992): 141–52.

Clifford, James, and Vivek Dhareshwar, ed. *Traveling Theories Traveling Theorists*. Special Vol. *Inscriptions* 5 (1989).

Eberon, Didier. *Conversations with CLS: Claude Levi-Strauss*. Trans. Paula Wissing. London and Chicago: University of Chicago Press, 1988.

Fanon, Frantz. *Black Skin, White Masks*. New York: Grove, 1967.

Forgacs, David, ed. *An Antonio Gramsci Reader: Selected Writings 1916–1935*. New York: Schoen Books, 1988.

Guha, Ranajit, and Gayatri Chakravorty Spivak, eds. *Selected Subaltern Studies*. New York and Oxford: Oxford University Press, 1988.

Gupta, Akhil, and James Ferguson. "Beyond 'Culture': Space, Identity and the Politics of Difference." *Cultural Anthropology* 7 (1992): 6–23.

Jameson, Fredric. "Third-World Literature in the Era of Multinational Capitalism." *Social Text* 15 (1986): 65–88.

Mani, Lata. "Multiple Mediations: Feminist Scholarship in the Age of Multinational Reception." *Inscriptions* 5 (1989): 1–23.

Mohanty, Chandra. "Cartographies of Struggle: Third-World Women and Politics of Feminism." In *Third World and the Politics of Feminism*. Ed. Chandra Mohanty, Ann Russo, and Lourdes Torres. Bloomington: Indiana University Press, 1991. 1–47.

———. "Under Western Eyes." In *Third-World Women and the Politics of Feminism*. Ed. Chandra Mohanty, Ann Russo, and Lourdes Torres. Bloomington: Indiana University Press, 1991. 51–79.

Moraga, Cherrie, and Gloria Anzaldua, eds. *This Bridge Called My Back*. San Francisco: Kitchen Table: Women of Color Press, 1983.

Said, Edward. *Culture and Imperialism*. New York: Alfred A. Knopf, 1993.

———. *Orientalism*. New York: Vintage, 1979.

Shohat, Ella. "Notes on the 'Post-Colonial.' " *Social Text* 31/32 (1993): 99–112.

Spivak, Gayatri Chakravorty. *The Postcolonial Critic: Interviews, Strategies, Dialogues*. Ed. Sarah Harasym. New York and London: Routledge, 1990.

———. *Outside in the Teaching Machine*. New York and London: Routledge, 1993.

———. "Who Claims Alterity." *Remaking History*. Ed. Barbara Kruger and Phil Marianai. Seattle: Bay Press, 1989.

Thapar, Romila. *The Past and Prejudice*. Delhi: National Book Trust of India, 1975.

Thiong'o, Ngugi wa. "Interview with Sara Suleri." *Yale Journal of Criticism*. 4: 1 (1990): 269–93.

II

HISTORICAL SURVEY

Out of the Center: Thoughts on the Post-colonial Literatures of Australia and New Zealand

Ralph J. Crane

INTRODUCTION

"Post-colonial literatures" is now the accepted designation for what has in the past been referred to as "commonwealth literature" and the "new literatures in English." But while this term may be politically correct, it is not without its problems: the inclusiveness of the term has left it vulnerably vague and imprecise. The national identities of the various literatures gathered under the all-embracing post-colonial banner seem to emphasize diversity rather than homogeneity. Yet there is enough commonality to allow the myriad national literatures to be fruitfully considered alongside one another. That commonality is, of course, tied to the shared experience of colonization and the emergent interest in the effects of colonialism, an interest in the experience of the post-colonial condition itself. This is mediated in the various uses of the language of the colonial power, and language is the ultimate tool of colonialism, which has in turn been successfully colonized by the margins—as even a cursory glance in the direction of West Indian poetry shows. Or as Ian Wedde pleads in his introduction to *The Penguin Book of New Zealand Verse*: "The History of a literature with colonial origins is involuntarily written *by* the language into its location, to the point where English as an international language can be felt to be original *where it is*" (23). Alan Riach suggests that the converse may be as true, too—that as the international language of domination and exploitation English is the ultimate symbol of the colonial process, and that it is a perpetual foreigner (70).

The literatures of Australia and New Zealand are both distinct in themselves, yet indistinct enough from each other to make the homogenizing term "Australasian Literature" a useful if not always a desirable one. Whether or not one wishes to accept the notion of a federated literature, the literatures of the two countries share enough in common to warrant their parallel consideration in this essay. I'm thinking here of their common settler culture, their shared language question, and their similar relationship to the two major literary movements, Romanticism and Modernism.

What follows is a brief and inevitably incomplete historical survey of the gradual shift from a colonial to post-colonial consciousness in the literatures of Australia and New Zealand.

ABSENT SIGNIFIERS AND SIGNIFICANT ABSENCES: THE COLONIAL CONDITION

Early Australian and New Zealand literature (leaving aside the oral literatures of the aboriginal peoples of Australia and the Maori in New Zealand for the moment) inevitably came from the pens of the colonizers. As elsewhere, the writers whose hands directed those pens frequently sought to explain their new environments through references to the homes they had left behind. In New Zealand Edward Tregear's poem "Te Whetu Plains" is an example of this:

> All still, all silent, 'tis a songless land,
> That hears no music of the nightingale,
> No sound of waters falling lone and grand
> Through sighing forests to the lower vale,
> No whisper in the grass, so wan, and grey, and pale. (O'Sullivan, 1)

This stanza illustrates the way the poem laments an absent landscape instead of celebrating the present one; the land, of course, would not have been silent, but it would have been without the familiar birdsong of the center, which for the poet effectively renders the land songless. Similarly, in Australia there was much nostalgia and sentimental longing for the center evident in the poetry of the mid-nineteenth century, and even though the subjects of the poems were often inspired by the Australian landscape, the form and style of the poetry were distinctly English—as is the case, for example, with Henry Kendall's "The Rain Comes Sobbing to the Door." Poets like Kendall and his contemporary Adam Lindsay Gordon failed to find a distinctly Australian voice in their verse, and instead succeeded only in mimicking the narrative and lyrical poetry of the center. In other words, in the early colonial poetry of Australia and New Zealand the center was privileged over the periphery to the extent that Australia and New Zealand are effectively absent, while Britain is omnipresent. Or at least discrete parts of it are. While the literatures of Australia and New Zealand are not yet post-colonial literatures, they are already the literatures of dispossessed people, but rapidly evolving into the literature of a homogenized "cosmopolitan Anglocentrism."

In much of the early convict prose fiction of Australia, like James Tucker's *Ralph Rashleigh* (probably written 1844–45, first published in 1929), in which the convict system is described in all its horrific detail, there is none of the explicit criticism of the center, which is such a common trait of revisionist historical fiction and post-colonial literatures in general today. Tucker, a privileged convict at the

Port Macquarie penal settlement when he wrote the novel, was in some respects writing as the "plaything" of the colonial power. But there is explicit criticism of the convict system, and by extension the center, in what is perhaps the best-known Australian convict novel, Marcus Clarke's *For the Term of His Natural Life* (revised and first published in book form in 1874). Meanwhile, across the Tasman, what Lawrence Jones labels "Pioneer" or "Early Colonial" literature (107)—which includes the first novel published in New Zealand, Henry Butler Stoney's *Taranaki: A Tale of the War* (1861)—for the most part set out to celebrate the pioneer experience, and was often heavy with pro-colonial values.

In short fiction of this period the pioneer spirit was likewise celebrated, and much of merit to be found in Australia and New Zealand had British origins. But this colonial myopia, while apparent in a great many novels and short stories of the time, was by no means universal. In his convict tales William Astley (who wrote under the name Price Warung) set out to expose the evil and injustice of the convict system. In the satiric story "Parson Ford's Confessional" (1892), to cite just one example, it is clear that the colony of Tasmania is populated by rogues, and that the greatest rogues are not the convicts, but those who govern the colony.

Also noticeable in the poetry and prose of the early colonial period is the manner in which the indigenous peoples are frequently represented as savage, and entirely lacking in the work ethic so prized by the colonists. Although their customs are sometimes described, as in Tucker's *Ralph Rashleigh* or the New Zealand novel *Te Rou; or, The Maori at Home* (1874) by John White, Aborigines and Maori are often portrayed as Other in a way which was designed to highlight (by contrast) the noble qualities of the invaders.

The literature of this period, in European terms, was entirely the product of the settler culture. In Australia and New Zealand there had been a tradition of oral literature dating back to well before the arrival of the European invaders; but unlike some of the other colonies, notably India, there had been no tradition of written literature. Consequently, whereas in countries like India the educated upper classes began at an early stage to write in the language of the colonizers, and to contribute to the body of colonial and post-colonial literatures, this stage only took place much later in Australia and New Zealand, and as a result Aboriginal and Maori literatures in English are largely without that early body of work which sought to mimic the center at the expense of its own identity.

NATIONALIST TRADITIONS AND BEYOND: BREAKING AWAY FROM THE CENTER

Periods of nationalism, in the 1890s in Australia and four decades later in the 1930s in New Zealand, marked the beginning of a rejection of the predominantly Anglocentric perceptions of the two countries that had previously characterized Australasian Literature. Instead the focus was shifted to the internal (but not necessarily indigenous) cultures of the two antipodean countries. In Australia this frequently manifested itself in celebrations of the land and its people without recourse to the previously defining Anglo- or Eurocentrism, while in New Zealand it began the slow process of reinterpreting the country as a Pacific island. The earlier move toward a national identity in Australian literature probably has much to do with the considerable percentage of convicts and otherwise dispossessed people who inhabited the country and bore little love for the English center, while in New Zealand the free settlers who made up the majority of New Zealand's early European population had less cause to reject the Anglocentric hegemony that had fed rather than starved them.

In Australia the Sydney *Bulletin* under the guidance of J. F. Archibald and A. G. Stephens was instrumental in taking the first faltering steps towards the creation of a distinctly national Australian literature and the hand-in-hand rejection of the center. Other important early steps on the path toward what we now refer to as post-colonial literature can be seen in the poetry of Henry Lawson, in the stories of Barbara Baynton, and in novels like Louis Stone's *Jonah* (1911), in which an authentic Australian urban landscape is inhabited by characters like the larrikin Jonah who are convincing Australian, rather than colonial, types. Baynton's stories are particularly interesting in the context of this essay. A story like "Billy Skywonkie," in which the bush itself appears to bring out the brutal racial and sexual discrimination which confront the unnamed female protagonist when she journeys to the "Never-Never," anticipates some essential post-colonial concerns.

This move away from the center toward an identifiable Australian (post-colonial) literature was continued in, for example, the work of the poet Mary Gilmore, and later in the work of the "Jindyworobaks," the group of poets who are frequently associated with a second phase of Australian nationalism which began in the 1930s. In the work of these poets an interest in Aboriginal culture and the environment came to the fore, and perhaps paved the way for an understanding of the grim realities of white settlement in Australia which was to come in later Australian literature.

In the 1930s, across the Tasman Sea in New Zealand the Auckland University College student literary magazine *Phoenix* and the writers associated with it—including the poets Allen Curnow, A.R.D. Fairburn, and Denis Glover, who became known as the *Phoenix* generation—set out to foster a recognizable *New Zealand* literature. The same motivation was also behind the journal *Landfall*, launched fifteen years later, in 1947, under the editorship of Charles Brasch. Though nationalist in intent the New Zealand writers of this generation were nevertheless essentially Anglocentric in their outlook, borrowing many of their ideas from the center they were supposedly rejecting, as their identification with the poets of the Pylon School—principally W. H. Auden, Cecil Day-Lewis, Louis MacNeice, and Stephen Spender—illustrates. Another writer who did not seem to be interested in subscribing to a national literary tradition was John Mulgan. Nevertheless, his novel *Man Alone* (1939) is widely regarded as a founding novel in the New Zealand canon, one which set out to show the country as it really was, and one which deliberately challenged the cozy romanticism of

Anglophile New Zealand writers of the previous generation like his own father, Alan Mulgan. The stories of Frank Sargeson, taken together, also present a remarkable picture of New Zealand, inhabited by distinctly New Zealand characters.

Although Australia and New Zealand are generally accepted as post-colonial countries (despite the fact that in neither country has the colonizing power left or in any real fashion relinquished the power acquired by invasion), much of the fiction produced by Australian and New Zealand writers does not address post-colonial issues. There is a well-nourished body of fiction in both countries which deals with universal themes such as human relationships (the novels of Elizabeth Jolley or Maurice Gee, for example), and other various aspects of contemporary society—the drug culture, as in Helen Garner's *Monkey Grip* (1977), French nuclear testing in the Pacific, which is the subject of Maurice Shadbolt's *Danger Zone* (1975), and so on. These books are only to be considered as post-colonial in the sense that they are written *out of* this condition. In fact much contemporary Australian and New Zealand fiction has more in common with contemporary American fiction than South American or West African fiction. The New Zealand poet and novelist Ian Wedde, for example, has as much in common with, say, the American writer William Gaddis as he does with the Nigerian writer Ben Okri. Nevertheless, there is also an equally well-nurtured body of fiction in each country that *does* confront the post-colonial condition, that does challenge the beast.

THE NATURE OF POST-COLONIALITY IN AUSTRALIA AND NEW ZEALAND

In post-colonial discourses the center-periphery model has provided a useful framework for exploring the relationship between the ex–colonial power and an ex-colony. In the "settler colonies" like Australia and New Zealand the challenge to the center has often manifested itself in the form of revisionist historical fiction, which, in reinterpreting history, either by taking the perspective of the periphery or by including the perspective of the periphery, effectively challenges or subverts the hegemonical center. In Australia writers like Thomas Keneally in novels such as *The Chant of Jimmie Blacksmith* (1972) and *The Playmaker* (1987), Mudrooroo Narogin (formerly Colin Johnson) in *Doctor Wooreddy's Perscription for Enduring the Ending of the World* (1983), and Kate Grenville in *Joan Makes History* (1988)—which challenges the patriarchal perspective of history—to choose some diverse examples, have successfully used historical fiction to write back to the center. Similarly in New Zealand, writers like Maurice Shadbolt, in his trilogy of the New Zealand Wars, *Season of the Jew* (1986), *Monday's Warriors* (1990), and *The House of Strife* (1993), and Witi Ihimaera in *The Matriarch* (1986) have used historical fiction to challenge the hegemony of the center. But in both countries historical fiction which has challenged the center and given voice to the previously silenced periphery has constructed a further periphery-center dichotomy in itself, and in this context, it has often failed to give adequate voice to the other. Indeed, as Joanne Tompkins explains, white literature in Australia and New Zealand has often only included indigenous versions of history for the purpose of humor (485). In some respects the historical situation in the settler colonies has meant that the center, rather than becoming the ex–colonial power, has been absorbed into the periphery, pushing the indigenous peoples, the Aborigines and the Maori, into what is effectively an outer periphery.

Central to the literature of this outer periphery is the desire to reclaim the histories of the indigenous peoples, and to educate non-indigenous readers about Aboriginal and Maori cultures. And herein lies the major difference between the post-colonial literatures of the "settler colonies" (including South Africa) and the post-colonial literatures of the "non-settler colonies." While it may be convincingly argued that white Australian writers and Pakeha writers in New Zealand do write back to the center, they do so from the privileged position of the settler, whereas indigenous writers are frequently not writing back to the absent (British) center so much as writing back to this present and dominant "settler cultures," which have maintained a Eurocentric perspective at the expense of a deliberately muted indigenous one.

Recovering silenced indigenous histories is a central concern of much Aboriginal literature in Australia and Maori literature in New Zealand. Traditionally history has been told from the perspective of the colonizers, deliberately denying colonized or indigenous peoples their place as a consequence. In *Doctor Wooreddy's Perscription for Enduring the Ending of the World* and *The Matriarch* (to continue with the same examples) Mudrooroo Narogin and Witi Ihimaera deliberately set out to "recapture our history and culture," as Mudrooroo Narogin explains in the essay "White Forms, Aboriginal Content" (29). They also set out to expose the lies of history sanctified by the center, as a telling passage from *The Matriarch* illustrates:

All New Zealand schoolchildren were taught about Captain James Cook's discovery of New Zealand and his historic landfall at Poverty Bay in the *Endeavour* in October 1769. They are told that the event was quite glorious—that a lad at the masthead shouted "Land Ahoy!" at 2 p.m. on 7 October 1769, a curly-headed youth after whom the landform that he had sighted, Young Nick's Head, was named. They are asked to imagine the sight as the *Endeavour* anchored off the mouth of the Turanganui River. They are told, to some amusement, that the reaction of the Maori people on shore was one of awe for the huge white bird, the floating island, and the multicoloured gods who had come on the bird. Ah yes, the stuff of romance indeed!

But what the schoolchildren are not told is that Cook's first landing was marked by the killing of a Maori called Te Maro, shot through the heart by a musket bullet, Monday 9 October, 1769. Then on the morning of Tuesday 10 October, 1769, another Maori called Te Rakau was shot and killed, and three others were wounded. During the afternoon of that same day a further four Maoris were murdered in the bay merely because they had showed fight when molested, and three of their companions were taken captive.

Captain James Cook claimed New Zealand for Britain. The *Endeavour* finally left Poverty Bay on Thursday 12 October, 1769. The glorious birth of the nation has the taste of bitter almonds when one remembers that six Maoris died so that a flag could be raised and that the *Endeavour* had lain in Poverty Bay for only two days and fourteen hours. (36–37)

Here, as elsewhere in the novel, the "accepted" Eurocentric/Pakeha version of history is recounted, only to be challenged and rejected in favor of a revised version which retells the story from a Maori perspective. Thus Ihimaera (and Narogin in Australia, too) reverse the past trend of black (hi)stories being rejected in favor of white ones.

Moreover, white histories have tended to be told in a linear fashion which does not necessarily reflect Aboriginal or Maori views of time. To counter this, in *Tangi* (1973), the first Maori novel in English, and again in *The Matriarch* Witi Ihimaera rejects the linear narrative in favor of a circular structure or pattern which is distinctly Maori in order to wrest the past from the strangling grip of the center; throughout the novel stories of the past wash over and rearrange our perceptions of the present in much the same way as waves, continually advancing and retreating, rearrange the sand on a beach. Thus the past is seen literally to shape the present; it continues to be a tangible presence in the present, just as ancestors are a tangible presence in Maori life. And here we glimpse what has been called the educative purpose of indigenous literatures which seek to show what it is like to be Aboriginal/Maori in Australia/New Zealand (see for example, Arvidson, 117). As Patricia Grace explained in an interview: "I hope [my] stories show aspects of a way of life that is essentially Maori and they give some insight into what it is to be a Maori" (Arvidson, 117–18). And in the post-colonial context this educative function helps Maori and Aborigines to promote a visible sense of identity within the larger New Zealand and Australian societies.

Many Maori and Aboriginal writers, like Ihimaera or Narogin, whose *Doctor Wooreddy's Perscription for Enduring the Ending of the World* is set in Tasmania in the early part of the nineteenth century and deals with the historical figures of Wooreddy, the last male Aborigine from Bruny Island, and George Augustus Robinson, use history to challenge the discourse of the center and/or the periphery. Other indigenous writers focus more on recent historical events, as Patricia Grace does in her novel *Potiki* (1986), which is partly based on a dispute over Maori land at Ragland on the west coast of New Zealand's North Island.

But indigenous writers do not by any means only focus on the past in their fiction. Narogin's *Wild Cat Falling* (1965), the first novel to be published by an Aboriginal writer, tells the story of an Aboriginal youth who is denied the privileges of the white-dominated society he is forced to live in because of his racial background. His fight against that society is seen as futile, but it does lead him into the company of an old Noongar, from whom he learns a new sense of pride in his cultural identity. Similarly, in her most powerful short stories, which focus on Maori identity in contemporary New Zealand society, Patricia Grace, like Mudrooroo Narogin, combines an educative purpose with a political one, and clearly challenges the dominant periphery. In "The Hills," for example, Grace begins by reminding the reader of the colonial connotations of the word "boy," which effectively marginalizes the boy in this story, confirms him as other in a still white-dominated "settler culture":

> "Boy" means little kid, "boy" means dirty with a filthy mind. It means "smart arse". A "boy" is a servant and a slave. . . . Anyway, I'm not a slave or a servant. I'm just myself. One day I'll call myself a man, and I won't just be an old "boy" like my father. (65)

But outside the marginalized framework, the word "boy" also has an apolitical meaning that signifies youth and innocence:

> When the mist comes down to cover the hills I don't think grey. I think of parcels and coloured wrapping, and clothes and tits and bums. Then I have a good laugh at myself and think that I'm only a boy after all. I don't mean a servant or a slave or a smart brat. I just mean "boy" in a different, youngish way.
>
> Then something can happen to you that's too much for a boy. You can't be a boy any more afterwards. (66)

What happens to the Maori youth shows that in a society born of imperial aggression, in which many of the prejudices of the center linger, those two different meanings of the word "boy" are linked after all, as Grace emphasizes as she draws the story to a close:

> Later that day I went outside and walked up the street, and when I got to the top of the road I wouldn't look out at the hills. The hills could've been clear, or the mist could've been down or it could've been just lifting off. I turned and went back home. I remember wondering if I would ever look there again. (69)

It is because of this prejudice, the legacy of a colonial past, that the narrator will never again be able to call himself a "boy" in a youngish way, nor, ironically, will he ever be prepared to accept the role of "boy" as servant or slave, which is the role that the dominant white culture is trying to impose on him.

In my introduction I referred briefly to the power of language and commented on the way the English language has in turn been successfully colonized by post-colonial writers, in the West Indies and elsewhere. In Australia and New Zealand the pattern is somewhat different: the language of the center has never been as successfully colonized because the cultures of the antipodean countries are essentially born of the center, and much of what we now refer to as Australian English or New Zealand English has its origins in the various shires of England, or the various regions of Scotland, Wales, and Ireland. Indigenous writers, however, have used language for clear political ends. (It is worth remembering that in New Zealand most Maori writers are bicultural and make serious attempts to bridge the two cultures, whereas most Pakeha writers are monocultural and subsume the cultural differences they have inherited as white New Zealanders.) In Witi Ihimaera's early works like *Tangi* we find the English language being molded by the rhythms of the Maori language, and the spiraling patterns of the oral narrative as performed by storytellers. More significantly, perhaps, Maori writers, like Ihimaera, Grace, Hone Tuwhare, Keri Hulme, Apirana Taylor and others, and also some Pakeha writers, notably the poet James K. Baxter (in poems like "He Waiata mo Te Kare" and "Te Whiore o te Kuri"), have increasingly used untranslated Maori words in their fiction, which inscribes difference by suggesting that certain cultural experiences can't be reproduced in the language of the center or white periphery (see Ashcroft et al. 53). And this use of Maori words also challenges the cultural hegemony of English itself, as well as making deliberately muted voices heard. Similarly Aboriginal writers like the poet Kevin Gilbert (whose play *The Cherry Pickers* was, in 1971, the first play by an Aboriginal playwright to be performed in Australia) regularly use words from their own indigenous languages in their work, though in Australia the situation has been complicated by the often all-too-thorough genocide carried out against Aboriginal tribes and languages by the colonizers. Thus in the work of a poet like Lionel Fogerty, the only Aboriginal words the reader encounters tend to be place names or tribal names as in the poem "Nyarki's Place." As Narogin explains, to understand Fogerty's poetry one must leave behind the safety of language and explore the Aboriginality that is inherent in a poem like "Free Our Dreams" (*Writing from the Fringe*, 54–59).

CONCLUSION

In Australia and New Zealand white writers have begun to write back to the center in an attempt to exorcise some of the Eurocentrism that has fashioned so much of the literature of the dominant culture in the two countries. In turning away from the center white writers in Australia and Pakeha writers in New Zealand are beginning instead to redefine themselves in relation to the indigenous cultures of their countries.

Post-coloniality in Australia and New Zealand thus involves not only writing back to the center, but also recognizing and accepting the cultural heterogeneity which defines the post-colonial national identity of each country.

The work of the Australian poet Les Murray brings out this sense of a post-colonial national identity. His poetry, which is often very local, antimodern, is also attentive to the cultural differences in his own makeup. His poetry pays attention to Scotland, thus recognizing his European ancestry, and also to Aboriginal culture, which is part of his identity as an Australian. Writing from the periphery, Murray includes both the center and the outer periphery in his work, providing a synthesis of what at times have appeared to be the disparate elements of the post-colonial condition in Australia and New Zealand.

WORKS CITED

Arvidson, Ken. "Aspects of Contemporary Maori Writing in English." In *Dirty Silence: Aspects of Language and Literature in New Zealand.* Ed. Graham McGregor and Mark Williams. Auckland: Oxford University Press, 1991. 117–28.

Ashcroft, Bill, Gareth Griffiths, and Helen Tiffin. *The Empire Writes Back: Theory and Practise in Post-Colonial Literatures.* London and New York: Routledge, 1989.

Grace, Patricia. *Electric City and Other Stories.* Auckland: Penguin, 1987.

Ihimaera, Witi. *The Matriarch.* 1986. Auckland: Picador, 1987.

Jones, Lawrence. "The Novel." *The Oxford History of New Zealand Literature.* Ed. Terry Sturm. Auckland: Oxford University Press, 1991. 105–199.

Narogin, Mudrooroo [Colin Johnson]. "White Forms, Aboriginal Content." *Aboriginal Writing Today.* Ed. Jack Davis and Bob Hodge. Canberra: Australian Institute of Aboriginal Studies, 1985. 21–33.

Narogin, Mudrooroo. *Writing from the Fringe.* Melbourne: Hyland House, 1990.

O'Sullivan, Vincent, ed. *An Anthology of Twentieth Century New Zealand Poetry,* 3rd ed. Auckland: Oxford University Press, 1987.

Riach, Alan. "Stranger Eyes: Charles Olson, 'Pacific Man' and Some Aspects of New Zealand Poetry." *Landfall* 43.1 (1989): 57–73.

Tompkins, Joanne. " 'It All Depends on What Story You Hear': Historiographic Metafiction and Colin Johnson's *Doctor Wooreddy's Perscription for Enduring the Ending of the World* and Witi Ihimaera's *The Matriarch.*" *Modern Fiction Studies* 36.4 (1990): 483–98.

Wedde, Ian. "Introduction" In *The Penguin Book of New Zealand Verse.* Ed. Ian Wedde and Harvey McQueen. Auckland and Harmondsworth, England: Penguin, 1985. 23–52.

"A Terrible Beauty Is Born": Irish Literature as a Paradigm for the Formation of Postcolonial Literatures

Ian Crump

During the recent outpouring of theory and criticism dealing with postcolonial literatures, critics who have not ignored Irish literature have largely been inclined to dismiss its significance. The authors of *The Empire Writes Back* argue, for example, that Ireland's "complicity in the British imperial enterprise makes it difficult for colonized peoples to accept [Irish literature's] identity as post-colonial"; these authors are quite willing, however, to allow that "the literature of the USA should be placed in this category" (Ashcroft et al. 33). More pointedly, Gay Wilentz claims that "the historicity of the situation in Ireland belies easy comparison to imperialism in the New World, since the components of race and slavery do not enter into the colonization of European peoples" (Lawrence 265). Yet since its emergence at the end of the nineteenth century, Irish literature has self-consciously defined itself as primarily a national(ist), anti-colonial literature. Moreover, precisely because of its many (re)constructions of Irish racial, linguistic, and sexual identities, this literature offers an especially potent paradigm for the postcolonial condition in all its multiplicity.

As Ella Shohat has recently argued, "The globalizing gesture of the [phrase] 'post-colonial condition,' or 'post-coloniality,' downplays multiplicities of location and temporality" in the struggles against colonialism (104); further, it conflates the very different historical situations of colonialism, post- (that is, after) colonialism, and neocolonialism (106–7). Yet rather than reject the term "postcoloniality," we should follow the lead of critics who have begun to explore its many permutations, especially as they apply to writers. Responding to the European decolonization of the 1950s and 1960s, Frantz Fanon describes "three levels" in the anti-colonial "evolution" of the "native writer" (178):

> In the first phase, the native intellectual gives proof that he has assimilated the culture of the occupying power. . . . In the second phase we find the native is disturbed; he decides to remember what he is. . . . But since the native is not a part of his people, he is content

to recall their life only. . . . Finally in the third phase, which is called the fighting phase, the native . . . shake[s] the people. . . . He turns himself into an awakener of the people. (178–79)

Reacting to the rise of neocolonialism, and thus less convinced than Fanon that colonialism can be defeated once and for all, Kwame Anthony Appiah details two stages, the first of which combines Fanon's first two phases. In this stage, which occurs before and just prior to independence, European-educated writers produce, for a European audience, "realist legitimations of nationalism" in which they "authorize a 'return to traditions' " by celebrating themselves "as Other," "while at the same time recognizing the demands of a Weberian rationalized modernity" (150, 156). In Appiah's second, or postcolonial, stage, writers "are no longer committed to the nation . . . but [to] Africa—the continent and its people"—which they represent in "novels of delegitimation" (152).

While these levels, or stages, prove useful, we must differentiate further stages if we hope to comprehend fully the multiplicities of the postcolonial condition. To that end, Irish literature provides an example of a postcolonial literature that can be divided into five stages of development. Writers from the first stage produce a radically conservative national(ist) literature that revives the indigenous, precolonial culture in an effort to celebrate a concept of racial difference which they originally derive from their colonizers. This literature is often intended more for an audience of the colonizers than of the colonized. In the second stage, writers forge a literature of delegitimation which is transnational or continental in vision. These writers frequently choose to write from exile. In the third stage, after the colony achieves political independence, writers attempt to demythologize the literature of the first stage, which eventually fosters neocolonialism and cultural conservatisism in the new nation. Yet their efforts prove, finally, to be so dependent on the literature which these writers seek to invalidate that they become constrained in what they can write. To counteract this dependence, writers from the fourth stage continue the process of demythologizing, but try to avoid the earlier writers' trap by creating a literature that also espouses the continental vision of the writers from the second stage. And in the fifth stage, women writers challenge the "double colonialism" which they have endured by producing a literature that rewrites the male canon and offers an explicitly female perspective.

The self-consciously Irish national(ist) literature that writers from the first stage of postcoloniality began to produce in the 1880s corresponds to other national(ist) literatures, such as Italian or Hungarian, which emerged contemporaneously across Europe in support of political nationalisms. Yet in Ireland, this national(ist) literature emerged only after the indigenous Gaelic culture had been largely destroyed. This destruction was initiated systematically with the Act of Union (1800–1), which legislated the absorption of what had been, essentially, a self-governing colony into the United Kingdom of Great Britain and Ireland. Writing in 1800, Maria Edgeworth recognized that "When Ireland loses her identity by an union with Great Britain," "individuals . . . [would acquire] new habits and a new consciousness," but she failed to foresee that rather than learning to "bear to be rallied for their past follies and absurdities" (x), the Irish would experience an unsettling sense of cultural deracinization in the face of growing British political, linguistic and economic hegemony. The Potato Famine (1845–48), which "hit the Gaelic-speaking areas worst," exacerbated this feeling of uprootedness; the Irish population decreased by half in ten years through starvation or emigration (McHugh and Harmon 96, 86).

The writers of the Irish Literary Revival attempted to redress this cultural "erasure" by reclaiming Ireland's Celtic past. They translated or retold the ancient Celtic myths and found inspiration in Irish folk and faery lore because, as Standish O'Grady declared, "The[se] legends represent the imagination of the country; they are that kind of history which a nation desires to possess" (27).[1] Using for their poetry, fiction, and plays "a speech as beautiful as that of Morris, . . . a dialect of English [as true as the one] Burns wrote in," an Irish-English which they "heard among the country people of Ireland" or from servant girls through "a chink in the floor of [an] old Wicklow house" (Gregory 12; Synge 3),[2] the Revivalists created a deliberately national literature, with which they meant to foster a spiritual, rather than an anticolonial, identity for Ireland.[3] This literature would articulate the long-hidden Celtic essence which would reinvigorate and unite the Irish so that they could transcend the divisiveness of their nationalist squabbles and material desires.

The Revivalists located this Celtic essence not only in the ancient Celtic legends, which they translated, but also in the few remaining Gaelic-speaking regions of western Ireland, such as the Aran Islands. As John Millington Synge represents it in *The Playboy of the Western World* (1907), this is a wild and, beneath the veneer of Catholicism, essentially pagan world where traditional representatives of civil authority, the priest and "the peelers" (10), are effectively absent. Here, Christy Mahon can dominate his father—even if he fails to kill him—and "make [him]self a hero in the sight of all" the villagers "with his mighty talk" (Synge 45, 77). William Butler Yeats evokes, in such early poems as "The Stolen Child" (1889), "The Lake Isle of Innisfree" (1893), "The Man Who Dreamed of Faeryland" (1893), and "The Song of the Wandering Aengus" (1893), a melancholy, yet peaceful, antimaterialist world which resonates "in the deep heart's core" (Allt and Alspach 117) and so provides an antidote to the modern urban world, which is "full of weeping" (Allt and Alspach 87). The man who dreams of faeryland is so tormented by his vision that he cannot even find solace in the burial ground. And, unconcerned with having to earn a living, Aengus, the Celtic god of poetry, beauty, and love, can devote himself to searching for a faery fish-girl who once called his name.

Writing during the same period as, and originally allied with, the Revivalists was a more loosely organized group of nationalist writers, including Douglas Hyde and Patrick Pearse, who were affiliated with the Gaelic League, which promoted the revival of the Gaelic language. The writers also wanted to articulate an Irish identity, but were critical of the Revivalists—whom they viewed suspiciously as members of the Ascendency, the Protestant colonial elite—for avoiding the issues of language and religion. The Revivalists' Celt spoke English, albeit an English shaped by Gaelic linguistic patterns, and was spiritually linked to pre-Catholic Ireland because the Revivalists wished to advance an Irish identity that would include them. Hyde, Pearse, and the other Gaelic League writers offered, instead, a more narrowly defined identity for the Irish, that of the Gael, who spoke only Gaelic and was profoundly Catholic.

Although a member of the Ascendency, Hyde came to be regarded, because of his founding of the Gaelic League and publishing of the bilingual *The Love Songs of Connacht* in 1893, as "the archetype of the Catholic Protestant, cunning, subtle, cajoling, superficial and affable" (qtd. in Foster 72). With *The Love Songs*, Hyde intended, as he noted in his preface, not only to preserve "the poetry of the Irish country people" but also to make it better known in its original language. This work differs from O'Grady's or Lady Gregory's translations of the bardic legends as well as from Yeats' early poetry because it means to present directly "the way in which the Connacht peasant puts his love-thoughts into song and verse, whether it be hope or despair, grief or joy, that affects him" (106): although "there remains nothing of the people who composed [most of the poems] in grief and tribulation, except the songs" themselves, they express the essence of "the Gaelic nature," which is neither heroic nor quaint, but which is given to "excessive foolish mirth, or [to] keening and lamentation" (2, 1).

Pearse, more actively nationalist than Hyde, articulated an ideal of Catholic rebellion in which the self-sacrifice of the rebel, who "come[s] of the seed of the people /. . . . of the blood of serfs," is explicitly equated with that of Christ, Who, to save all people, "died naked, suffering shame" (25–6). In his posthumously-published play *The Singer* (1917), Pearse depicts the title character, MacDara, as "some great hero that has come back again to lead the people against the Gall [the British], or maybe an angel, or the Son of Mary Himself that has come down on the earth" (108–9). Not content to be a poet or singer, who "is only a voice that cries out, a sigh that trembles into rest," MacDara resolves to "suffer and do" as "The true teacher must": "He must break bread to the people: he must go into Gethsemane and toil up the steep of Golgotha" (117). His aim is not to defeat the British, but to inspire the Irish: "One free man can free a people as one Man redeemed the world. I will take no pike, I will go into battle with bare hands. I will stand up before the Gall as Christ hung naked before men on the tree!" (124–5). Although this play is a less accomplished work than Yeats's own seditious, yet secular *Cathleen ni Houlihan* (1902), *The Singer* acquired a powerful nationalist authority once Pearse was executed by the British after he led the Easter 1916 Rising.

Ironically, however, the Celtic and Gaelic identities which these national(ist) writers promoted were both derived from Matthew Arnold's idea of Celtic racial difference.[4] In his lectures *On the Study of Celtic Literature* (1867), Arnold describes "the impressionable Celt" as "social, hospitable, eloquent, figuring away brilliantly. He loves bright colors, he easily becomes audacious, overcrowing, full of fanfaronade" (76–77). Because of his sentimental nature, he is "always ready to react against the despotism of fact" and is "peculiarly disposed to feel the spell of the feminine idiosyncrasy" (77, 82). Arnold's thesis is that the British needed to acquire these Celtic traits "to give us delicacy, and to free us from hardness and Philistinism"; but by urging the Celts to abandon the Gaelic language because it is "the badge of a beaten race" and to bow to the "fusion"—made inevitable by the Act of Union—"of all the inhabitants of these islands into one homogeneous English-speaking whole" (133, 5, 9), he reveals that he is also eager to assimilate the Irish, as a temperamentally different, yet finally a racially similar people, into the United Kingdom of Great Britain and Ireland.[5] Significantly, Arnold delivered these lectures, in which he implicitly rejects the long-standing British opinion that the Irish were mere savages who needed to be dominated militarily, on the eve of the "scramble for Africa." Consciously or not, he justifies co-opting the white Irish for the colonization of black Africans, whom both the British and the Irish regarded as racially inferior.

By adopting Arnold's definition of Celtic identity, these writers from the first stage of postcoloniality made the same Manichean gesture Léopold Sédar Senghor and Aimé Césaire made when they promoted the idea of Négritude: they celebrated themselves as Other. Pearse's and Yeats' works equally engage in the revival of a moribund culture. Hyde's works, written in Gaelic to encourage its revival, appealed in practice to the same metropolitan audience which admired Synge's celebration of Celtic culture as "exoticized other" (Appiah 156). Few Irish could speak Gaelic, and fewer Gaelic speakers from western Ireland could actually read the language, and thus it was British cultural tourists like Haines in *Ulysses* who purchased copies of *The Love Songs of Connacht*.[6] By embracing this idea of their own Otherness, no matter how they developed or redefined it, these Irish writers perpetuated in themselves and the Irish people feelings of inferiority, dependency, and nostalgia, which resulted in Ireland's transformation, upon independence, into a neocolonial and culturally reactionary state. Writing at the same period as these two groups, James Joyce refused to join with either not only because they reaffirmed British authority by celebrating themselves as Other but also because one group ignored, while the other pledged its loyalty to what he viewed as the equally insidious authority of the Catholic church.[7] As a writer from the second stage of postcoloniality, he rejects, in his fiction, the concepts of the Celtic and the Gaelic nation-people, which he found too exclusive, archaic, rural, and pious to suit the modern, urban Irish; instead, he celebrates Dublin and its citizens as European, much as Salman Rushdie celebrates Bombay in *Midnight's Children* as a microcosm of the Indian subcontinent. Writing from exile on the Continent, where he moved to escape the spiritual and the political binds peculiar to colonialism and neocolonialism in Ireland, Joyce produced a literature of delegitimation, in which he "forge[d] . . . the uncreated conscience of my race" (*Portrait* 253) by abdicating his literary authority, reinventing the English language, and representing a more inclusive, European identity for the Irish.

Keenly aware that the Irish liked to "entrust their wills and minds to others that they may ensure for themselves a life of spiritual paralysis" (*Stephen Hero* 146), Joyce used increasingly radical narrative techniques—represented speech and thought (or *style indirect libre*), interior monologue and dream monologue—to develop an authorityless style which would cause his readers to become independently minded interpreters of his works. In *Dubliners* (1914) and *A Portrait of the Artist as a Young Man* (1916), he represents the double "catalepsy" (JanMohamed 5), or what he calls the paralysis, of the Irish colonial subject. Cut off from their Gaelic culture, and ruled by London and Rome, Joyce's characters experience alienation and a loss of authority. In "Counterparts," Farrington beats his son because he has been humiliated by his Ulster boss and by an English circus strongman. Similarly, in "The Boarding House," Bob Doran is maneuvered into a marriage in part because of the prevailing Victorian and Catholic moralities. Yet at the same time, these characters feel trapped by the political, linguistic, and religious demands of Irish nationalism: Stephen Dedalus announces to his friend Davin that "When the soul of a man is born in this country there are nets flung at it to hold it back from flight. You talk to me of [Irish] nationality, [the Gaelic] language, [Catholic] religion. I shall try to fly by those nets" (*Portrait* 203).

In *Ulysses* (1922) and *Finnegans Wake* (1939), Joyce depicts characters who, even though they remain in Ireland, are not limited by, but rather transcend, its political and spiritual colonialisms. As an incarnation of both the Wandering Jew and the epic hero Ulysses, Leopold Bloom stands outside Gaelic culture, yet within all European culture. He is not troubled, as Stephen is, that English, "so familiar and so foreign, will always be . . . an acquired speech" (*Portrait* 189), because the English he speaks embraces Irishisms, misquotations from Italian operatic libretti, and Greek words. Likewise, as a son, a husband, a father, a friend, and a lover, Bloom is, like his heroic model, a "complete all-round character" (Budgen 15–16). As the sleeper in *Finnegans Wake*, HCE is so universal that he can dream himself simultaneously "Here Comes Everybody" and "Nomon . . . imparticular" (32, 374, 602). His dreams about Celtic myths, Irish politics, European history, and British literature are recorded in a "nat language" (83), which, because it fuses the linguistic rubbish of Europe and beyond, but is spoken with a Dublin accent, may be less familiar than English, yet is less foreign. The difficulty of Joyce's works of delegitimation has meant, however, that they have gone largely unread until recently in Ireland; therefore, in failing to become independently minded readers, as he had hoped, the Irish have not learned how to circumvent the other forms of authority in their lives.

After most of Ireland achieved its political independence as the Irish Free State in 1922, which resulted from the struggle that Pearse and others initiated with the Easter Rising, the myth of the Gael was enshrined as the national ideology. In reaction, Yeats and several younger writers, who constitute what Terence Brown calls the Counter Revival (Deane *Field Day* 3: 89), initiated the third stage of postcoloniality, which is characterized by angry disillusionment and caustic demythologizing. Although Yeats cannot be included with the Counter Revivalists because, despite turning away from Celticism, he continued to champion

Revivalist ideals, he became a critic of the state shortly after independence. Earlier, he had been willing, in "Easter, 1916," to acknowledge the modern heroism of the rebels, even if he did not particularly like some of them or approve of their aims. He recalls the disillusionment of the heroic MacBridge figure by simultaneously castigating him for being a "vain-glorious lout" and valorizing "him in song." Yet sickened by the new nation's divisive party politics, he declares that "if it had played a larger role in the wars, Irish identity would not have been compromised. Angered by the Catholic majority's growing intolerance of the Anglo-Irish and by its lack of concern for its aesthetic sensibilities, he condemns Ireland for getting caught in other matters and forgetting those 'Monuments of unageing intellect' " (Allt and Alspach 407). Dismayed that the Irish had become preoccupied with material wants, he reminds them that sons of Ireland are forgetting their rich heritage and hankering after a belated modernity. Yeats has correctly been criticized for his flirtation with the Blue Shirts in the 1930s, yet this fascist organization appealed to him because he believed that it was a suitable ally in his struggle to preserve his ideals in the face of the restrictive censorship and cultural isolation which the Free State adopted to protect its Gaelic identity.

Younger than Yeats, the Counter Revivalists experienced even stronger feelings of anger and disillusionment about the ideals of the two Revivals precisely because they had been nurtured on them. These feelings—similar to those Ngugi wa Thiong'o articulates in works such as *Devil on the Cross*—were occasioned by their perception of a growing discrepancy between these ideals, which had led to independence, and the realities of the Irish Free State (and after 1949, the Republic), that remained dominated economically by Britain and that wanted to preserve, rather than develop, its culture. Exposing the horrible, human consequences of Pearse's Catholic-inspired Republican ideology of blood sacrifice, Sean O'Casey shows, in plays such as *Juno and the Paycock* (1924) and *The Plough and the Stars* (1926), how such women as Juno Boyle and Bessie Burgess suffer for the actions of boastful, cowardly men. Parodying the Literary Revival's wish to reinvigorate the Irish with translations of Celtic legends, Flann O'Brien juxtaposes, in his novel *At Swim-Two-Birds* (1939), the legend of King Sweeney, Irish cowboy yarns, and realistic descriptions of the squalid conditions in Dublin in the 1930s. And in his bleak poem "The Great Hunger" (1942), Patrick Kavanagh undermines the glorification of the pious Gaelic peasant by depicting Paddy Maquire as a farmer who never marries because he obeyed his mother for "prais[ing] the man who made a field his bride" (35). Instead, he leads a lonely life by fantasizing and erotizing his lover and quenching his thirst with a "drink the next Saturday" (43). Ultimately, however, these Counter Revivalists realized that, unlike Ngugi, who has discovered an empowering inspiration in choosing to write in Gikuyu so that he could reach a wider Kenyan audience,[8] they had become so dependent on the literature whose power they so angrily wished to break that they could write about little else: Kavanagh and O'Brien turned to journalism, while O'Casey occupied himself with his autobiography.

Like the Counter Revivalists, Samuel Beckett attacked the Celtic and Republican pretensions of the Free State in his early novel, *Murphy* (1938). But by exiling himself, like Joyce, to the Continent; by choosing to write primarily in French; and by continuing his dissection of Cartesianism—which he had already begun in *Murphy*—he managed to avoid becoming trapped in the Counter Revivalists' sterile dead end. Instead, in such works as *Waiting for Godot* (1953), *The Unnamable* (1953), and *Company* (1980), he pares away all extraneous preoccupations, including the political, so that he can expose how the subject, that "Devised deviser" (*Company* 46), devises its own comforting prison with deadening habits, linguistic sleights-of-hand, and self-distracting fictions. Thus, even when it is faced with the realization that "They give birth astride of a grave, the light gleams an instant, then it's night once more" (*Waiting* 57), this devised subject can assert, "I can't go on, I'll go on" (*Three Novels* 414).

The fourth and fifth stages of postcoloniality, which have occurred contemporaneously, have resulted from Ireland's growing economic independence since the 1960s and its decreasing cultural isolation since its entry into the European Community in 1972. The Irish writers in the fourth stage have been forced by the Troubles in Northern Ireland to reexamine not only the long-festering colonialism in British-ruled Ulster but also the lingering effects of neocolonialism in the southern Republic, much as Hanif Kureishi uses the London race riots to confront Pakistani as well as British bigotries in films such as *Sammie and Rosie Get Laid.* Like the Counter Revivalists before them, these writers have remained in Ireland for the most part while trying to dismantle its Revivalist and Republican ideologies, which they believe have perpetuated the island's partition. In 1980, Brian Friel and the actor Stephen Rea founded the Field Day Theatre Company with the belief that it "could and should contribute to the solution of the present crisis by producing analyses of the established opinions, myths and stereotypes which had become both a symptom and a cause of the current situation" (Deane *Ireland's* vii). In *Translations* (1980), his play about the British army's mapping of Ireland and Anglicizing of Gaelic place names in the 1830s, Friel implicitly attacks the Republic's outdated pieties about the Gaelic language. Hugh, the hedge-school master, describes Gaelic somewhat ironically as "a rich language . . . full of fantasy and hope and self-deception—a syntax opulent with tomorrows. It is our response to mud cabins and a diet of potatoes" (418), but then warns that

> words are signals, counters. They are not immortal. And it can happen . . . that a civilization can be imprisoned in a linguistic contour which no longer matches the landscape of . . . fact. . . . We must never cease renewing those images [embodied in language]; because once we do, we fossilize. (419, 445)

Yet the writers of this fourth stage have also been trying to avoid the Counter Revivalists' dead end by formulating, like Joyce, a Continental, or universalist, vision for Ireland through explorations of the personal. In his long poem "Station Island" (1985), for example, Seamus Heaney confronts his guilt at friends and relatives murdered in the Troubles, asking one ghost to "forgive" him for being inattentive to the nationalists' call and being chastised by a second because he withdrew into the ivory tower of art. Yet in the final section of the poem, he is visited by the ghost of Joyce, who lays to rest Heaney's anxieties about the language question and colonialism by announcing that "The English language" is not solely the province of the imperial agent. Instead, this ghost insists that he remain true to his own, individual concerns by using the English language and his "signatures" to write an eloquent speech for the nationalist cause (92–94). Like Heaney or Friel, the women writers from the fifth stage of postcoloniality have tried to demolish what they regard as oppressive Irish ideologies. Yet unlike their male contemporaries, they find themselves subject to what Marilyn Reizbaum calls "the phenomenon of 'double exclusion' suffered by women writing in marginalized cultures . . . where the struggle to assert a nationalist identity obscures or doubly marginalizes the assertion of gender" (Lawrence 165).[9] They feel constrained—in ways that Irish men cannot—by the enduring, Catholic-inspired dichotomous image of women as either madonnas or whores and by the political image of Ireland as an old crone, Cathleen ni Houlihan, who, in an act of reverse vampirism, is made young and beautiful by the blood sacrifice of male revolutionaries. In a gesture reminiscent of Jean Rhys' rewriting of Rochester in *Wide Sargasso Sea* or of Maxine Hong Kingston's redefinition of the Woman Warrior, Irish women writers have responded to their "double colonialism" by rewriting the male canon and articulating a highly personal, female vision. In *Country Girls Trilogy* (1960–4), for example, Edna O'Brien replaces Joyce's account of Stephen's development with that of two Irish girls. Growing up in Catholic Ireland, Kate and Baba lead more circumscribed lives than Stephen does. While he can weigh and reject different vocations, they can hope merely for a good marriage. While he can dream of artistic independence, they can dream only of love. Yet while he flees Ireland alone and friendless, Kate and Baba remain supportive of each other while living in London. Eavan Boland, in her poem "The Woman Turns Herself into a Fish" (1982), rewrites Yeats' "Song of the Wandering Aengus" from the fish-woman's perspective to expose how his romantic image deprives the woman of her identity: that is stripped of everything (Deane *Field Day* 3: 1396). Medbh McGuckian writes poetry that she describes as "mostly moody and menstrual in a way that a man's poetry never is" (McCracken 20). Although she admits that "the [Ulster] crisis informs my work, naturally," McGuckian claims that she cannot confront it in her poetry because "it is too complex"; instead, "I just suggest an attitude of compassion in what is part of a universal tragedy" (McCracken 21). Thus, in the poem "The Blue She Brings with Her," McGuckian expresses the private emotions of "a mother whose son was destroyed" (McCracken 21). Yet despite her disabling grief, this woman finds the strength to survive her son's senseless sacrifice because "Beauty lives . . . [because it bears] the mark of my fingers in the morning" (McCracken 30). Unlike Yeats' "terrible beauty," which paradoxically celebrates both the nationalists' self-sacrifice and the transcendence of physical struggle, this beauty escapes yet leaves a bruise as the tangible sign of the postcolonial realities that remain to be transcended.

As this account of Irish literature suggests, a literature does not cease to be postcolonial once a colony has attained its independence, any more than its politics, its economics, or its history does. The struggle against colonialism, neocolonialism and "double colonialism" is an ongoing one, and postcolonial writers remain engaged in efforts to create a beauty which shapes this struggle even as it escapes from these postcolonial realities which bruise them. And although the five stages of postcolonial writing detailed here should be considered neither rigid nor comprehensive—we will undoubtedly discern further stages as the struggle continues—they do enable us, in the meantime, to understand better the complexities of the postcolonial condition, which has manifested itself in so many different forms while unfortunately proving so enduring.

NOTES

1. Similarly, William Butler Yeats writes in his Preface to Lady Gregory's *Cuchulain of Muirthemne*, "We Irish should keep these [Celtic] personnages much in our hearts, for they lived in places where we ride and go marketing, and sometimes they have met one another on the hills that cast their shadows upon our doors at evening. If we will but tell these stories to our children the Land will begin again to be a Holy Land, as it was before men gave their hearts to Greece and Rome and Judea" (16).

2. Although Seamus Deane criticizes Synge for trying to give "the exhausted English language . . . a new vitality [by] its recourse to famous beauty-spots in the Irish language" (56), the Revivalists' enriching of English by using Gaelic words and linguistic patterns parallels that by such contemporary postcolonial writers as Sandra Cisneros, who by "incorporating the Spanish . . . create[s] new expressions in English. . . . All of a sudden something happens to English, . . . a new spice is added to the English language" (Jussawalla and Dasenbrock 289).

3. According to one of its members, AE (George Russell), the Literary Revival's purpose was "to create the Ireland in the heart" (qtd. in Cairns and Richards 70).

4. As Deane suggests, Arnold seems an "unlikely [grandparent] to the Irish Literary Revival. But the facts of the case seem to warrant this conclusion" (27); furthermore, "The immense cultural influence of Arnold's thought is pervasive enough to embrace Pearse" (66).

5. Arnold was so intent on assimilation that he dismissed all differences between the Irish and the English: "*Aliens in speech, in religion, in blood!* said Lord Lyndhurst; the philologists have set him right about the speech, the physiologists about the blood; and, perhaps, taking religion in the wide but true sense of our whole spiritual activity, those who have followed what I have been saying here will think that the Celt is not so wholly alien to us in religion" (134–5).

6. Deane claims that Hyde's *Love Songs*, among other works, "helped to consign Gaelic poetry to the bookshelf, transforming it into one of the curiosities of English literature" (34).

7. In a lecture given in Trieste in 1907, Joyce proclaimed somewhat grandiloquently, "I confess that I do not see what good it does to fulminate against the English tyranny while the Roman tyranny occupies the palace of the soul" (*Critical Writings* 173).

8. Ngugi's use of Gikuyu would be reminiscent of Hyde's or Pearse's revival of Gaelic

except that, because a larger proportion of Kenyans speak Gikuyu today than Irish spoke Gaelic at the turn of the century, Ngugi has not had to revive a nearly dead language.

9. A recent example of this "double exclusion" is provided by the three volume *Field Day Anthology of Irish Writing*, in which women writers are underrepresented; fortunately, the editors have corrected this error by commissioning an additional volume on women writers.

WORKS CITED

Allt, Peter, and Russell K. Alspach, eds. *The Variorum Edition of the Poems of W. B. Yeats.* New York: Macmillan, 1987.

Appiah, Kwame Anthony. *In My Father's House: Africa in the Philosophy of Culture.* New York: Oxford University Press, 1992.

Arnold, Matthew. *On the Study of Celtic Literature and on Translating Homer.* New York: Macmillan, 1883.

Ashcroft, Bill, G. Griffiths, and Helen Tiffin. *The Empire Writes Back: Theory and Practice in Post-Colonial Literatures.* London: Routledge, 1989.

Beckett, Samuel. *Company.* New York: Grove Press, 1980.

———. *Three Novels: Molloy, Malone Dies, The Unnamable.* Trans. Patrick Bowles and Samuel Beckett. New York: Grove Press, 1965.

———. *Waiting for Godot.* Trans. Samuel Beckett. New York: Grove Press, 1954.

Budgen, Frank. *James Joyce and the Making of Ulysses.* Bloomington: Indiana University Press, 1960.

Cairns, David, and Shaun Richards. *Writing Ireland: Colonialism, Nationalism and Culture.* Manchester: Manchester University Press, 1988.

Deane, Seamus. *Celtic Revivals: Essays in Modern Irish Literature, 1880–1980.* Winston-Salem, N.C.: Wake Forest University Press, 1987.

———, ed. *Field Day Anthology of Irish Writing*, 3 vols. Derry: Field Day, 1992.

Deane, Seamus, et al. *Ireland's Field Day.* Notre Dame, Ind.: University of Notre Dame Press, 1986.

Edgeworth, Maria. *Castle Rackrent.* New York: W. W. Norton, 1965.

Fanon, Frantz. *The Wretched of the Earth.* Trans. Constance Farrington. New York: Grove Press, 1963.

Foster, R. F. "Anglo-Irish Literature, Gaelic Nationalism and Irish Politics in the 1890s." In *Ireland after the Union.* Oxford: University Press, 1989. 61–82.

Friel, Brian. *Selected Plays.* Washington, D.C.: Catholic University of America Press, 1984.

Gregory, Lady Augusta. *Cuchulain of Muirthemne.* Gerrards Cross, England: Colin Smythe, 1973.

Heaney, Seamus. *Station Island.* New York: Farrar, Straus, Giroux, 1985.

Hyde, Douglas. *The Love Songs of Connacht.* Dublin: Dun Emer Press, 1904.

JanMohamed, Abdul R. *Manichean Aesthetics: The Politics of Literature in Colonial Africa.* Amherst: University of Massachusetts Press, 1983.

Joyce, James. *The Critical Writings.* Ed. Ellsworth Mason and Richard Ellmann. New York: Viking, 1959.

———. *Finnegans Wake.* New York: Viking, 1939.

———. *A Portrait of the Artist as a Young Man.* Harmondsworth, England: Penguin, 1976.

———. *Stephen Hero*, rev. ed. Ed. Theodore Spencer, John J. Slocum, and Herbert Cahoon. New York: New Directions, 1963.

Jussawalla, Feroza, and Reed Way Dasenbrock, eds. *Interviews with Writers of the Post-Colonial World.* Jackson: University Press of Mississippi, 1992.
Kavanagh, Patrick. *Collected Poems.* New York: Norton, 1973.
Lawrence, Karen R., ed. *Decolonizing Tradition: New Views of Twentieth-Century "British" Literary Canons.* Urbana: University of Illinois Press, 1992.
McCracken, Kathleen. "An Attitude of Compassion." *Irish Literary Supplement.* 9, no. 2 (Fall 1990): 20–21.
McGuckian, Medbh. *On Ballycastle Beach.* Winston-Salem, N.C.: Wake Forest University Press, 1988.
McHugh, Roger, and Maurice Harmon. *Short History of Anglo-Irish Literature from Its Origins to the Present Day.* Totowa, N.J.: Barnes and Noble, 1982.
O'Grady, Standish. *Selected Essays and Passages.* Dublin: Talbot Press.
Pearse, Patrick. *The Literary Writings.* Dublin: Mercier Press, 1979.
Shohat, Ella. "Notes on the 'Post-Colonial.'" *Social Text* 10 no. 2–3 (1992): 99–113.
Synge, John M. *The Complete Plays.* New York: Vintage, 1935.

Caribbean Writing in English: Intimations of a Historical Nightmare

P. S. Chauhan

Turn where you will in the territory of Caribbean literature, from George Lamming's *In the Castle of My Skin* through V. S. Naipaul's *The Middle Passage* to Derek Walcott's *Omeros*, you encounter reports of a historical nightmare, varying accounts of "the day after" the reign of a cruel colonial night. Nor is it patriarchal works alone that crackle with reports of a seared human landscape. Open Jean Rhys' *Wide Sargasso Sea*, thumb through the pages of Merle Hodge's *Crick Crack, Monkey*, or glide through Jamaica Kincaid's *Annie John*, the daughters' narratives about their motherlands/mothers' lands tell virtually similar tales—of the lives trapped in fields of desolation left behind by the departed colonizer. Stripped of their native histories and wrenched from their traditional homes, descendants of various peoples try in vain to eke out a parody of a sensible existence among institutions the Empire sloughed off.

Yet this is not how the life and the landscape of the Caribbean islands made their first appearance in European languages. The Caribbean world sprang into European letters with Christopher Columbus' report of 15 February 1493 about his discoveries to the monarchs of Spain, Ferdinand II and Isabella. The islands that he had taken possession of "for their Highnesses, done by proclamation and with the royal standard unfurled" (191), were, like the lands of a Utopia, "fertile to a limitless degree" (192). In the island he had named Española, among the trees of the temperate zone, the "marvelous pine groves . . . and fruits in great diversity," surprisingly enough, he found, too, that "the nightingale was singing" there (192). Europe had finally found a local name and a habitation for its romantic imagination, for there it met the perfect colonial hosts, too, who were "so guileless and so generous . . . that they refuse[d] nothing that they possess[ed]" (194). The French essayist Michel de Montaigne followed the famous Spanish report with "Des Cannibales," which, published as the thirtieth piece in *Essais*, fixed the image of the New World that was opening up for European exploration and its exploitation as a plentiful preserve that had "great store of fish and flesh, that ha[d] no resemblance to those of ours," where no person was "paralytic, blear-eyed, toothless, or crooked with age," and among whom "the very words that signify lying, treachery, dissimulation, avarice, envy, detraction, pardon, [were] never heard of," and whose entire ethics could be summed up in two articles: "resolution in war, and affection to their wives" (93–94). The denizens of this "brave new world" were not, in Montaigne's view, savages; rather, it were the Europeans who deserved to be called wild "whose natures we have changed by our artifice, and diverted from the common order" (93). After such a spirited endorsement the natives, poised at the brink of large-scale destruction by the aliens they had considered Heaven-sent, pass into a metaphor of uncorrupted tribes of Edenic origins. The widespread importation of slaves from Africa, an institution backed by European capital and goaded by a greed for profits, did not deter the European writers from dreaming of these islands as idyllic sites. Aphra Behn's novel *Oroonoko, or the Royal Slave*, for example, tells how Imoinda was forcibly separated from her fiancé, Oroonoko, and then transported in chains to Surinam, where by a twist of fate she is joined by her African prince. The tragic story of the love of Oroonoko and Imoinda re-inscribes the familiar medieval romance of *Tristan and Isolde*.

After being treated to the glowing European accounts of the life in the tropical islands, it is not without some shock that one encounters the "other" story, the confessions of the West Indian slaves, the first authentic voices from the region. *The History of Mary Prince, A West Indian Slave, Related by Herself*, for example, details how child slaves were often rendered "ragged and raw with licks. Licks—Licks" (7), or how women were stripped, tied upon a ladder and flogged till, mercifully for them, they passed out. The following account of the treatment meted out to an old slave, Daniel, who was lame in the hip, will make the horrors of the imaginary Purgatory feel light in comparison. Because Daniel could not, at times, keep up with the rest of the slaves, his master in Antigua would get him stretched out on the ground and "have him beaten with a rod of rough briar till his skin was quite red and raw." He would then order a bucket of salt "flung upon the raw flesh till the man writhed on the ground like a worm," screaming aloud with agony. His wounds, never healing, would often become "full of maggots, which increased his torments" (11). The terror inflicted upon generations of a race, whose descendants would later constitute the majority of the islands, was bound to determine the complex of the writing that would issue from the West Indies. When the repressed rage finally found words, it could hardly be too sweet or too amiable to European masters.

In sum, then, for centuries the tropical islands at the western edge of the Atlantic had been viewed by Europeans as the mythic magical islands, as the lost Atlantis. What Père Labat said of Granada ("to live there was to live in Paradise") seems to have been the burden of the musings of Chapman and Spenser, Montaigne and Shakespeare, about the life in the West Indian islands. Shielded by European security and lulled by their national achievements, the Western writers remained oblivious of the ruthless political rivalries, the brutal slave trade, and the blind exploitation that had been let loose into the Caribbean basin by the European colonizers. But the natives, who had tasted the whip and suffered inhuman indignities, remembered the degradation of their ancestors at the hands of planters and their overseers. The modern Caribbean discourse is, therefore, generated by a dialectical interaction between a pastoral nostalgia and a national nightmare. Much of its fiction, whether it be Jean Rhys' *Wide Sargasso Sea* or V. S. Naipaul's *The Mimic Men*, lies at the intersection of the twin tendencies. Sometimes, within the same work, as in George Lamming's *Of Age and Innocence*, one can discern a schizophrenic split between the love for the soil but hatred for its history. Derek Walcott's *Omeros*, dragging up the island history and dressing up the catch in Greek mythology, a poetic performance no less momentous than *Ulysses*, is still divided between the two poles of the Caribbean imagination. Naturally, the reader who seeks to cruise by the cavalcade of, say, the Caribbean novel is bound to come upon sudden heaves in the human landscape. In moving from the European fictions about the Caribbean to the native writers' reports about their lives and societies, or from the diaries of governors' wives to the confessions of slave women, one moves from comfortable suburban fantasies to discomfiting urban ghettos as it were, from a well-fenced order to spilling chaos. Lately, it is the latter that seems to have been sweeping through Caribbean literature.

What is widely recognized as Caribbean literature today is the product of the late twentieth century. "Few Negroes in the nineteenth century cultivated," as Kenneth Ramschand says, "the art of reading imaginative literature, and fewer attempted to write it" (31). Though Mary Prince's life story appeared before the abolition of slavery in the British colonies in 1834, and Mary Seacole's *Wonderful Adventures of Mrs. Seacole in Many Lands*, a vivid biography of Florence Nightingale's Jamaican colleague, appeared in 1857, the first piece of fiction by a West Indian writer, Thomas Henry MacDermot ("Tom Redcom"), understandably an Englishman, was published under the title *Becka's Buckra Baby* in 1903. It is roughly at the end of World War II, though, when the islands developed some sense of a common West Indian culture, that West Indian novels begin to tumble out in a quick succession. Part of the explanation for a spurt in literary creativity can be found in the seminal works of the West Indian intellectuals of the 1930s. They came to provide, besides an indigenous viewpoint, unifying frames that could hold the past history and island cultures in focus. If Léon Damas' *Pigments* and Aime Cesaire's *Cahier d'un pays Natal* invested the educated with the proud notion that Négritude was a distinct essence of a race, C.L.R. James' *The Black Jacobin: Toussaint L'Ouverture and the San Dominto Revolt* presented them with a mythical hero, who while championing the cause of African slaves could also feel at home with the contemporary European thought. James' work, which later on inspired *Capitalism and Slavery* by Eric Williams, provided a Marxist interpretation of the West Indian history, taking it out of a purely racial dimension and linking up the happenings of the last five hundred years in the Caribbean to a capitalist design unfolding over the globe and hurting the colored peoples of the world. Whatever the limitations, or the worth, of such socioeconomic explanations, they not merely rearranged the authors' perceptions but also set up the West Indian writers and thinkers on the world stage, most of whom had begun to move to Western metropolises with a new-found pride and confidence. From the position of a marginalized eaves-dropper, then, the West Indian writer came to occupy a privileged position in the intellectual dialogue going on in Western parlors. A stranger neither to the European languages nor to their idiom of thought, the West Indian novelist was ready to meet his audience abroad.

The main body of the West Indian novel in English consists of more than 250 works. The chief of them—productions, that is, of Lamming, Naipaul, Rhys, and Wilson Harris—justifiably recognized for their linguistic vitality as well as for the formal complexity, belong with the best work done in English since the generation of Lawrence, Joyce, and Virginia Woolf passed away. The second generation, which consists mainly of women writers from the Caribbean—Jean D'Costa, Rosa Guy, Merle Hodge, Jamaica Kincaid, and Paule Marshall, to name but a few—have sustained the quality established by the first generation of West Indian writers.

Understandably, the fictions of the authors from various islands and different races do not make up a seamless web. Besides the inevitable differences dictated by personal values, tones, and temperaments, there are others occasioned by the differing importance the authors attach to the signifier or the signified, to language or to mimetic reality. No less remarkable are the contrasts caused by the personal choices the authors make regarding the subject or the fictional form. If Wilson Harris is a mythicist, discovering primitive myths in aboriginal and modern existence alike, Naipaul is an analyst, by turns coldly rational and self-reflexively comic. If Jean Rhys' women characters continually haunt the island world, Jamaica Kincaid's protagonists are constantly straining to escape the borders of mothers' lands. Individual differences between works, marks of a mature community of artists, would under normal circumstances subvert any categorical or general remarks about the entire body of the West Indian fiction. But neither the West Indian communities nor their fictions developed under normal human political circumstances. Though separated by distances and distinguished by differing demographics, they were presided over by similar histories of cruelty and exploitation. Whatever the size of their economies, they were like wards of absentee landlords whose affairs were managed by self-serving overseers accountable to no local authorities in particular. "The men who ruled the country and made its laws," says Orlando Patterson in *The Sociology of Slavery* (1967), "were themselves the planters who were the masters of the slaves" (70). Personal lives, even human ties, of the people torn from their lands and communities across the oceans and thrust into an alien environment were subject to the will of an autocratic plantocracy. The common history of deprivations and inhuman treatment, of underdeveloped economy and exploited natural resources has tended to bend individual talents to similar meditations upon their past and the present. Despite individual differences, therefore, some patterns of emphases are clearly discernible in West Indian fiction.

Most of the male writers of the West Indies—Harris, Lamming, Naipaul, and Walcott, alike—intrigued by the contemporary desolation of island societies have, for example, turned to history for an explanation. And for them history means neither the glories of the past, nor a narrative of national achievements; it means, rather, a reconstruction of the factors that led Europeans to mount a large-scale plunder of a little-known corner of the world, and the decimation of its local population, which was to be replaced by imported mercenaries and slaves. Naipaul devotes nearly four hundred pages to demonstrate, in *The Loss of El Dorado*, how at first the Spaniards destroyed the native institutions and civilizations, ostensibly in the name of Christianity (but, in fact, out of greed), and then how the English, for the glory of the British arms, dispossessed the Spaniards and introduced slavery into the region. Watching with ironic, almost Olympian detachment, the narrator finds in the eminent family's misery a fitting end to the adventurism of the conquistador Antonio de Berrio, who broke upon the peace of Chibchas, roughly the modern Colombia, in 1580. At the end of the eighteenth century, people would point out a ragged shepherd boy, a descendant of the once mighty Gonzales Ximenes de Quesada, the brother-in-law of Berrio, of one who had dreamt of finding the mythical El Dorado. The progeny of the conquistadors who, in their quest for El Dorado, laid a continent to waste could not hold on even to ordinary existence. "On both sides of the Gulf [of Paria]," so ends the book with irony, "Spanish Empire, after three hundred years, had inheritors" (368). The inheritors were, of course, English; but they, in their own turn, would vanish from Trinidad at the liberation of the colony, uncovering in their wake the ultimate design of human history: the mighty of the world pass away, leaving behind those who will till the soil or tend to sheep. No different is the ending of George Lamming's *Natives of My Person*, an allegorical history of the people of Lime Stone (England), whose chief ambition is to "plant some portion of Lime Stone in the virgin territories of San Cristobal" (11), Lamming's imaginary West Indian island homonymous with Christopher Columbus' Spanish name, Cristobal Colon. The journey of the ship *Reconnaissance* ends in a crushing humiliation of the commander. Of course, the novel seeks to ferret out the various natives that dwell inside each desperado who, abandoning hearth and home, embarks upon a hazardous journey only because he must find "the mines and rivers [that will] yield the yellow fortune" (11). The novel is offered not as a psychological case history, but as an allegory of the political intrigues at home that issued in adventurous expeditions first to pick up slaves in New Guinea and then to clear, with their help, the land where they hoped to start a new colony across the Atlantic. Mixed and complex are the motives of the people who, in search of fortunes in strange and inhospitable lands, leave their homes and wives behind—some of them abandoned in asylums for good. If they by their own acts had deprived themselves of a chance for ordinary peace and happiness, destiny tricks them out of fame and fortune, leaving them wrecked or buried in unmarked graves. Such ironic endings of the fictional histories appease the West Indian writers with the notion of a natural justice from whose clutches no one remains safe for too long.

The consolations of history, thus, turn out to be especially satisfying to the dispossessed of the earth, for time, as Naipaul repeatedly reminds us—in *The Enigma of Arrival* as in *A Bend in the River*—humbles those who once humbled others. Some of the important novels of the West Indies powerfully rehearse the tale of the Ozymandiases of human history, offering wisdom, instead of propagating anger, about the trespassers of the world.

Wilson Harris and Derek Walcott, too, make raids upon history, but they do so for entirely different purposes. Like his painter-narrator Da Silva da Silva, Harris, through an act of memory, draws together scattered bits of the past to make them converge upon a picture of either Guyana and Brazil, or Peru. For Harris, no place is too humble, no act too small, to catch the echoes of perpetual human myths. Poseidon, the haunting figure of *The Secret Ladder*, who, wraith-like, emerges from his lair in the rain forest, is seen by many "as the black king of history whose sovereignty over [the] past was a fluid crown of possession and dispossession" (22). Beauty and greatness did not happen "once upon a time": they happen everyday; the passion of an Othello may be concealed in the gestures of a surveyor in the backwoods of Guyana. The mythical epiphany of Harris' fiction redeems the sordidness of the life of the Caribbean folk. Similarly, by constantly uncovering parallels between the life in the Aegean isles and that in the Caribbean islands, Walcott's poetry not only obliges the reader to take another look at the existence of, say, ordinary fishermen but also enhances the value of the life lived in the Caribbean. That which was condemned as pathetic by the departing masters now becomes transformed as something majestic. Walcott, like Synge, confers dignity upon what had for long been considered wretched. There is nothing for pity here in the island of St. Lucia. The mantle of classical history now dignifies what might have passed without notice.

It is a fair guess to say that Lamming and Naipaul, Harris and Walcott, like the nineteenth-century founders of the American literature, Irving and Cooper, Hawthorne and Melville, have sought either to create new myths for their respective national literatures or to transplant older myths to their native shores, transforming, thereby, a neglected corner of the world into a prized colony of intellectual performance. Such a conception alone can explain the universal prestige of the West Indian writing in the contemporary world of letters.

The next generation of West Indian authors, most of them women, advances Caribbean literature in a new direction. From the political programs of Claude McKay and Lamming, the attention now shifts to personal relations; from the national stage to home, the scene of family battles. Of course, the struggle of female narrators to define themselves by revolting against their mothers, as Jamaica Kincaid's protagonists do, can be explained in terms of feminist psychology. To do that, however, is to set up a binary opposition between male and female discourses. Those refusing to be caught among stereotypes may well discover that the shadow of dying colonial politics weighs as heavily in the domestic scenes inscribed by the Caribbean women writers as it does in other political arenas. The political past of the island history, seldom implicated in the principal subject of the protagonist's commentaries of meditations, is nevertheless very present in women's fiction. At the head of the long line of Caribbean women writers of the twentieth century stands Jean Rhys, whose work bridges the division between the world of the colonial Dominica and the imperial England, between Coulibri and the Boulevard du Montparnasse. But whether it is the pastoral world of Coulibri or the metropolitan scenes of London or Paris, the tale that unfolds across the Atlantic is always about the desolate life of a woman used and abused, a telling symbol, if you would, of the Caribbean isles exploited and abandoned by the European master.

Sasha, the narrator of Rhys' *Good Morning, Midnight*, speaks for most of the women characters who will, decades later, troop through the pages of Merle Hodge, Jamaica Kincaid, and Rosa Guy. Sitting in a tabac near the Panthéon, and musing over a glass of Pernod, Sasha, reviewing her past, says: "Every word I say has chains round its ankles; every thought I think is weighted with heavy weights. Since I was born, hasn't every word I've said, every thought I have thought, everything I've done, been tied up, weighted, chained?" (106). Such has been the burden of the stories that Caribbean women writers tell of the lives of the daughters of the islands, of an existence full of drudgery and slavery to local customs and traditions. In voicing their heroines' disgust with the inherited way of life, the women writers imply a judgment, too, upon the historical past that has left in the backwaters of the world the twisted lives of countless sisters.

In Merle Hodge's *Crick Crack, Monkey*, Cyntie, the orphaned daughter, is happily installed with her country aunt, Tantie, whose "company was loud and hilarious and the intermittent squawk and flurry of mirth made [one] think of the fowl-run when something fell into the midst of the fat hens" (4). To be civilized, she is taken away by Aunt Beatrice, who can boast of Anglicized tastes besides her wealth. At her new home, Cyntie continues to be treated with contempt by her cousins, till they hear that Cyntie's father, who had migrated to England seven years ago, has sent her an air ticket to join him in London. Between the arrival of the news and her actual departure, "my standing," she says, "was like that of a pariah who has suddenly inherited a title" (109). The remotest connection with England, the mother country, confers dignity in the eyes of the colonial subjects. But the latter had never felt the glory of England on their own pulses; they had just dreamt about it. Cyntie, who has never been away from the tropical island, considers the imagined world of England to be superior to her own: Books would transport her into "the familiar solidity of chimneys and apple trees," where, she imagines, "real Girls and Boys . . . went a-sleighing and built snowmen, ate potatoes, not rice," and what is more, "went about in socks and shoes from morning until night" (61). The colonial's servitude comes in for various kinds of digs here. Sir, the inimitable teacher who had some training in England, drills his pupils in the ways of English schoolboys: "One afternoon a week [they] spent getting up and sitting down, getting up and sitting down," practicing the Art of Noiselessly Rising from the seats. And they had to go through the meaningless drill for Sir had read or imagined that this is how "the little choir-boys of Westminster Abbey" were "trained to do this" (55–56). So by leaving aunt Beatrice and the bullying Sir behind, Cyntie takes leave of the island life overburdened with English limitations. Better the harsh reality of the British scene than the island fakery of its imagined charms. For a reader familiar with the reception of the West Indian immigrant in England, the ultimate irony of the novel may lie in Cyntie's belief that by escaping her island world she would escape perversity and cruelty. She has little idea of what she is truly moving toward.

Nor is it the political underpinning alone that links Caribbean women's fiction with their male counterparts'. The West Indian novelists, irrespective of gender, tend to write of the folk life and its practices. The shapes of their plots share similar features, too. Like the heroes of Lamming and Naipaul, the heroines of Rhys, and Hodge, and Kincaid bring their life stories to a closure by embarking upon a journey that takes them away from their island homes. Journeys, in fact, crisscross the varying fabric of the West Indian fiction. The journey motif, it can be said, signifies the instability of existence in the West Indies, whose humanity, haunted by dreams of a better future, must drift toward Europe, the old colonizer, or toward North America, the new equalizer. The arrivals and the departures, with which the lives of the characters of the West Indian novel are punctuated, indicate an inescapable desire to flee not only an oppressive past or present but also an oppressing psyche, the need to break out of a choking self that is urgent in most protagonists. The compulsive obsession that frantically drives innumerable people away from their homes and the world of their affections is the hallmark of the colonial psyche, a feature not easily forgotten by the Caribbean writer. At the eve of her departure for England, Kincaid's Annie John confesses to herself that "the whole world into which I was born had become an unbearable burden and I wished I could reduce it to some small thing that I could hold underwater until it died" (128).

The Caribbean characters' loathing for their own world derives, at least partially, from their recognition that while the distant world happens to be excellent, their own have been utterly demeaning. In their self-consuming hatred, one can, therefore, read the history of colonial oppression. One can note, too, that what had been outbound violence in the earlier fiction has, in the post-colonial writing, become an inner conflict. The shift clearly marks a new stage in the development of the West Indian novel, which is still in the making.

WORKS CITED

Behn, Aphra. *Oroonoko: Or the Royal Slave.* New York: W. W. Norton, 1973.

Columbus, Christopher. *The Journal of Christopher Columbus.* Trans. Cecil Jane. New York: Clarkson N. Potter, 1960.

de Montaigne, Michel E. *The Essays,* I. Trans. Charles Coton. *Great Books of the Western World,* vol. XXV. Ed. Robert Maynard Hutchins. Chicago: Encyclopaedia Britannica, 1978.

Harris, Wilson. *The Secret Ladder.* London: Faber and Faber, 1963.

Hodge, Merle. *Crick Crack, Monkey*. Oxford: Heinemann, 1970.
Kincaid, Jamaica. *Annie John*. New York: Plume, 1985.
Lamming, John. *In the Castle of My Skin*. New York: Schocken Books, 1983.
———. *Natives of My Person*. Ann Arbor: The University of Michigan Press, 1972.
Naipaul, V. S. *The Loss of El Dorado: A History*. Harmondsworth, England: Penguin Books, 1969.
———. *The Middle Passage*. New York: Vintage Books, 1962.
Patterson, Orlando. *The Sociology of Slavery*. London: MacGibbon & Kee, 1967.
Prince, Mary. "The History of Mary Prince." In *Six Women's Slave Narratives*. Oxford: Oxford University Press, 1988.
Ramchand, Kenneth. *The West Indian Novel and Its Background*. London: Faber and Faber, 1970.
Rhys, Jean. *Good Morning Midnight*. New York: W. W. Norton, 1986.
———. *Wide Sargasso Sea*. New York: W. W. Norton, 1982.
Walcott, Derek. *Omeros*. New York: Farrar Strauss Giroux, 1990.

South African Writing in English

John C. Hawley

As commentators such as Lewis Nkosi and Malvern van Wyk Smith have noted, even though writers from South Africa occasionally engage in an exploration of traditional African values (as has preoccupied the writers of many other countries), their truly characteristic impetus is to focus readers' attention on the conflict between white masters and black servitors. As Bernth Lindfors and Reingard Nethersole have shown, South African writers have had a national obsession to describe in committed detail the practical implications of apartheid, and consequently have produced a literature that is unabashedly didactic. Those who choose to write "metapolitical" fiction are generally attacked as collaborators in injustice.

This, of course, had not always been the case, and the literature of South Africa can be divided roughly into five periods: the early frontier writing and that of the late nineteenth and early twentieth century, the period following the Nationalist election victory in 1948, that following the explosive response to the Sharpeville massacre in 1960, the new consciousness following the Soweto school rising of 1976 and the death of Steve Biko in detention in 1977, and the present transitional period away from apartheid.

In his description of the country as a "violent arcadia," poet Sydney Clouts (1926–82) nicely encapsulates an early, but still enduring, vision of a postlapsarian Eden that would not easily bend to the newcomers' wills.[1] While many implicitly yearned for the European comforts they had, it was hoped, only temporarily left behind, others dug in for the long haul. Among this latter group, the earliest English writers identified the Boers, rather than the indigenous population, as their real opposition. It is true that one school of thought, led by J. A. Froude, saw the Boers as courageous warriors facing overwhelming odds; the opposing view that gradually gained dominance in the 1820s, however, portrayed them as brutish interlopers. By contrast to these Dutch immigrants, the Xhosa impressed writers like Sir John Barrow (1764–1848) as regal; others eventually extended this favorable description to the Zulus, as well. In both cases, however, these noble savages were also described as being in need of England's paternalistic governance, and midnineteenth century literature, especially in the "mother" country, elaborated this mixed message.

In format, the literature of this early period can be classified in two categories. The first is a type of rough pastoral fantasy, culminating in the works of writers like Rider Haggard (1856–1925) and John Buchan (1875–1940), who tended to stress the exotic nature of the wilderness; this is a style now echoed to some extent in Laurens van der Post (b. 1906). The second is a realistic settler narrative, culminating in the work of Olive Schreiner (1855–1920), for whose characters personal survival, both spiritual and physical, becomes an issue. In this respect, her approach has come to dominate white writing in South Africa.

In the latter half of the nineteenth century and the beginning of the twentieth, as the portrayal of blacks in much South African literature became either fearful and heavily negative or sentimentalized, portrayal of the Boers by the English was frequently more positive. In 1924, with the publication of *God's Stepchildren*, Sarah Gertrude Millin (1889–1968) offered the classic embodiment of a related obsession of white writers: miscegenation, a word that appeared first in 1864. This was followed in 1926 by William Plomer's (1903–73) slightly more nuanced *Turbott Wolfe*. In general, sexual relations between races are portrayed in white South African literature as a threat to the master's identity; the threat intensifies in the literature as blacks become socio-politically secure and increasingly vocal. Before then, such relations are seen as a sexual reflection of the subjugation of the land itself, and an implied symbol for the settler's mission: typical of much colonial discourse, the colonized land is seen as feminine. "Mixing" with those who appear to be taking on the trappings of some semblance of equality, however, leads in the literature to malaise and soul searching, a fearful occasion for the blurring of distinctions between master and slave. In proportion to the white population, the community of mixed racial origin in South Africa is uniquely large throughout the continent—about 3.2 million (Boyd 97).

In 1883, Schreiner published *The Story of an African Farm*, an antiromantic and proto-feminist settler novel that introduced many of the thematic ambiguities that have become central in subsequent colonialist discourse in South Africa. She set the tone for many white writers, including Alan Paton (1903–88) and Nadine Gordimer (b. 1923), in her liberal humanism and optimistic endorsement of human dignity and individual effort. As will be seen, a different approach was gradually taken by emerging black writers. Schreiner also recognized that the Boer Wars (1880–81, 1899–1902), described principally by residents of England, would transform South Africa into an urban, capitalist country in which the veld, a pastoral retreat for many and a testing ground for others, would recede as a locus for serious fiction. Overtaking the interest in both Buchan's entertaining romances and the popular settler novels, the locus now shifts away from the veld, first to stories dealing with the mines, and then to those focusing on the troubles of the cities; before long, the typical white South African story turns inward, painting interior landscapes of psychological turmoil, guilt, and split consciousnesses. The stories of Herman Charles Bosman (1905–51) offer early examples of these growing doubts.

Early poetry reached a high mark with Roy Campbell (1901–57), who founded the periodical *Voorslag* with William Plomer in 1926. He did much of his subsequent writing outside South Africa, but his principal works dealing with this country helped refashion writers' understanding of the myths of appropriation and renunciation that had set the terms for literary creation. This is especially true of *The Flaming Terrapin* (1924), a creation epic, and *Adamastor* (1930), a title that refers to Camoens' myth and the Cape itself as a symbol of the land, defiant yet conquered. Francis Carey Slater (1876–1958) played an important role in anthologizing indigenous literature and in popularizing aspects of Xhosa oral culture.

Unusual among early black writers,[2] Solomon T. Plaatje (1875–1932) made a strong appeal for the franchise in *Native Life in South Africa* (1916), and he was supported by John Tengo Jabavu (1859–1921), who began *Imvo Zabantsundu* in 1884, and by the brothers R.R.R. and H.I.E. Dhlomo. With Hertzog's "Native Acts" of 1936 the endemic discrimination against blacks was specified and legitimated in what amounted to an extended run-up to the elections of 1948. Such legislation and that which followed responded to the escalating sense of black pride, which was advanced by their participation in the Second World War. The publication of Peter Abrahams' *Mine Boy* in 1946, the first novel by a black since 1930, no doubt called international attention to the situation of blacks in South Africa, but also outraged elements within white society. The imposition of apartheid demanded a response from its victims, and resulted in a literature of anger and resistance. The impact on white writers was significant, as well; as van Wyk Smith notes, their literature "has increasingly become a literature of dread, in contrast to a black discourse of endurance and challenge" (67). This can be seen in Alan Paton's *Cry, the Beloved Country* (1948), which embodied the liberal realism, based unabashedly upon the Sermon on the Mount, that many sympathetic whites hoped might yet ameliorate an untenable and increasingly dichotomized situation. In *Too Late the Phalarope* (1953), centering around an act of interracial sexual relations, Paton examines the Boer (Afrikaner) mentality, again from an English point of view, and finds it to be rigid and self-righteous. In the short stories of Sheila Roberts, Peter Wilhelm, and Barney Simon, van Wyk Smith sees "records of internal exile," documents of the dilemma facing liberal white South Africans with "impoverished sensibilities living out of touch with a vibrant and fecund world around them" (96).

Nadine Gordimer's work, which culminates in her acceptance of the Nobel Prize in 1991, charts an experience shared by many like-minded white writers in South Africa: the gradual movement away from the hope, expressed in Paton's fiction, that well-intentioned whites, working alongside patient blacks, could improve the country's internal politics while still maintaining an imperialistic capitalist economy and a hierarchical structure. Humanist individualism, once the mainstay of such writers, eventually wears thin; in its place has come a silent despair, a retreat to fantasy or fiction that is not tied to South African concerns, or a nod to black writers to propose alternatives. The development can be seen from *The Lying Days* (1953), a mining story from the point of view of a woman gradually coming to an awareness of her disagreement with the ways of the world, to *Burger's Daughter* (1979), whose protagonist is forced to a similar self-exploration but now in a world of greater moral ambiguity, a world in which she worries that "no one knows where the end of suffering will begin" (356). In *A Sport of Nature* (1987) the solution seems to be to start over; in fact, in much of her fiction there is a fascination with time and human memory, notable, for example, in *The Late Bourgeois World* (1966). Most of Gordimer's fiction circles around questions of the resolution of guilt, the possibilities for recompense, and the consequences of past actions.

The 1950s saw a period of prolific output among black writers, principally in protest to the policies of the recently elected Afrikaner Nationalist party, yet not tied to a particular ideology of its own (Shava 29). But this was also a time of false hopes: a multiracial opposition seemed to suggest that a multiracial society was soon to be realized, but in retrospect this was merely a dream of the disenfranchised majority and a few liberal whites. While colonial rule was gradually coming to an end throughout much of Africa during this decade, in South Africa most whites were tightening their grip. Except in small "native reserves" blacks could not own land and were thereby rendered economically dependent upon whites. Each main tribal group was provided with a "homeland" (a "Bantustan"), and they were encouraged by the white government to declare their independence. Consequently, within South Africa, where they worked, they could thereby be considered "foreign natives" and/or "immigrants" who had no political rights outside the homeland. This policy continued for decades, and by 1982 Bophuthatswana, Ciskei, Transkei, and Venda had declared this self-defeating independence (Boyd 98). Black writers sought to reverse this trend by alerting whites to their frustration, and by raising the consciousness of other blacks.

Protest gained a focus in 1953 in the government's bulldozing of the township of Sophiatown, a shanty-town with a unique character but with unsanitary conditions—that also happened to border white suburbs. For black writers the strong-arm tactics of the government came to symbolize the history of white domination in South Africa, the history of appropriation by the Europeans of the rights and property of the indigenous. Can Themba (1924–68), for example, writes, "I am itchingly nagged by the thought that slum-clearance should have nothing to do with the theft of freehold rights" (103).

Just as earlier white writers showed a preoccupation with the land of South Africa, fascinated by the notion of frontier, mythologizing on the Adamastor of the Cape, black and mixed-race ("coloured") writers, too, speak of "the tyranny of place," in the words of Es'kia Mphahlele (formerly Ezekiel, b. 1919). Increasingly, however, these black writers focused their attention not on the wilderness of the veld but on that of the city, in juxtaposition to the unique characteristics of their own township. Thus, the destruction of Sophiatown assumed great importance. In his stark autobiography, *Blame Me On History* (1963), Bloke Modisane emphasizes the township's charms, and Modikwe Dikobe, in his novel *The Marabi Dance* (1973), recreates the area by describing its removal. The townships, as Nadine Gordimer has noted, began as reservations inflicted upon blacks: "once more accurately called 'locations,' since they are sites chosen by whites to dump blacks outside the limits, after work, just as they choose sites well out of the way for the city trash heap" (English 141). Nonetheless, in an attempt to resist Verwoerdian attempts to "retribalize" urban blacks, a great deal of literature is devoted to what might be described as a sentimentalizing of the townships: they're not much, but they're ours. In poetry, Lionel Abrahams (b. 1928) brings this spirit of place to Johannesburg in his volumes *Thresholds of Tolerance* (1975), *Journal of a New Man* (1984), and *The Writer in the Sand* (1988).

Exile and expatriation have been significant features of South African writing. Most of the major figures of the 1920s and 1930s left the country (Pauline Smith, Campbell, Plomer, Van der Post). After the Second World War a great many others left, including Dan Jacobsen, Sydney Clouts, Christopher Hope, and Roy Macnab. This was often in protest to the racist environment and the oppressive atmosphere that discouraged criticism or creative work. Most significant, of course, has been the exile of an entire generation of black writers: Peter Abrahams, Dennis Brutus, Lewis Nkosi, Bloke Modisane, Alfred Hutchinson, Can Themba, Alex La Guma, Arthur Nortje, Daniel and Mazizi Kunene, Mongane Wally Serote, Bessie Head, and Njabulo Ndebele, and others. Dennis Brutus (b. 1924), in *Sirens, Knuckles, Boots* (1963) and *Thoughts Abroad* (1970), has been among those who argue that the most honest South African literature must be that of the exile, written, as it is, away from the compromises that have been necessary for publication within the country. The works of many of the exiles, including Todd Matshikiza, Mphahlele, Nkosi, Modisane, and Themba, were banned in their own country. Some have been criticized, however, for writing "as if life in South Africa froze with the trauma of Sharpeville." Referring to Alex La Guma (1925–85), Nadine Gordimer complains that "he cannot from abroad quite make the projection, at the deeper level, into a black political milieu that has changed so much since he left" (English 144).

Among this exiled group, autobiography is often the chosen genre for combining a sometimes eerie blend of elegiac remembrance of township life, family relations, urban violence, and resistance. Peter Abrahams' *Tell Freedom* (1954), Mphahlele's *Down Second Avenue* (1959) and its novelistic continuation *The Wanderers* (1971), Todd Matshikiza's *Chocolates For My Wife* (1961), and Bloke Modisane's *Blame Me On History* (1963) are among them. But a good number of writers did not fare well in exile—Nat Nakasa committing suicide, Can Themba drinking himself to death, Arthur Nortje dying of a drug overdose. Es'kia Mphahlele has written eloquently on the anguish of exile and of the choice to return to his native land (Chirundu ix–x), and the ambiguities of living "in-between" have been a significant issue among the writers (see Manganyi and Kunene).

After the Sharpeville Emergency of 1960, black protest appeared in such novels as Peter Abrahams' *A Night of Their Own* (1965), a depiction of the role of the Indian community in the underground resistance movement; Enver Carim also writes about the Indian community, in *Golden City* (1968), and in *A Dream Deferred* (1973) he explores the motives of a group of revolutionaries. Alex La Guma's *In the Fog of the Season's End* (1972) is the story of a strike in which the dangerous choice of opposition is shown to be the only avenue opening on progress. La Guma is still considered by many to be South Africa's best short story writer, evidenced in such collections as *A Walk in the Night* (1967). In the eyes of some, his principal competition seems to be Richard Rive (1931–89) in *African Songs* (1963). His *Emergency* (1964) is a gripping account of the three days between the Sharpeville shooting and the declaration of the first State of Emergency. Described as the finest bildungsroman in South African literature, it details its protagonist's developing consciousness and gradual commitment to direct political action. Nadine Gordimer's *Something Out There* (1984) offers a liberal white view of militancy.

Poetry was increasingly used by black writers as a vehicle to avoid censorship on such questions. Oswald Mtshali, Mongane Serote, Njabulo Ndebele, Mandlenkosi Langa, and Mafika Gwala are among these poets. James Matthews (b. 1929), in his verse and short stories, is looked upon by many of those mentioned as the trailblazer into the wilderness of literary resistance. Critics like Van Wyk Smith point to Matthews as typifying a pattern of ideological development in many black writers that varies from that of most white liberals: a movement from personal alienation, frequently to imprisonment, and then to the adoption of a communal voice (100–101). In the 1970s, influenced by the Black Consciousness movement in the United States, Matthews and others, like Don Mattera, angrily assert racial pride in a much more direct manner.

The 1970s also saw the advent of radical theater, something quite new on the scene. In the 1960s they were principally escapist musicals; the political content, in general, is subordinated to the demand for entertainment and the making of money. The most famous of these is *King Kong*, dealing with life in a shanty town. Others, however, though acted by blacks, were white-produced and far from innocent entertainment. *Kwa Zulu* and *Ipi Tombi*, for example, were used to confirm the stereotypes of unthinking whites. In the words of Piniel Shava, "*Ipi Tombi*'s stress on music and dance, its glossing over the oppression of blacks and its portrayal of bantustans as 'hospitable' landscapes to which blacks can conveniently return and resume their 'simple, rustic life,' obscure the politico-economic realities of black people" (128). In the 1970s, however, Athol Fugard (b. 1932) produced his most explicitly political plays: *Boesman and Lena* (1969), *Sizwe Bansi Is Dead* (1972), *The Island* (1973), *Statements after an Arrest under the Immorality Act* (1974), and then in 1982 with *"Master Harold" and the Boys.* He did this with the Serpent Players who, along with Phoenix Players and Workshop '71, used both black and white actors and were known as "town theatre" because they took place in town rather than in the black townships. Robert Mshengu Kavanagh describes the methodology of Workshop '71: "Its plays deal with the differences of its members and are performed before audiences whose responses are often conditioned by those differences" (66). An example of this approach is Credo Mutwa's *uNosilimela* [*sic*] (1973), a reassertion of black culture.

Black "alternative theatre" in the townships is represented each year at the Grahamstown Festival, and a small sampling of it has been published, notably Robert Mshengu Kavanagh's *South African People's Plays* (1981), but many of them were not scripted or written down. Some of the work of Gibson Kente (*Too Late*, for example), Mthuli Shezi (*Shanti*) and Zakes Mda is now available, and, in the view of Shava, "the radicalism of this theatre goes beyond that of Fugard in the sense that the theatre not only registers protest but also advocates change" (136). Noting the didactic nature of much of this drama, Shava concludes that it prepared "like the poetry of Black Consciousness, the theatre prepared the schoolchildren and workers for the uprising" (143). Since the activist 1970s, workshop collaborations like *Woza Albert* (1983) have become popular. *Sarafina*, a successful musical on Broadway, has since been made into a film.

There continue to be autobiographies, such as D. M. Zwelonke's *Robben Island* (1973), Molefe Pheto's *And Night Fell* (1983), Mark Mathabane's *Kaffir Boy* (1987), and Don Mattera's *Memory Is the Weapon* (1987), but their reminiscences over the townships have been considerably muted and replaced by a more urgent black consciousness. It might be said that the Soweto uprising of 1976 prompted a new direction in black writing, or a new audience. Now there was less attention paid to alerting the world, especially the world of whites, to the evils of apartheid; instead, black writers turned their attention to black readers and sought to raise their involvement in a growing resistance to the system. To a great extent, poetry became the preferred genre for this era. Leading the pack were Mbuyiseni Oswald Mtshali, whose *Sounds of a Cowhide Drum* appeared in 1971, and Mongane Wally Serote, with *Yakhal'inkomo* in 1972. Both focused on Johannesburg rather than rural parts of the nation, both showed the growing black pride, and both sought to extend their national consciousness to a sense of the African continent, as well. Later in the decade Mafika Pascal Gwala published *Jol'iinkomo* (1977), and Sipho Sepamla wrote both satire, in *Hurry Up to It!* (1975), and embittered frustration in *Children of the Earth* (1983). The death of Steve Biko in 1976, though, threw many of these writers into the dilemma of wondering whether silence might not be a more eloquent response in the face of such powerful inhumanity. In *Forced Landing* (1980), Mothobi Mutloatse offered a militant manifesto against Western forms of writing. In Ingoapele Madingoane's *Africa My Beginning* in 1979, however, we also begin to hear the new voice of poets-in-performance, something like political street theater that educates and inspires its audience. Again, the principal difference in the post-Soweto writing is that it now seeks not to win over the ruling whites by its confessional mode of personal suffering; it seeks, instead, to build a constituency among fellow sufferers, who can together bring about change.

The new sense of mission is best expressed in the writings found in *Staffrider*, the journal founded in 1978, which seemed, in some sense, to catch the contemporary spirit in the way that *Drum*, founded in 1951, had in an earlier era. *Drum* provided a home for an impressive array of black writers, and Nat Nakasa's *Classic*, founded in 1963, printed a great deal of their best work. Can Themba was associated with this group, as were Casey Motsisi, Modisane, Matshikiza, Mphahlele, and Bessie Head (1937–86).

Head's writing career was carried on almost entirely in Botswana, where she sought to find a sense of rootedness, in both space and time. *When Rain Clouds Gather* (1969) is her autobiographical novel, and *Maru* (1971) raises the question of racial prejudice to a universal plane of isolation by portraying intolerance between tribes. In her principal novel, *A Question of Power* (1974), which is also autobiographical, she places herself firmly in the tradition of the South African miscegenation novel; in doing so, however, she twists the genre into a study of schizophrenia and implied rejection of such a system's definition of sanity. Her collection of short stories, *The Collector of Treasures* (1977), significantly introduces the question of women's rights and their sense of double rejection by the world around them (Harlow 134–36).

Certainly several whites have shared intimately in the effects of opposing the oppressive regime. Breyten Breytenbach (b. 1939) has been recognized as the leading Afrikaner poet of his generation and became an expatriate in 1959. In Europe he was active in the anti-apartheid movement and, upon returning to South Africa in 1975, he was arrested and served seven years in prison for "terrorism." He himself recognizes the ironic position of such a writer, in his novel *The True Confessions of an Albino Terrorist* (1983). His prison experience gave him a clear view of the maintenance of the apartheid system even there: "Even the condemned man's last meal is subject to apartheid. Before being hanged, the white prisoner gets a whole roast chicken. The black prisoner gets a half a chicken. . . . It's like a kind of reaffirmation of apartheid in the final moment before the gallows" (24). His *Memory of Snow and of Dust* (1989) is a sophisticated and gripping account of an unjust imprisonment and employs poetry, drama, and letters in the course of its narration.

J. M. Coetzee (b. 1940) deals with myths of appropriation and dispossession in most of his fiction, frequently circling around a consciousness that has been warped by the demands of imposing an unjust social structure on others. He most resembles Kafka in his enclosed, paranoid worlds. Like Breytenbach, he reflects on the sense of being an interloper when he addresses issues more personally central to black South Africans, as in *White Writing* (1988). Speaking of himself in the third person, he elsewhere reflects on his condition as something other than narrowly South African: "At the age of twenty-one he departs South Africa, very much in the spirit of shaking the dust of the country from his feet. . . . Does he grow homesick for South Africa? Though he feels at home neither in Britain nor in the United States, he is not homesick, nor even particularly unhappy. He merely feels alien" (Interview 393).

André Brink (b. 1935) is another Afrikaner, who has won the most important South African literary prize (the CNA Award) three times and whose novels have been shortlisted for the Booker Prize twice. He has also won several other international awards, and now teaches Afrikaans and literary theory at the University of Cape Town. He has been compared to Camus in his existentialist description of the good man as one who does not align himself with the world's oppressors. His nine novels are highly accomplished narrative experiments and his latest, *An Act of Terror* (1991), has prompted some to compare him to García Márquez as embodying his entire culture.

Somewhat unique on the scene is Christopher Hope (c. 1944), who writes very funny satire. He left the country in 1974 and is ignored by some as being flippant in the face of intransigent problems. Nonetheless, novels like *A Separate Development* (1980) provide a welcome alternative voice. Following in this tradition is Damon Galgut (b. 1963), who writes novels, drama, and short stories. *The Beautiful Screaming of Pigs* (1991) takes the South African novel in new directions in the area of gender questions. Poet Mike Nicol's recent novels, *The Powers That Be* (1989) and *This Day and Age* (1992), offer another promising voice in fiction.

The acceleration of political change in South Africa in recent years will clearly have a great impact on the literature,[3] but it remains to be seen what "voice" these changes will take. It is premature to predict that the "grammar" of the nation's writing, its preoccupation with race distinctions, will be transformed overnight. In this context, however, one might suppose that black writers, as they are increasingly freed from the immediacy of political goals, may turn with more relish to the sort of fiction currently being written by whites—more allegorical, less realistic, and postmodern in its experimentation. This has always been a tricky political question in South Africa. As Thomas Banks has noted, "the term 'African,' when applied to the novel and other literary genres, does not ordinarily include the Arab states of the North or the peoples of European descent who may have settled in Africa. It refers to the black, indigenous population in the southern two-thirds of the continent" (2033). But such a policy would exclude literature that is central to South Africa's national identity and struggle.

NOTES

1. In 1652 the Dutch established their first colony at Cape Town; the British annexed the Cape of Good Hope in 1814. There are now about 38 million inhabitants of the country, and about 13 percent are white. Of that 13 percent, three-fifths are of Dutch origin (Afrikaners), and the other two-fifths are of British descent. There are also about 1 million Indians (Boyd 97). Early immigrants from Europe, like those in other areas of nineteenth-century empires, set about the task of appropriating their new land to the consciousness and mythology they had brought with them.

2. Although the African National Congress (ANC) was founded in 1912 and gave evidence of a growing black political consciousness, early black writing, sponsored for the most part by mission schools and training colleges, was rather tame. Some of the writing was altered by publishers and made to conform to the polite standard of white expectations.

3. In 1961 South Africa became a republic and withdrew from the British Commonwealth; during this decade Britain gave independence to Swaziland, Botswana, and Le-

sotho. International isolation became increasingly unavoidable between 1975 and 1980, as Portugal and white-ruled Southern Rhodesia no longer offered a buffer zone for South Africa's commerce and racial policies. In 1983 a new constitution guaranteed that real power would remain in the hands of the whites, but also provided for separate parliamentary chambers to be elected by the Indian and Coloured communities. But both communities supported blacks, who were still to be unrepresented, by refusing to vote. In reaction to the general unrest, the government called a nationwide State of Emergency in 1986. In the same year, the United States imposed economic sanctions against the nation. In 1989 Frederik de Klerk was elected president and significant changes were set swiftly in motion. In the next year he lifted the State of Emergency and released from detention Nelson Mandela, Walter Sisulu and other leaders of the now-legal African National Congress (ANC) (outlawed in 1961). Opposition between the ANC and Mangosuthu Buthelezi's Inkatha party (ISO) brought before the eyes of the world the serious rivalries among black factions within the country. Nelson Mandela was released from prison in February 1990. The black citizens of South Africa were granted franchise in 1994 and Mandela was elected President. Mandela and de Klerk were jointly awarded the Nobel Peace Prize in 1994.

WORKS CITED

Banks, Thomas. "African Long Fiction." In *Critical Survey of Long Fiction*, vol. 5. Ed. Magill. Englewood Cliffs, N.J.: Salem Press, 1984: 2033–58.

Boyd, Andrew. *An Atlas of World Affairs*. London: Routledge, 1991.

Breytenbach, Breyten, with Donald Woods. "A South African Poet on His Imprisonment." *New York Times Book Review* (1 May 1983): 3–25.

Coetzee, J. M. *Doubling the Point: Essays and Interviews*. Ed. David Attwell. Cambridge, Mass.: Harvard University Press, 1992.

Gordimer, Nadine. *Burger's Daughter*. New York: Penguin, 1980.

———. "English Language, Literature and Politics in South Africa." *Journal of Southern African Studies* 2: 2 (1976): 131–47.

Harlow, Barbara. *Resistance Literature*. New York: Methuen, 1987.

Kavanagh, Robert Mshengu. "Tradition and Innovation in the Theatre of Workshop '71." *Theatre Quarterly* 7:28 (Winter 77–78): 63–67.

Kunene, Daniel P. "Ideas under Arrest: Censorship in South Africa." *Research in African Literatures* 12.4 (1981): 421–39.

Lindfors, Bernth, ed. *Contemporary Black South African Literature: A Symposium*. Washington D.C.: Three Continents Press, 1985.

Manganyi, N. Chabani. *Exiles and Homecomings: A Biography of Es'kia Mphahlele*. Johannesburg: Raven Press, 1983.

Mphahlele, Es'kia. *Chirundu*. Westport, Conn.: Hill, 1979.

Nethersole, Reingard, ed. *Emerging Literatures*. Bern: Peter Lang, 1990.

Nkosi, Lewis. *Tasks and Masks: Themes and Styles in African Literature*. London: Longman, 1981.

Shava, Piniel Viriri. *A People's Voice: Black South African Writing in the Twentieth Century*. London: Zed Press; Athens: Ohio University Press, 1989.

Themba, Can. *The Will to Die*. London: Heinemann, 1972.

van Wyk Smith, Malvern. *Grounds of Contest: A Survey of South African English Literature*. Kenwyn, S.A.: Juta Press, 1990.

Postcolonial East African Literature: Toward a Literature *of* the People, *for* the People, and *by* the People?

Jeannine DeLombard

Addressing the topic of postcoloniality and its relationship to East African literature, one immediately faces a dilemma. Such a discussion must acknowledge in some depth the work of Ngugi wa Thiong'o—East Africa's most celebrated author and one of the continent's most outspoken and controversial critics of neocolonialism and cultural imperialism—without ignoring or slighting the work of other, lesser known but equally important authors from Ngugi's own Kenya, as well as neighboring Tanzania and Uganda. This essay will seek to resolve this dilemma by demonstrating how a crucial period in Ngugi's career as a writer and cultural critic encapsulates some of the major issues faced by other East African writers in the postcolonial era.[1]

In 1977, fourteen years after Kenya had achieved independence[2] and made English its official language, Ngugi wa Thiong'o was detained without trial for a year as a result of his participation in a community theater project, a production of *Ngaahika Ndeenda* (I Will Marry When I Want), the Gikuyu-language play he coauthored with Ngugi wa Mirii and the members of the Kamiriithu Education and Cultural Centre. Although this work is less critical of the hypocrisy, corruption and brutality of postcolonial Kenya than Ngugi's previous English-language novels, *A Grain of Wheat* and *Petals of Blood*, Ngugi was not only detained for his role in this allegedly subversive project, but also lost his post as the chairman of the University of Nairobi's Literature Department (which he helped to found). Ngugi's involvement in a second Gikuyu play, *Maitu Njugira* (Mother Sing for Me), in late 1981 led to the destruction of the Kamiriithu Centre, the prohibition of drama and theater activities in Kamiriithu, and, eventually, to Ngugi's exile from Kenya. In this same time period, during and immediately after his 1978 imprisonment, Ngugi authored two books, *Detained: A Writer's Prison Diary* and *Caitaani Mutharabaini* (Devil on the Cross). The former is an autobiographical meditation on Kenyan history, while the latter, according to its author, "was the first novel of its kind in scope and size in the Gikuyu language" (*Decolonising* 63), a sign of Ngugi's growing commitment to writing in African languages.

Although Ngugi's detention, his work with the Kamiriithu Centre, and his decision to write in Gikuyu have attracted a great deal of international attention, he would be the first to acknowledge that his experiences are anything but unique in East Africa. Ngugi is not the only, or even the first East African writer to stress the importance of writing in African languages. Nor is he the only East African intellectual to collaborate with everyday people in a popular theater project. Nor, unfortunately, is he the only East African author to be imprisoned, censored, or driven into exile for his writing.

This essay will use Ngugi's experiences in 1977–78 as a point of departure from which to examine three issues that have dominated postcolonial East African language: the language debate, the role of popular literature, and the emergence of testimonial literature in response to government repression.

LANGUAGE

Since 1981, when Ngugi bade a formal "farewell to English as a vehicle for any of [his] writings" in *Decolonising the Mind* (xiv), the language issue has dominated the critical discourse on African literature, with intellectuals like Abiola Irele defending and expanding Ngugi's position and others, like Chinua Achebe, Wole Soyinka, and Lewis Nkosi, challenging the efficacy, relevance, and political expediency of writing literature in African languages.[3] Still, the basic tenets of Ngugi's argument, as outlined in *Decolonising the Mind* and *Moving the Centre*, remain compelling: that, by writing in English, French or Portuguese, African authors enrich these languages and cultures at the cost of impoverishing or even endangering their own; that European languages are not only inadequate for expressing African concerns and experiences, but also carry with them the ideological baggage of slavery and colonialism; and that Europhone African literature automatically excludes the majority of African people from its audience.

Although Ngugi successfully has brought the language debate into the global spotlight, he is by no means the first to raise the issue. In a 1963 article, "The Dead End of African Literature," Obiajunwa Wali anticipated Ngugi by arguing that authentic African literature must be written in African languages, sparking a continent-wide debate over the issue (cited in Westley 171). That such a statement should have appeared in *Transition*, an East African literary journal based in newly independent Uganda, was more than a little ironic. Uganda was, after all, the home of Makerere University, the birthplace of anglophone East African literature (Bakari and Mazrui 876).

Uganda was also the adopted home of Sudanese writer Okot p'Bitek, the acclaimed Acholi author/poet. Okot struggled with the question of language throughout his career. Okot's lyrical *Wer pa Lawino*, the lament of a traditional Acholi woman about her politician husband's corrupt, Westernized ways, was an immediate critical success when the author's English translation was published as

Song of Lawino in 1966. The Acholi original was not published until 1969. But as Ugandan cultural critic and author Taban lo Liyong has observed, "Okot did not translate *Wer pa Lawino* into *Song of Lawino*. He wrote two books: *Wer pa Lawino* (a very deep, philosophical book in Acholi; a book of morals, religion, anthropology and wisdom) and a second light book, *Song of Lawino*" (88). In a 1978 interview Okot himself discusses the impossibility of translating both his Acholi novel *Lak Tar* and the last verse (chapter 14) of *Song of Lawino* into English (Nichols 244–45). Okot partially resolved this dilemma by publishing a volume of poetry, *Horn of My Love*, in which the Acholi originals appear alongside the author's English translations. Although *Lak Tar* was eventually published in English as *White Teeth*, and although Okot himself authored several works of poetry and prose in English, his experiences illustrate the complexity of the language issue. For, while Ngugi's stress on the importance of African authors' writing in African languages is supported by Okot's insistence of the inadequacy of European languages to express certain aspects of African experience, Ngugi's faith in translation as the key to a viable Afrophone literature is called into question by Okot's contention that important components of African languages (i.e., praise names) cannot be translated into Western languages.[4]

Language choice has been a highly contested issue in East African literature ever since coastal poets made the switch from Arabic to Kiswahili in their literary compositions.[5] In the late eighteenth century Abu Bakari concluded his epic poem *Utenzi wa Katirifu* by stating that "his purpose had been to tell an Arabic tradition in the vernacular (Ki'ajami)" (Gerard 98).[6] At the time, Arabic, as the language of a foreign imperialist power and world religion, was to Kiswahili as English, French, Portuguese are to it and other African languages today. That the switch from Arabic to Kiswahili was soon followed by "The Golden Age of Classical Swahili Literature" (Gerard 98) augurs well for the proposed move from a Europhone to an Afrophone African literature.

Under colonialism, East African authors not only continued to write in Kiswahili, they began writing in other African languages that had been reduced to writing by European missionaries. The government-sponsored vernacular newspaper became an important forum for this writing. The earliest, *Msimulizi* (Storyteller), appeared in German Tanganyika in 1888; the most significant for East African literary production was *Mambo Leo* (Issues of the Day), founded by the British in 1923 (Gerard 134). Just as missionaries discovered that the easiest way to reach potential African converts was through their own languages, the British colonial administration often used such vernacular publications in an attempt to win the hearts and minds of its East African subjects.

Here the case of Kenyan author Gakaara wa Wanjau bears mentioning, illustrating as it does the different political purposes vernacular literature has been made to serve. Gakaara was arrested and detained on October 20, 1952, the eve of the State of Emergency (declared by the British colonial government in an attempt to gain control of the quickly spreading insurgent Mau Mau movement).[7] Although he was not tried nor given any reason for his arrest, Gakaara learned that he had been detained for his pro–Mau Mau and nationalist writing in Kiswahili and Gikuyu. After four years of being subjected to an intensive program of government brainwashing in what the British authorities, after World War II, called "concentration camps," Gakaara once again began writing in Gikuyu. This time, however, he wrote anti–Mau Mau propaganda designed both to weaken his fellow prisoners' resistance and to prove his own "rehabilitation." As well as editing a weekly camp newspaper, *Atiriri! Gitugi kia Muccii* (The Pillar of the Home), Gakaara also composed and directed a series of anti–Mau Mau plays and concerts to be performed by and for detainees (Gakaara 179–197). In 1961, after his release from detention and restriction, Gakaara resuscitated the publishing company he had founded before the Emergency. As Ann Bierstecker has noted in her survey of Gakaara's post-independence short fiction published in his Gikuyu language *Gikuyu na Mumbi* magazine, Gakaara's writing has become increasingly critical of the postcolonial Kenyan government and elite. This may explain why he was detained in 1986 "for alleged association with 'Mwakenya' underground movement, but was released after signing an officially prepared false 'confession' in which he repudiated his works, including his prize winning diary [documenting his experiences in colonial detention camps]" (Bierstecker 75).

Gakaara's colonial detention experience suggests that vernacular literature does not necessarily help to decolonize the African mind, but, in fact, may actively assist in its colonization. On the other hand, Gakaara's literary activities before and after the Emergency—and the repressive manner in which both the colonial and postcolonial Kenyan government responded to these activities—testify to vernacular literature's potential as a form of cultural resistance to imperialism.

POPULAR LITERATURE

To raise the question of language is to raise the question of audience. In East Africa, as in other areas of the continent, language unites and divides along not only ethnic, but class lines. By writing in a European language an African author automatically addresses an exclusive minority urban, educated, often elite local audience, as well as a larger, more diverse international one. Indeed, Ngugi's decision to write exclusively in Gikuyu and Kiswahili was motivated by his experiences with the Kamiriithu Centre and his desire to reach the masses of East African peasants and workers.

But does writing in an African language necessarily guarantee that one is speaking to the masses? Is vernacular literature de facto popular literature? Or is popular literature by definition an apolitical, unliterary genre—"what the unsophisticated reader has chosen for pleasure"?[8] Which is more "popular"—a Gikuyu novel that is read in bars in exchange for beer by professional readers (and eventually banned and confiscated)[9] or the English language romances that can be found in "the satchel of any teenage [African] girl" (Versi, "Romantic" 4)?

Since independence, a strong tradition of popular literature in the latter, "unsophisticated" sense has developed in both English and Kiswahili in East Africa.

According to Knight, Kenya in the early 1970s saw "a positive flood of literature often printed in the form of series designed to cater [to] the low-brow taste of the recently literate urban reader" ("Kenya" 909). These books, by Charles Mangua (*Son of Woman, A Tail in the Mouth*), Mwangi Ruheni (the *What a Life* series), David Maillu (*Unfit for Human Consumption, The Ayah*) and the more self-consciously literary Meja Mwangi (*Kill Me Quick, Carcase for Hounds*, and *Going Down River Road*), tend to have sentimental or melodramatic plots, an urban setting, stereotyped characters, and a considerable amount of slangy dialogue (Knight, "Kenya" 911). The same could probably be said of the more recent spate of Kiswahili popular literature in Tanzania, such as Ben R. Mtobwa's *Pesa Zako Zinanuka* (published in English as *Give Me Money*), *Tutarudi na Roho Zetu!* (published as *Zero Hour*) and *Dar es Salaam Usiku* (Dar es Salaam at Night) or Agoro Anduru's *Laana ya Pesa* (The Curse of Money) in Tanzania, although much work remains to be done on this genre.

Postcolonial economics and the contradictions of the international publishing business have conspired to render such indigenous adventure novels and romances relatively unpopular among East African readers, especially those in Kenya, since "imported books of the James Hadley Chase and Harold Robbins type [are] often cheaper than local works of a similar nature" (Knight, "Kenya" 910). Given this, it will be interesting to see how the Heinemann Heartbeats series of English language African romances fares. So far, only one of these, Jessica Maji's *The Place of Gentle Waters* (which reportedly couples British colloquialisms with faulty Kiswahili), is set in East Africa (Versi, "Romantic" 7).[10] Ironically, in postcolonial Kenya at least, such Western popular fiction in European languages is often more easily available, more widely read, and therefore literally more "popular" than locally produced fiction about the East African populace.

Defining East African literature as that which was written in languages understood by the majority of the people in a given community poses equally knotty problems. A case in point is the translation of *Julius Caesar*, by Julius Nyerere, the first president of Tanzania, which was published in 1963, the same year Obiajunwa Wali issued his call for an Afrophone African literature (Gerard 134). The translation powerfully demonstrated not only Kiswahili's suitability as a literary language, but also the newly independent government's commitment to Kiswahili as Tanzania's official language. Today, however, in the context of the language debate, Nyerere's linguistic appropriation of Shakespeare's play also highlights the distinction that some East African scholars have drawn between linguistic and formal accessibility: chances are, the translated *Julius Caesar* will seem no more approachable to the Kiswahili-literate masses than the original does to the majority of English speakers today. In the same vein, critics like Simon Gikandi have questioned the efficacy of Ngugi's decision to write in Gikuyu while retaining the formal properties of the nineteenth-century European novel in his fiction.[11]

But again, Ngugi is not alone in addressing these issues. In particular, heirs to the Swahili literary tradition have had to negotiate among language choice, formal sophistication, and audience accessibility. Alain Ricard summarizes the difficulties encountered by Ebrahim Hussein, Tanzania's premier playwright:

> Hussein has paid dearly for his accomplishments. . . . On the one hand they have fostered the impression that he is a difficult, esoteric writer who has lost contact with the socialist masses; his more recent works have created a gulf between himself and the principal audience for Kiswahili writing in Tanzania, and his resignation from his teaching post at the University of Dar es Salaam marked the culmination of his gradual shift away from the mainstream of Tanzanian society. On the other hand, his works have failed to attract the attention of foreign critics because a knowledge of Kiswahili is not sufficiently widespread among them to permit a wider appreciation of his work in the original language or to stimulate the urge to translate it. (176–77)

Ebrahim Hussein's "predicament" is shared by postcolonial Swahili poets. A recent essay by Kenyan poet/playwright Alamin Mazrui traces the debate over the form of Swahili poetry that has been waged since independence. On one side are the "conservationists," who favor "a prosodic norm that combines meter and rhyme in a variety of largely fixed patterns"; on the other are the "liberalists," who are "more inclined toward free verse" (Mazrui 67).[12] Interestingly, each camp claims its poetry is authentically African, accusing the other of mimicking foreign formal conventions: the conservationists believe "the introduction of free verse into Swahili poetry constitutes yet another case of African artists capitulating to European cultural colonization," while liberalists insist that "prosodic poetry is merely a form of Arabic cultural imperialism" (Mazrui 67, 68). Not surprisingly, each camp also insists that it is writing for "the people" and that the other addresses a privileged elite. As Mazrui points out, however "part of the . . . problem depends upon the kinds of audiences for which the two schools of poets are composing" (73). The "common" Swahili audience could be the coastal, ethnic Swahili who are familiar with the prosodic tradition as well as other classical conventions such as the use of Arabisms, archaisms, contractions and dialect; or it could be the masses of mainland Africans for whom Kiswahili is a second language and who are familiar with free-verse Bantu oral traditions. As Mazrui (himself a free-verse poet) concludes, however, the question of audience has become a moot point:

> Ironically, what was intended to be "the common language of the people" in Swahili free verse has turned out to be as incomprehensible as the "specialized language" of classical poetry. If prosodic poetry has been accused of being a restricted dialogue within a small group of literary conservationists or "organic intellectuals," free verse might now be regarded as having assumed the character of a specialized discourse within a small circle of "inorganic intellectuals." (75)

The issues raised by both the Swahili poetry debate and Ebrahim Hussein's predicament suggest that, in the East African context, questions of form are at least as pressing—and contested—as the question of language is at the international level. Such questions also complicate any notion of popular literature, for they suggest that the linguistic and cultural diversity of postcolonial East Africa precludes the possibility of writing or composing for a monolithic popular audience.

One Tanzanian playwright and novelist, Penina Muhando Mlama, has responded to the predicament of multiple audiences by "operat[ing] as an artist with two faces—one as a playwright for urban audiences and the other as an oral creator and performer for rural audiences" ("Creating" 11). In the latter capacity Mlama has discovered that "writing in the mother-tongue is not enough," and that in order for their work to be meaningful on the local level, "African writers must extend their interest to areas outside the realm of literary creations," and to theater in particular ("Creating" 13). Here again, formal considerations come into play. In order to be truly popular, Mlama insists, such theater must arise from indigenous "oral literary and performative forms," rather than imported Western dramatic traditions. Mlama and other African intellectuals like Ngugi and Mlama's fellow Tanzanian playwright Amandina Lihamba have collaborated with everyday African people, many of whom are illiterate and live in rural areas, to produce a literature that is popular in its origins as well as its destination.[13]

POLITICAL REPRESSION AND TESTIMONIAL LITERATURE

After participating in a number of popular theater projects, Penina Muhando Mlama realized that their "mode of operation assured that problems related to the oppression and exploitation of women would be raised," although the projects had not been originally formulated to do so ("Women" 44). Because they give women and other traditionally marginalized people, such as African peasants and workers, a forum in which to testify to the harsh circumstances of their lives—and, ideally, to make the first step toward changing these circumstances—these popular theater projects constitute a kind of testimonial literature.

Although testimonial literature usually takes the form of an autobiographical narrative composed by a representative marginalized person (see Beverley, "Margin" 93; Gugelberger and Kearney 4), many of the genre's constitutive characteristics resemble those of East African popular theater. Like popular theater, testimonial literature is marked by an emphasis on the collective rather than the individual, an incorporation of the oral into the written literary text, and a commitment to social change. This literature is often collaborative,[14] multivocal, and documentary. Written from the perspective of the marginalized and oppressed, testimonial literature is intended to serve as a corrective to official, hegemonic versions of history (see Gugelberger and Kearney). Although scholarship on testimonal literature has tended to focus on that produced in response to the Holocaust or in postcolonial Latin America, testimonial literature based on the Mau Mau uprising has flourished in Kenya since the colonial period.[15]

Ugandan writer and critic Peter Nazareth has characterized Mau Mau as the "anti-colonial war and corresponding myth" that has given Kenyan literature its focus (9). Indeed, an extraordinary volume of Mau Mau–themed novels, plays, poetry and memoirs have been produced since independence.[16] It would be wrong, however, to see this outpouring as "the literary exorcism of the Mau Mau experience" (Knight, "Kenya" 899). This observation is particularly erroneous with respect to the memoirs published since the mid-1960s by former freedom fighters and other Mau Mau participants. By composing and publishing their memoirs men[17] like J. M. Kariuki, Gakaara wa Wanjau, Karari Njama, Gucu Gikoyo, Joram Wamweya and Koboi Muriithi (to name but a few) sought not to exorcise or forget the past—as the newly independent Kenyan government urged them to[18]—but, quite the contrary, to break the national silence that has been imposed on the subject of Mau Mau and to erect a literary memorial to their struggles in the absence of a physical one.[19] Likewise, prison memoirs by Ngugi and Koigi wa Wamwere, as well as Abdilatif Abdalla's collection of poetry *Sauti ya Dhiki* (Voice of Agony, written while the author was in prison), also illustrate the continuities between what Ngugi has called "the colonial culture of fear and silence" (*Detained* 106) and the repressive postcolonial regimes of Jomo Kenyatta and Daniel T. Arap Moi.[20]

The extremely repressive conditions in postcolonial Uganda under first Idi Amin then Milton Obote, and the resulting mass exodus of both Asians and intellectuals from the country (the former against their will), would seem to be fertile ground for a national testimonial literary tradition on par with that of Kenya. Indeed, one poem by Ugandan author and cultural critic Taban lo Liyong counsels the nation's youth to fight with a pen instead of a sword. Despite this, however, as George Heron has observed, "It is conspicuous that Ugandan writers in exile failed, or more probably, refrained to comment through art on their country's tragedy" (947). Perhaps, like Okot p'Bitek, they have found the experience simply too overwhelming to relate. Heron sees Okot's discussion of his experience writing *Song of a Soldier* as representative: "It is a very terrible book because I lost quite a lot of relatives in the Uganda coup, a lot of friends, too, and after I write a few lines, I drop it because it causes a lot of tears" (cited in Heron 947). With the passage of time—and with the passing of the kind of debilitating personal grief described by Okot—a literary tradition that testifies to the brutality of the first two decades of the postcolonial era may still emerge in Uganda.

CONCLUSION

This essay has focused on how the issues raised by Ngugi's involvement with the Kamiriithu Centre and his subsequent detention by the Kenyan authorities are representative of those faced by other East African authors in the postcolonial era. These issues—the language debate, the question of popular literature, and the impact of political repression on a nation's literature—are all manifestations of a single underlying question: What are the role and the responsibility of the author/intellectual in postcolonial East Africa? Like Ngugi, many East African authors have responded to this question by working to create a literature that is not only *about* everyday East African people in all their diversity, but *for* and, in some cases, *by* them. For many this has meant composing and publishing in African languages, using indigenous literary and cultural forms, and/or collaborating with collectives of (often) illiterate peasants and workers. Too often, however, these efforts are stunted or silenced by neocolonial economics or government repression.

Although Kenya, as its tradition of testimonial literature attests, is currently the most repressive of the three East African nations, the 1990s have seen Uganda and Tanzania resorting to similar measures in order to intimidate and silence dissident voices. Since February 1990 the government of Uganda's President Yoweri Museveni has routinely harassed, arrested and detained journalists merely for doing their job.[21] And, although economic liberalization has led to an increase in publishing possibilities for Tanzanian writers and to the growth of an independent press, in the past few years several political dissidents have been detained, broadcast and print journalists have been harassed, and two Swahili newspapers have been banned under the 1976 Unwholesomeness Act, apparently for political rather than moral reasons (see "Voices" and Tagama). It is soon to ascertain what effect, if any, the revived East African community will have on these conditions, or on literature in general.

Ironically, the answer to some of postcolonial East African literature's dilemmas may lie in another medium, namely, film. Although almost prohibitively expensive and as susceptible to censorship as books are, film is capable of reaching wide audiences, does not require literacy, can be translated through subtitles or dubbing, and has already proven a popular medium in urban East Africa. Like theater, film lends itself easily to collaboration and collective participation. Although, since independence, West Africans have dominated this medium, the tide may be turning. Already Tanzanian Flora M'Mbungu Schelling's Swahili film *Kumekucha* has received international critical attention (Versi, "Africa" 10–11), and Kenyan filmmaker Anne Mugai won several awards at the 1993 Pan-African Festival of Film and Television for *Saikati*, her fourth film (Msoka 28). But perhaps the most auspicious sign of things to come is that Ngugi wa Thiong'o—following in the footsteps of Sembene Ousmane, the acclaimed Senegalese author who effectively ceased writing in French to make films in Wolof and French—has begun to experiment with filmmaking.

NOTES

1. Elizabeth Knight takes a similar approach when she observes that "the history of Kenyan literature since independence can largely be summarized by reference to [Ngugi's] career" (Knight, "Kenya" 916). But while Knight focuses on thematic and aesthetic trends, my concern here is to explore how the political issues faced by Ngugi in the late 1970s and the 1980s and their subsequent effect on his literary production are representative of the experiences of other East African writers.

2. Tanzania gained its independence in 1961, Uganda in 1963.

3. The recent surge of government-sponsored ethnic violence in Kenya complicates this issue even further. See "Spectre."

4. For further criticism of Ngugi's faith in translation and a discussion of the effect of English translation on his own work, see Gikandi, "Epistemology."

5. It is unclear exactly when this occurred. While Gerard states that there is no "objective support" for oral traditions identifying "a warrior-poet named Liyongo Fumo who is alleged to have been active on the island of Lamu (c. 1150–1204)" (93–94), Shariff has asserted the validity of these traditions. As Shariff states, there are "a number of poems which are attributed to Fumo Liyongo . . . [in which he] uses Arabic and Swahilized Arabic phrases" ("Liyongo" 159). Gerard notes that "when Ibn Battuta visited Kilwa [in present-day Tanzania] . . . in 1332, he reported meeting with native poets, who composed lyric and epic works in Swahili" (95). Gerard himself claims that the "earliest surviving manuscript in Swahili was written for the Sultan of Pate in 1728. Composed by the author who identified himself as Mwengo bin Athumani, the poem is known as *Chu cha Tambuka* ("The Book of the Battle of Tabuk") or as *Utenzi wa Herekali* ("The Epic of Heraklios" Gerard 96).

6. For a further discussion of *ajami* (vernacular literature in Arabic script) as it developed in West Africa see chapter 3 in volume 2 of *European-Language Writing in Sub-Saharan Africa*, edited by Gerard.

7. Considerable debate surrounds the history of Mau Mau, making it difficult to define the movement in simple terms. Loosely speaking, Mau Mau was a militant grass-roots movement for "land and freedom" that was composed predominantly (but by no means exclusively) of the Agikuyu, and which had its roots in nationalist organizations like the East African Association (founded in 1919), the Young Gikuyu Association (1920), the Kikuyu Central Association (1925), and the Kenya African (Study) Union (1944; in 1947 the word "Study" was dropped). See also Barnet and Njama.

8. Victor E. Neuberg cited in Knight, "Popular Literature" 177. Gakaara wa Wanjau's serialized Gikuyu wa-Nduuta stories are of particular interest because they are both vernacular and popular, both "entertaining" and politically oriented.

9. Ngugi describes the reception of *Caitaani Mutharabaini* (Devil on the Cross) in Kenya:

> [An] example of the community's collective appropriation of the novel was the emergence of professional readers in bars. Someone would start reading the novel aloud while drinking his beer, and when the beer was finished, he would just put the novel down. And of course the other customers would have to offer him another round to get him started again. (Ngugi, "On Writing" 154)

After a similar reception, *Matigari*, Ngugi's second Gikuyu novel, was confiscated by the police and subsequently banned in Kenya. See Ngugi, "Moving."

10. Despite the Swahili pen name, the nationality of the author is unclear, a point which Versi, unfortunately, does not address.

11. Gikandi argues persuasively that for Ngugi "writing in Gikuyu did not constitute an epistemological break, and it did not result in the creation of a new kind of African novel. What Ngugi's linguistic conversion did accomplish, however, was significant; it brought the conventions of the European novel to the Gikuyu reader, and brought the Gikuyu language into the orbit of the global novelistic tradition" ("Ngugi" 143).

12. For an account of this debate from the conservationist perspective see Shariff, *Tungo*.

13. See also Mlama, *Popular Theatre*. Mlama notes that because "women are often the

most talented practitioners of the community's traditional theater forms . . . [w]ithout having to acquire new skills and techniques of the mass media [as required by other development projects which tend to ignore or exclude women], they gain access to a powerful tool of communication" in such theater for development projects. Likewise, Mlama points out that "popular theater is one of the few communication media in which women are active participants. . . . It offers them a voice generally denied to them by radio, television, film and print media" ("Women" 45). It would be interesting to compare the impact on women of this kind of popular literature with that represented by the Heinemann Heartbeats series, which appears to be targeted at a female audience.

14. Usually, but not always, this is a collaboration between the intellectual and the so-called masses. John Beverley has warned that we should not misread testimonial literature as the coming to voice of the silenced subaltern but, rather, as "the union of a radicalized (Marxist) intelligentsia with the subaltern . . . a discursive space where the possibilities of such an alliance can be negotiated without too much angst about otherness or 'othering' " (Beverley, "Through" 4). This observation would appear to obtain with respect to the East African popular theater projects in which both Ngugi and Mlama have been involved.

15. In reference to the testimonial literature of the Holocaust, see Felman and Laub; in reference to Latin America, see Jara and Vidal and *Voices of the Voiceless: Latin American Testimonial Literature*, the two-volume special issue of *Latin American Perspectives* edited by Gugelberger and Kearney; in reference to Africa see Harrow and Harlow.

16. For a partial list see Knight, "Kenya" 896–900.

17. So far, full-length firsthand accounts of female freedom fighters are lacking, although women were actively involved in every aspect of the movement. For descriptions of Mau Mau from a female perspective, see Waciuma, Muthoni and Davison.

18. In 1964, President Jomo Kenyatta informed Kenyans that "the past is . . . dead," and urged, "Let . . . all of us commit ourselves to erase from our minds all the hatreds and difficulties of those years that now belong to history. Let us agree that we shall never refer to the past" (Slater 241).

19. In his memoir Gakaara describes how after independence

> Mau Mau fighters . . . subdued their agonised spirits and learned to work and live with . . . Government administrators and workers who had been faithful servants of British imperialism and colonialism but were now conveniently serving an African nationalist Government. . . . [The fighters'] aspiration for active participation in the nationalist Government, which they had been instrumental in making a reality, fell into the river of history. And national gratitude in the form of magnanimous gestures to individual Mau Mau fighters or in the form of memorials to the movement was quite absent, for such gestures had few champions and many detractors (211).

Twenty-five years earlier, J. M. Kariuki prophetically concluded his memoirs: "The future historian of these times may well find it difficult to get our side of the story. . . . May this book and our new state be a small part of [the freedom fighters'] memorial" (182).

20. See "Culture of Fear and Silence." An important but little-known popular prison memoir, Michael Karanja Ngugi's *Miaka 52 Jela* (Fifty-Two Years in Jail), the autobiography of a common criminal who spent most of his life in colonial and postcolonial prisons, also illustrates, from the perspective of one of Kenya's dispossessed, this continuity.

21. See "Uganda: Journalists" and Rake. In 1992, however, Museveni, in a refreshingly novel approach to journalistic dissidence, penned a lengthy response to *Uganda Confidential*, a Kampala newsletter that had been critical of him (Musoke 17).

WORKS CITED

Abdalla, Abdilatif. *Sauti ya Dhiki.* Nairobi: Oxford University Press, 1973.

Anyidoho, Kofi. "Language and Development Strategy in Pan-African Literary Experience." *Research in African Literatures* 23.1 (1992): 45–63.

Bakari, Mohamed, and Ali A. Mazrui. "The Early Phase." In *European-Language Writing in Sub-Saharan Africa*, vol. 2. Ed. Albert S. Gerard. Budapest: Akademia Kiado/UNESCO, 1986. 863–86.

Barnett, Donald, and Karari Njama. *Mau Mau from Within: An Analysis of Kenya's Peasant Revolt.* New York: Monthly Review Press, 1966.

Beverley, John. "The Margin at the Center: ON Testimonio (Testimonial Narrative)." In *De/Colonizing the Subject: The Politics of Gender in Women's Autobiography.* Eds. Smith and Watson. Minneapolis: University of Minnesota Press, 1992. 91–114.

———. " 'Through All Things Modern': Second Thoughts on Testimonio." *Boundary* 2 18.2 (1991): 4.

Bierstecker, Ann. "An Alternative East African Voice: The Wa-Nduuta Stories of Gakaara wa Wanjau." *Research in African Literatures* 22.4 (1991): 63–78.

"Culture of Fear and Silence." *Index on Censorship* 12.4 (1983): 20–23.

Davison, Jean, and the Women of Mutira. *Voices from Mutira: Lives of Rural Gikuyu Women.* Boulder, Colo.: Lynne Reiner, 1989.

Felman, Shoshana, and Dori Laub, M.D. *Testimony: Crises of Witnessing in Literature, Psychoanalysis and History.* New York: Routledge, 1992.

Gakaara wa Wanjau. *Mau Mau Author in Detention.* Trans. Paul Ngigi Njoroge. Nairobi: Heinemann Kenya, 1988.

Gerard, Albert S. *African-Language Literatures: An Introduction to the Literary History of Sub-Saharan Africa.* Washington D.C.: Three Continents Press, 1981.

Gikoyo, Gucu. *We Fought for Freedom: Tulipigania Uhuru.* Nairobi: East African Publishing House, c. 1972.

Gikandi, Simon. "The Epistemology of Translation: Ngugi, *Matigari*, and the Politics of Language." *Research in African Literatures* 22.4 (1991): 161–67.

———. "Ngugi's Conversion: Writing and the Politics of Language." *Research in African Literatures* 23.1 (1992): 131–44.

Gugelberger, Georg, and Michael Kearney. "Voices for the Voiceless: Testimonial Literature in Latin America." *Latin American Perspectives: A Journal on Capitalism and Socialism* 18.3–18.4 (1991): 3–14.

Harlow, Barbara. *Barred Women: Women, Writing and Political Detention.* Hanover, N.H.: Wesleyan University Press, 1992.

———. *Resistance Literature.* New York: Methuen, 1987.

Harrow, Kenneth. "The Poetics of African Litterature de Temoinage." *African Literature Studies: The Present State.* Ed. Stephen Arnold. Washington D.C.: Three Continents Press, 1985. 135–49.

Heron, George. "Uganda." In *European-Language Writing in Sub-Saharan Africa*, vol. 2. Ed. Albert S. Gerard. Budapest: Akademia Kiado/UNESCO, 1986. 922–48.

Jara, Renee, and Hernan Vidal. *Testimonio y Literatura.* Edina, Minn.: Society for the Study of Hispanic and Lusophone Revolutionary Literatures, 1986.

Kariuki, Josiah Mwangi. *Mau Mau Detainee: The Account by a Kenya African of His Experience in Detention Camps 1953–1960.* Nairobi: Oxford University Press, 1975.

Knight, Elizabeth. "Kenya." *European-Language Writing in Sub-Saharan Africa*, vol. 2. Ed. Albert S. Gerard. Budapest: Akademia Kiado/UNESCO, 1986. 887–921.

———. "Popular Literature in East Africa." *African Literature Today 10: Retrospect and Prospect*. Ed. Eldred Durosimi Jones. New York: Africana, 1979. 177–90.

Koigi wa Wamwere. *Conscience on Trial—Why I Was Detained: Notes of a Political Prisoner in Kenya*. Trenton, N.J.: Africa World Press, 1988.

Mazrui, Alamin. "Conservationism and Liberalism in Swahili Poetry: The Linguistic Dimension." *Research In African Literatures* 23.4 (1992): 67–76.

Mlama, Penina Muhando. "Creating in the Mother-Tongue: The Challenges to the African Writer Today." *Research in African Literatures* 21.4 (1990): 5–14.

———. *The Popular Theatre Approach in Africa*. Uppsala, Sweden: Scandinavian Institute of African Studies, forthcoming.

———. "Women's Participation in 'Communication for Development': The Popular Theater Alternative in Africa." *Research in African Literatures* 22.3 (1991): 41–53.

Msoka, Valerie. "The Image of an African Woman." *New African* (November 1993): 28–29.

Muriithi, J. Kiboi, and Peter N. Ndoria. *War in the Forest: The Autobiography of a Mau Mau Leader*. Nairobi: East African, 1971.

Musoke, David. "Museveni Strikes Back." *New African* (June 1992): 17.

Muthoni, Likimani. *Passbook Number F.47927: Women and Mau Mau in Kenya*. London: Macmillan, 1985.

Nazareth, Peter. "Waiting for Amin: Two Decades of Ugandan Literature." In *The Writing of East and Central Africa*. Ed. G. D. Killam. Nairobi: Heinemann Educational Books, 1984. 7–35.

Ngugi, Michael Karanja. *Miaka 52 Jela*. Nairobi: Heinemann, 1989.

Ngugi wa Thiong'o. *Decolonising the Mind: The Politics of Language in African Literature*. Portsmouth, N.H.: Heinemann, 1981.

———. *Detained: A Writer's Prison Diary*. Exeter, N.H.: Heinemann, 1984.

———. *Moving the Centre: The Struggle for Cultural Freedoms*. Portsmouth, N.H.: Heinemann, 1994.

———. "On Writing In Gikuyu." *Research in African Literatures* 16.2 (1985): 151–55.

Nichols, Lee, ed. *Conversations with African Writers: Interviews with Twenty-Six African Authors*. Washington D.C.: Voice of America, 1981.

Rake, Alan. "Who Is in Charge of Uganda?" *New African* (April 1992): 14–15.

Ricard, Alain. "Ebrahim's Predicament." *Research in African Literatures* 23.1 (1992): 175–78.

Shariff, Ibrahim Noor. "The Liyongo Conundrum: Reexamining the Historicity of Swahili's National Poet-Hero." *Research in African Literatures* 22.2 (1991): 153–67.

———. *Tungo Zetu: Msingi wa Mashairi na Tungo Nyinginezo*. Trenton, N.J.: Red Sea Press, 1988.

Slater, Montagu. *The Trial of Jomo Kenyatta*. London: Secker & Warburg, 1956.

"Spectre of Civil War." *New African* (January 1994): 26.

Taban lo Liyong. "On Translating the 'Untranslated': Chapter 14 of *Wer pa Lawino* by Okot p'Bitek." *Research in African Literatures* 24.3 (1993): 87–92.

Tagama, Herald. "Curbing the Press." *New African* (April 1993): 41–42.

"Uganda: Journalists Imprisoned for Asking Questions." *New African* (May 1990): 21.

Versi, Anver. "Africa at the Pictures." *New African Life* (June 1993): 9–11.

———. "The Romantic African." *New African Life* (June 1993): 4–8.

"Voices of Dissent." *New African* (December 1990): 15.
Waciuma, Charity. *Daughter of Mumbi*. Nairobi: East African, 1969.
Wamweya, Joram. *Freedom Fighter*. Nairobi: East African, 1971.
Westley, David. "Choice of Language and African Literature: A Bibliographic Essay." *Research in African Literatures* 23.1 (1992): 159–171.

Between Cultures: Insights on West African Writing in English

Anthonia Kalu

The legacy of writing in English by African scholars is considered one of the most controversial issues of the western educated community in all of Africa. The impact of this legacy is at its most poignant within West African communities, where those who write have not always necessarily been a part of the educated elite. Fraught with questions and issues of language, identity, political and economic independence and all kinds of individual and community freedoms, writing in English in West Africa remains a very controversial endeavor even though it continues to enjoy popularity as the most enhancing vehicle of communication in this postcolonial segment of the African continent.

To a certain extent, engagement in postcolonial discourse presupposes a certain willingness to subsume postcolonial geographic spaces and people within a framework that views the world, even for a brief moment, through observation lenses colored by a vision of the after-effects of independence. For instance, in his *Resistance in Postcolonial African Fiction*, Neil Lazarus' analysis of Aŷi Kwei Armah's works begins with the conclusive title "Great Expectations and the Mourning After: Decolonization and African Intellectuals." Framing his work around the idea of a postcolonial environment that fails to deliver certain types of goods to a newly independent Ghana, Lazarus indicts Armah and other African writers like Ngugi wa Thiong'o and Chinua Achebe as working from points of view that originate from an imagined "outside," effectively transforming these writers into intellectuals with messianic projects. Important to this project of transformation is the refusal and/or inability to admit that the creative African writer, writing in English, is in fact an artist. This exclusion of the postcolonial writer and writing from the arena of authentic creative endeavors presumes the African writer's willingness to relocate the African self to a postcolonial homeland that is essentially different from the precolonial. It is a relocation that assumes that the postcolonial ideal represents something that is different because it is better than the precolonial. For West Africa, in particular, this viewpoint insists on the transformation, through independence, of African nations and peoples from primitive to modern social, political, economic and other arenas of action and interaction. For the most part, postcolonial thought infers the birth of a new Africa whose period of gestation is colonialism, and whose natal moment is signaled by independence and the transfer of power from colonial rulers.

The problem with the situation described above is that it presupposes that the colonial enterprise involved a transfer of power from the colonized to the colonizer for the purposes of correcting precolonial African existence, liberating it from the toils of primitivism and lack of vision. Consequently, the agenda of the school of thought involves applauding the African writer as a director of Africa's ideological vision rather than as an artistic and creative narrator of events for the purposes of interrogating social norms and values across historical time and space. However, even while writing from viewpoints that consistently criticize African nations' stagnation despite the lessons of colonialism, most African writers remain consistent in their use of African thought in the exploration of the sources and locations of conflict and transition. The point here is that postcolonial African literature, rather than reflecting messianic postures or postures of those learned during the colonial encounter, should be read primarily as creative texts which purposefully assume the role of interrogating (a) the presence of a disabling new dispensation, (b) the apparent willingness of Africa and Africans to dismiss a meaningful precolonial African past with or without apology, and (c) the absence of a will to explore a future within which Africans could successfully exist as postcolonial people and simultaneously as Africans with a meaningful precolonial heritage.

The intersection of these discursive locations within the African experience after the achievement of independence from colonial rule remains one of the most important points of reference in the discussions of the origins, direction and development of analytical tools, language use, and the future of African literature. It is at this intersection that Achebe starts his exploration of the African experience in *Things Fall Apart* (1958), his first work of fiction. In other words, effective analysis of postcolonial African literature is not possible without a good understanding of the dynamics of the various positions and dynamics at this intersection of Africa's collision with the west.

For the West African writer, the identification of this location coincides with the identification and recognition of the African self poised in the exploration of both that self and the dynamics of the relationship between it and this multidimensional location. Within West African fiction, Amos Tutuola's *The Palm-Wine Drinkard* (1953) is the first work to posit and explore the feeling of estrangement engendered by the colonial encounter. However, Tutuola's work has not been discussed within the postcolonial tradition of West African fiction. It is the contention of this work that the very fact of Tutuola's use of the English language in writing *The Palm-Wine Drinkard* and other works places his works within this frame of reference and evaluation of African works. Published in 1953, *The Palm-Wine Drinkard* has not been evaluated or analyzed as a postcolonial work. However, if one looks at it from the point of view of language and the import of English language acquisition for the British West African colonial subject, not only Tutuola's work but all the works written in English during colonialism and after can be seen as having been written with postcolonial imperative. Simply put, this means that writing in English enabled the West African writer not only to explore the disabling features of colonialism but also to evoke a postcolonial future within the colonial present.

This evocation becomes obvious when postcoloniality is seen as a process and not as a moment within the Euro-African encounter. Locating postcolonial activities within colonized territory enables in-depth discussion of the African writer's involvement in the postcolonial discourse. Paul Feyerabend's discussion of incommensurable viewpoints in *Against Method* (1975) is helpful in understanding the shift in explanation that this work posits. In his work, Feyerabend uses examples of "simple" shapes which contain a number of "pictures" to illustrate the ways in which "every picture with a modicum of perception" (227) allows us "to compare two attitudes in our *memory but not while attending to the same picture*" (226). Using these pictures, he is able to show how "our perceptual apparatus" is able to give "rise to perceptual objects which not just *negate* other perceptual objects—thus retaining original categories—but prevent the formation of any object whatsoever" (227). Feyerabend's assertion regarding incommensurable viewpoints allows for a discussion of the shift in perception that is needed to understand West African writers' engagement of postcolonial issues within and during colonialism. This is not to say that postcolonialism and colonialism are the same or even similar. Rather, it is a repositioning that allows for a reevaluation of the African writer's perspective, the artistic perspective of the colonized within frameworks that are dictated by the colonizer's worldview and agenda. Language is a major tool of the West African writer in English, yet this very language imposes a framework of logic and usage that falls prey to the intensive interrogation of the anticolonial and postcolonial writer. The perspectives inherent in language itself reveal the problems confronted by these writers in their projects of national and individual quests for liberation.

In light of the foregoing, Tutuola's *The Palm-Wine Drinkard* is seen here as starting with a presentation of the problem. The protagonist is a palm-wine drinkard who is totally dependent on his father's favor and the wine tapster's skills. He has no training in any profession or skill and is absolutely dependent on these two men—the benevolent patriarch and the skilled workman. When both die within six months of each other, the protagonist whose name turns out to be "Father of gods who could do anything in this world," cannot tap his own wine. He leaves his "nine miles square, 560,000 palm tree farm" to go on a long journey to Deads' Town to bring his dead tapster from the transitional world of "the dead who . . . were [still] living in one place somewhere in this world" (9) back to the world of the living. He arrives in Deads' Town after an eventful journey that takes many years but discovers that he cannot take his tapster back with him because "a dead man could not live with alives and their characteristics would not be the same" (100). This incommensurable nature of the relationship between the two realities which Tutuola's work explores is finally articulated by the dead tapster when the protagonist and the tapster meet in Dead's Town.

The mediation of the situation, that is, a change in perspective, is facilitated with the gift of an egg from the dead tapster to the protagonist and his wife, who then go back to the palm-wine drinkard's hometown to resume the former life of dependence on the tapster's knowledge and skills. However, this time they are indirectly dependent on the tapster. The new relationship, represented in the egg, is delicately construed. According to Feyerabend, the logic of such relationships cannot be maintained except in memory (226). Tutuola portrays this difficulty in the presentation of the new relationship on the tapster's gift of the fragile egg, which breaks during the course of the first major conflict. Thus within a framework like colonialism which has built-in perceptual viewpoints that allow for the coexistence of incommensurable ideas, it becomes necessary to articulate differences such that some of the underlying relationships are exposed.

Generally, the creative artist's work involves this process of articulation of difference. Consequently, for the West African writing about the postcolonial experience in English, not only creativity but the form, style and very tradition in which the product is rendered become areas of contestation. Along with these arise issues of ownership. For instance, is the novel, poem or play written in English about West Africans on authentic West African literary work? Does it explore West African life and experiences and is the exploration complete or authentic? Should and can African people see themselves, their lives and experiences through the mirror of a non-African language? Should African presses publish and distribute such works to Africans? What is the status of authenticity itself in the emerging arena of postcolonial discourse? The questions are endless.

Significant to the main idea of this work is that these questions continue to be asked about other areas of the African encounter with the West that continue to maintain postures which favor the transfer of Western forms and ways of knowing to Africans. Exploration and expression of the multi-dimensional nature and impact of this encounter and the consequent relationship occupy a central position in African writing in general and West African writing in particular. Understanding the integral relationship that language bears to individual and community expression and exploration is necessary to objective portrayal, research and analysis of the intricate dimensions of African colonial and postcolonial experiences and thought. From the beginning, West African writing in English probed this relationship because upward mobility in the new dispensation was associated early with mastery of the English language. However, those who became involved in learning the language also realized early the untenable nature of their positions as straddlers of two or more cultures among which the English language and Western culture remained dominant.

For creative writers in West Africa, this situation continues to provide material for the exploration and portrayal of postcolonial thought and experience. Tutuola's *The Palm-Wine Drinkard* and Onitsha Market literature explore the West African's dilemma in this regard. However, rather than being applauded as pioneers in the portrayal of the African's experience during these periods of conflict and transition, these works have mostly received criticism that express "embarrassment and hostility at Tutuola's 'bad English' (or 'young English,' as Dylan Thomas called it)" (Chinweizu 263). On closer examination, Tutuola's work can be seen as a serious evaluation of a society in conflict and transition, and whose major problem is one of growing economic and political dependence on a seemingly benevolent system. It is the protagonist's father and the tapster who insist on the maintenance of habits of dependency of the palm-wine drinkard, and the father who provides a nine-square-mile palm-wine orchard, and the tapster who taps the 225 kegs of palm-wine that the palm-wine drinkard needs to consume daily.

Though highly dependent on the oral narrative tradition for the core stories, Tutuola signals his interrogation of the colonial moment through his references to the postcolonial imperative and in his authorial commentary and choice of titles. For instance, the titles to two important episodes are "On Our Way to the Unreturnable Heaven's Town" (57) and "Our Life with the Faithful Mother in the White Tree" (69). Like the oral narrator, most of the comments are built into the narrative description and are left open to the reader's interpretation. For example, after the protagonist and his wife leave the Faithful-Mother, the protagonist says,

> But as we were travelling along in the bush, we met a young lady who was coming towards us, but as we saw her, we bent to another way, but she bent to the place too, then we stopped for her to come and do anything she wanted to do, because we had sold our "death" and we could not die again, but we feared her because we did not sell our "fear." (72)

It is important here to remember that at this point in the story, the protagonist/narrator and his wife are still alive but are traveling in Spirit-land. Tutuola reminds the reader of this fact often throughout the story. Working within the African oral narrative tradition to reveal its uses, it becomes possible to see the social commentary in the uses of "death" and "fear" in the preceding quotation.

An indication of the potentially destructive impact of colonialism on the moral and humanizing essence of the colonized at independence is signaled by the protagonist's response to the tapster's death at the beginning of the story:

> When we reached the farm, we began to look at every palm-tree, after a while we found him under the palm-tree, where he fell down and died. But what I did first when we saw him dead there, *was that I climbed another palm-tree which was near the spot, after that I tapped palm-wine and drank it to my satisfaction before I came back to the spot. Then* both my friends who accompanied me to the farm and I dug a pit under the palm-tree that he fell down as a grave and buried him there, after that we came back to the town. (8) (My emphasis)

This is the first serious indication that there is more to Tutuola's narrative project than experimentation with the English language. Not only is the palm-wine drinkard's indifference to the finding of the tapster's body strangely selfish and individualistic, what signals the problem is that his friends say nothing about his disrespect of the dead. In West African writing in English, this is the first typical portrayal of societal dysfunction in the face of blatantly unacceptable social behavior from an individual. Although the ceremonial nature of most African society's response to birth and death is neither dictated nor openly enforced, it is expected that by a certain age, members of each community know the rules governing such discourses in their immediate locality. When the palm-wine drinkard ignores the dead tapster's body not only to tap palm-wine but to "[drink] it his satisfaction before [coming] back to the spot," (8) his friends, who form a part of this knowledge base, have the responsibility and/or restore this lack. It cannot be argued that they are silent because of individual or collective expectation of profit because he does not share any palm-wine with them on this occasion. The nature of this silence is addressed later by Chinua Achebe in *Things Fall Apart* after the elders are released from prison.

> They neither spoke to anyone nor among themselves. . . . As they made their way to the village the six men met women and children going to the stream with their waterpots. But the men wore such heavy and fearsome looks that the women and children did not say "nno" or "welcome" to them . . . they walked silently. . . . The village was astir in a silent suppressed way. (182–183)

It is a silence that is fed by unmediated introduction of discordance into ordered existence and the absence of formulaic responses to transitional situations. For the West African writing in English, the writing of this silence is an evocation of the postcolonial imperative within the colonial act that would continue to suppress the African's need to explain the world according to African experience and life. One of the problems with the portrayal of this situation is that the writing and the silence occur in two different languages which exist in incommensurable positions within the African experience that is being forced to assume a transitional posture. Again, according to Feyerabend, "A direct judgement is impossible. We may compare the two attitudes in our *memory*, but *not* while attending to the *same picture*" (226). In other words, the memory and the physical picture *are not the same*. Things do indeed fall apart. However, as Achebe's interpretation of Yeats' "The Second Coming" implies, even though "the center can no longer hold," neither the falcon nor the falconer is obliterated. The natal moment of the postcolonial imperative coincides with the time T_1 from which the revolution of the gyre, the new system, must be measured. My point here is that Achebe's, Tutuola's and Yeats' visions insist on the formation of new perspectives from which elements of the old, because they are not untenable in the new, must be re(con)figured in order to make sense of the new.

Consequently, Tutuola's protagonist has to go on the multifaceted quest in the attempt to bring his dead tapster back to the world of "Alives," while Achebe's Okonkwo kills the white man's court messenger in the attempt to restore Umuofia to life. In light of the foregoing, for the inherent tensions in postcolonial writing in West Africa to make sense, the works have to be read and analyzed from the point of view of the failure of elements from the precolonial and the colonial experiences to cohere with the workings of, not the elements within, the new system. Such interrogation of the system allows West African (and other African) writers the freedom to participate in the creative process the same way that the oral narrative performer participates in the oral traditions, that is, as one of many performers who delineate a viewpoint inherent in a certain version of the narrative or within another art form or art tradition rather than as a member of "a messianic middle-class [with] a specific conception of decolonization as a revolutionary process" (Lazarus ix). In other words, this artist must not be viewed as an outsider who must correct centuries'-old misconceptions.

In *Arrow of God*, Achebe explores the meaning of the would-be intellectual's position through the character of Ezeulu's son, Oduche, whose mandate from his father is "I want one of my sons to join these people as be my eye there. If there is nothing in it you will come back. If there is something there you will bring home my share" (51). Neither the Oduches of postcolonial Africa nor their children were expected to become carriers of the colonial or postcolonial burden. Neither scapegoats nor messiahs, they had the task of exploring possibilities within the new world order. From their point of view, Ezeulu, his people and their gods do not see the Oduches of colonial West Africa as redeemers because their concept of their world is not predicated on a wrong act that needs correction. By the same token, Tutuola's palm-wine drinkard is involved in a quest for his dead tapster not because he wants to redeem his society or himself from anything but because he realizes that the sudden and permanent break with the tapster through the latter's accidental death leaves him with the task of negotiating a new world order as a consumer of a way of life whose knowledge base is incomprehensible to him. The problem is not that the palm-wine drinkard does not know how to tap palm-wine but that he does not have the training that will enable him to tap enough to satisfy his cultivated need for this product.

It is important here to note that Tutuola works consistently within a recognizable oral narrative tradition, modifying versions of oral narratives that deal with the hero's journeys to distant and unknown lands and his subsequent return with either a coveted prize or versions of it. Consequently, Tutuola's portrayal of a protagonist who returns with a problematic prize questions the colonial agenda for the enlightenment of the minds of the inhabitants of a dark continent and its promise of a better civilization. In order to understand this aspect of the writing project in English by West African writers, it is necessary to appreciate the fact that the questions these writers ask about colonialism and postcolonialism are not new questions. Not only the oral narrative tradition but the oral traditions of most African cultures are replete with examples of the kinds of questions that are reframed within the contemporary and written tradition. However, since colonial education found these traditions incompatible with its project, it became necessary for the subsequent postcolonial educational systems to require that these traditions be obliterated or held in memory by the colonized. Consequently, the postcolonial subject with a modicum of understanding of both cultures was confronted with the problem of creating meaningful images within a written tradition whose survival, for a long time, depended on the negation of the validity of the life which had to be held in memory even as it was being lived. It is this phenomenon that Achebe refers to when he describes the relationship between the Christian and non-Christian parts of his family and the strategies that had to be adopted by the colonial subject to negotiate the new dispensation.

> When I was growing up I remember we tended to look down on the others. We were called *in our language* "the people of the church" or the "association of God." The others we called, with the conceit appropriate to followers of the true religion, the heathen or even "*the people of nothing*." (65) (my emphasis)
>
> We lived at the crossroads of cultures. . . . On one arm of the cross we sang hymns and read the Bible night and day. On the other my father's brother and his family, blinded by heathenism, offered food to idols. . . . I knew without knowing that it was too simple a way to describe what was going on. Those idols and that food had a strange pull on me in spite of my being such a thorough little Christian that often at Sunday services at the height of the grandeur of the *Te Deum Laudamus* I would have dreams of a mantle of gold falling on me as the choir of angels drowned our mortal song and the voice of God Himself thundering: This is my beloved son in whom I am well pleased. Yes, despite those delusions of divine destiny I was not past taking my little sister to our neighbour's house when our parents were not looking and partaking of heathen festival meals. I never found their rice and stew to have the flavour of idolatry. (67, 68)

The ability of the food from the hearths and homes of those designated "the people of nothing" to continue to sustain members of both groups constituted one of the major obstacles of colonialist enterprise. If food is here used to refer to any material or abstract component of both cultures, one of the difficulties encountered by the postcolonial with reference to language use becomes evident. The nature of this intricate link is not always immediately evident to people who have no experience of colonial domination. In the case of English-speaking West Africa, for instance, it is always necessary at this point to make reference to the fact that the relationship between Christianity and colonialism is seamless. Consequently, in the dichotomous relationship between indigenous West African and Western traditions and cultures, one is credited with idolatry, darkness and evil, while the other becomes Christian, illuminating and good.

The problem that this situation poses for the West African writer is this: How should the African use words from the language of a culture that posits African inferiority to claim African dignity and strength? Does knowing the English language transform and authenticate the West African writer? In other words, does knowing the language transform the West African writer into "my beloved son in whom I am well pleased," that is, an English writer, a messiah? According to

Achebe, the answer is an unequivocal "No." In "African Literature as Restoration of Celebration," Achebe says:

I went to a good school modelled on British public schools. I read lots of English books there. I read *Treasure Island* and . . . I did not see myself as an African to begin with. I took sides with the white men against the savages. In other words I went through my first level of schooling thinking I was of the party of the white man in his hair-raising adventures and narrow escapes. The white man was good and courageous. The savages arrayed against him were sinister and stupid or, at most, cunning. I hated their guts. . . . But . . . [later] I realized . . . I was not on Marlowe's boat steaming up the Congo in *Heart of Darkness.* I was one of those strange beings jumping up and down on the river bank, making horrid faces. Or, if I insisted on the boat-ride, then I had to settle perhaps for that "improved specimen", as Conrad sarcastically calls him, more absurd than a dog in a pair of breeches trying to make out the witchcraft behind the ship's water-gauge. (7)

The main thrust of the writing project in postcolonial Africa has been the authentication of "those strange beings jumping up and down" but on their own terms: from the Africans' view of their world. It is significant to note here that the nature of the incursion of western thought into African life and experience made it difficult for women to participate early and fully in the writing project. This does not mean that women were absent in the early explorations of male writers. Tutuola's protagonist in *The Palm-Wine Drinkard* gets married in the course of his travels. Even a cursory analysis of their relationship shows a deep concern for the woman's welfare in this metaphorical colonial misadventure. For example, in one of the episodes during the Palm-wine Drinkard's travels, the beautiful daughter of the head of the town is lured away and taken prisoner by the "Complete Gentleman" who turns out to be nothing but a Skull that had hired other body parts to make himself complete and so handsome that

if this gentleman went to the battle field, surely, enemy would not kill him or capture him and if bombers saw him in a town which was to be bombed, they would not throw bombs in his presence, and if they did throw it, the bomb itself would not explode until this gentleman would leave that town, because of his beauty. (25)

The beautiful woman is made to sit on a large frog and a single cowrie is tied around her neck. This cowrie around her neck makes a terrible noise which alerts her captors whenever she attempts to escape. Worse than this, however, is that she loses her voice and cannot speak as long as the cowrie is tied around her neck. After the protagonist rescues her from the Skull's Town and cuts the string that holds the cowrie around her neck, "it only stopped the noise, but I was unable to loose it away from her neck" (29). Eventually, he has to go back to the Skull's Town to learn the secret that would restore the woman's voice. The answer is in the leaves of two plants. Tutuola's commentary on the nature of incommensurability within systems is rendered in one of the most difficult passages in South African literature written in English. The protagonist goes back to Skull's Town.

When he sees the Skull, he changes himself into a lizard and hides in a tree. The passage is worth quoting in detail.

He [the Skull] stood before two plants, then he cut a single opposite leaf from the opposite plant; he held the leaf with his right hand and he was saying thus:—"As this lady was taken from me, if this opposite leaf is not given her to eat, she will not talk for ever," after that he threw the leaf down to the ground. Then he cut another single compound leaf from the compound plant which was *in the same place as with the opposite plant* he held the compound with his left hand and said that if this single compound is not given to this lady, to eat, the cowrie on her neck would not be loosened away for ever and it would be making a terrible noise for ever "(. . . . and I saw the place that he threw the leaves separately) then I changed myself as a man as before, I went to the place that he threw both leaves, then I picked them up and I went home. But at the same time I reached home, I cooked both leaves separately and gave her to eat; to my surprise the lady began to talk at once. After that, I gave her the compound leaf to eat for the second time and immediately she ate that too, the cowrie which was tied on her neck by the Skull, loosened away by itself, but it disappeared at the same time." (30)

The difficulty presented by this passage lies in the contradictory logic of the simplicity of the language and the apparently magical nature of the leaves implicit in and addressed by the oral tradition. Rather than magic, the situation here is one that deals with the problems of obtaining the right (or at least useful) answers. One of the many assumptions evident in the oral narrative tradition is that one first has to assume a viable posture. Tutuola's protagonist's transformation of himself from a man to a lizard which then hides itself in a tree solves the first part of the problem. After he acquires the key to the problem, he has to "change [himself] to a man as before" (30). The emphasis on keeping the leaves separate, cooking them separately and eating each one separately is reminiscent of Feyerabend's caution about the tendency for the smaller picture to merge or even disappear into the larger one if one holds one's gaze on the large picture for too long. Within the quest for a meaningful relationship between vehicular language and the West African writer, the realization of the nature and extent of the damage incurred through the loss of the female voice came late. However, most West African women writers' works have yet to be subjected to the careful analysis of the nature of the previous or current silence in a way similar to what Tutuola's protagonist insists on within the oral tradition.

How then should the West African postcolonial writer of West African language in English hold the leaves? Tutuola's protagonist marries the beautiful woman after she regains her voice. She joins him in his quest for the dead tapster. However, their marriage does not make their life easier. Together, they encounter many dangers before they find the tapster and start for home, but, as has been stated earlier in this work, the dead tapster's response/solution proves inadequate to their needs. And that's the point. For the West African writer in English, all the issues have to be addressed one at a time, separately but with utmost speed, because we work in a world community where those who have the power to construct and maintain the rules for what is beautiful and complete (as in the Complete Gentleman) are not obligated to reveal the rules for their construction. More importantly, they do not have the key to our self-reclamation. According to Tutuola's protagonist, even when the leaves are found and brought home, we have to cook them in our own cooking pots and eat them, separately. In the final analysis, the key is not in the recognition of difference. Postcolonialism itself is the result of the admission of difference. Rather, the key is in the West African writer's recognition and acceptance of the various strategies that facilitate the achievement of true independence within both the indigenous culture and the culture of the vehicular language through which we must speak our silence.

WORKS CITED

Achebe, Chinua. *Arrow of God.* New York: Doubleday and Company, 1969.

———. *Things Fall Apart.* New York: Fawcett Crest, 1959.

———. *Morning Yet on Creation Day.* London: Heinemann, 1975.

Feyerabend, Paul. *Against Method.* London: Verso, 1975.

Lazarus, Neil. *Resistance in Postcolonial African Fiction.* New Haven, Conn.: Yale University Press, 1990.

Petersen, Kirsten Holst and Anna Rutherford, eds. *Chinua Achebe: A Celebration.* Oxford: Heinemann International, and Dangeroo Press, 1990.

Tutuola, Amos. *The Palm-Wine Drinkard.* New York: Grove Press, 1953.

Language, Identity, and Nation in Postcolonial Indian English Literature

Aparna Dharwadker and Vinay Dharwadker

Indian literature in English is a product of the institutionalization of English education in colonial India in the early nineteenth century but has achieved maturity and viability as a body of writing only in the postcolonial period. This cryptic description of the origin and evolution of a literary tradition contains a double historical paradox. First, when English was introduced in British India through the Charter Act of 1813, and then more systematically through Lord Bentinck's English Education Act of 1835, its intended functions were educational and administrative, not literary. Yet the first two Indian literary "masters" of English, Rammohun Roy (1772–1833) and Henry Derozio (1809–1831), had already completed their careers before Bentinck's Act, and poems, plays, novels, and polemical prose in English were to become an important part of Indian literary production soon afterwards (Iyengar 22–98; Naik, *History* 7–113). Second, following the decolonization of the subcontinent in 1947, a spontaneous overflow of powerful nationalist feeling could well have uprooted the colonial language. But the political, cultural, and literary status of English in India in fact has continued to improve in the last four decades. As David McCutchion observed in mock-astonishment in 1964, "far from dying out, the yield grows annually richer!" (7). These two contradictions ensure that Indian literature in English is a particularly complicated referent in the discourse of nationhood, national identity, and cultural self-definition in the postindependence period.

To deal adequately with the unusual contexts of English in India, we will therefore approach postcolonial Indian English literature by means of two pertinent discourses: the political-cultural arguments that accompanied the introduction of English in India in the nineteenth century; and the polemic that has surrounded the literary use of English since independence. This will allow us to relate the contemporary situation in India to the larger processes of colonization and decolonization. We will then focus on several emergent generic and thematic features of lyric poetry and prose fiction, the two dominant postcolonial forms in this literature.

THE ARRIVAL OF ENGLISH

Raja Rammohun Roy's letter of 1823 to Lord Amherst (Governor-General of the East India Company), which supported English over Sanskrit or Arabic education, shows that for nineteenth-century Indian reformists English held mainly the promise of an up-to-date, useful, and "modern" knowledge. Acting as a public spokesman, Roy urged the government to employ "European Gentlemen of talent and education to instruct the Natives of India in Mathematics, Natural Philosophy, Chemistry, Anatomy, and other useful Sciences, which the Natives of Europe have carried to a degree of perfection that has raised them above the inhabitants of other parts of the world" (31). Roy acknowledged that the sciences and the literature of Europe were both worth emulating, but the disciplines he actively promoted were all scientific ones. Moreover, like Macaulay twelve years later, Roy envisioned the exchange of knowledge as a unilateral transaction between unequal cultures: the best knowledge would proceed from the European nations to India, with no possibility of a comparable reciprocation.

Macaulay's 1835 Minute on Indian Education reinforced the one-sidedness of the cultural exchange and marginalized literature and the arts even more decisively. Indeed, for Macaulay (representing the "Anglicist" position in the debate over English), the choice for colonial policymakers in India lay precisely between promoting literature, composed in the Indian languages, and promoting science, which would be accessible only in the enlightened languages of Europe—his own opinion being that the "dialects of India" contained "neither literary nor scientific information" (240). For Macaulay, moreover, the purpose of English education would not be to instruct "the great mass of the population" but to create "a class who may be interpreters between us and the millions whom we govern; a class of persons, Indian in blood and colour, but English in taste, in opinions, in morals, and in intellect" (249). The insignificance of specifically literary concerns in the cultural argument for English was clear in 1835, though "Orientalist" scholars like H. H. Wilson warned the East India Company's policymakers even then that the introduction of English would "annihilate native literature" and degrade the Indian people by making them "dependent upon a remote and unknown country for all their ideas and for the very words in which to clothe them" (Wilson 14). In fact, between the 1850s and 1890s alienated "hybrid" Indians—the first full-fledged representatives of an "unhoused sensibility" in the colonized nonwestern world—appeared in most of the local and regional Indian-language cultures, ironically justifying the opposing visions of both Macaulay and Wilson (Mukherjee, "Macaulay" 34–36).

However, to consider English as the weapon only of "deracination" and linguistic-cultural "denationalization" is reductive. In her recent study of English education in India, Gauri Vishwanathan aims at "elucidating the relationship between the institutionalization of English in India and the exercise of colonial power, between the processes of curricular selection and the impulse to dominate and control" (3). But where the disciplines of language and literature are concerned, this position seems to be a description of the Company's intentions rather than actual effects. For once Indian students had been subjected to the new medium of instruction in colonial schools and colleges, the English language and its literature transformed the conditions of writing and reading on the subcontinent, permanently altering the subjectivity of the Indian writer in unanticipated ways. For the subjects of the colony, English became a language to write *in*, to translate *from* and *into*, generating powerful and durable new strategies of appropriation, amplification, assimilation, and synthesis which cannot be contained now by a simple narrative of domination and control. As Sara Suleri reminds us, colonial facts "frequently fail to cohere around the master-myth that proclaims static lines of demarcation between imperial power and disempowered culture, between colonizer and colonized" (3). A language imposed merely from the outside cannot survive, and a literary culture cannot flourish without the active "complicity" of "native" authors.

The facts of nineteenth-and early-twentieth century Indian writing in English bear out the complexity of the cultural exchange between English and India. The dominant genres in this body of writing are lyric and narrative verse, as practiced by Henry Derozio, Kashiprasad Ghose, Michael Madhusudan Dutt, Toru Dutt, Romesh Chunder Dutt, Manmohan Ghose, and Aurobindo Ghose (Iyengar 22–98; Naik, *History* 7–113). The narrative poems, moreover, are based principally on legendary, historical, or epic Indian material, as in Derozio's *The Fakir of Jungheera*, Madhusudan Dutt's *The Captive Ladie* (1849), Toru Dutt's *Ancient Ballads and Legends of Hindustan* (1882), R. C. Dutt's *Lays of Ancient India* (1894), and Sri Aurobindo's *Urvashi* (1896) and *Savitri* (1946). R. C. Dutt also produced abridged translations of the *Ramayana* and the *Mahabharata* (four-thousand lines each), and Aurobindo Ghose translated shorter selections from the two epics. In contrast with this large, conspicuously intercultural output of poetry, original Indian drama in English is undistinguished (notwithstanding the plays of Aurobindo Ghose), and original fiction in English is rather slight until the generation of Mulk Raj Anand, Raja Rao, and R. K. Narayan. In fact, the plays, short stories, and novels of Rabindranath Tagore in translation provide the most interesting late-colonial examples of drama and fiction in English, prefiguring the importance of bilingualism and translation in postcolonial Indian English literature. As a translator of his own work (including the *Gitanjali*) into English, as occasionally an original writer in English, and as an international spokesman for Indian literature and culture, Tagore, as numerous post colonial critics have pointed out, is also unquestionably the most powerful model for bilingualism from the preindependence period.

The conflicts and contradictions inherent in the emergence of an English literary "tradition" in India, however, manifest themselves in two separate parts which provide a bridge between the colonial and postcolonial periods. First, the status of Indian writing in English remains ambiguous for more than a century because, as Meenakshi Mukherjee notes, even early-twentieth century critics "use the term 'Anglo-Indian' to cover all writing in English about India without making any distinction between Indians writing in English and Englishmen using India as material" (*Twice Born* 9). Second, as a linguistic and literary medium English becomes deeply implicated in the cultural politics of nationalism. Mahatma Gandhi's *Hind Swaraj* (1909), for example, formulated an anticolonial politics principally in terms of a rejection of everything "foreign," from European food, clothing, and other manufactured goods to the English language itself (Raghavendra Rao 66–69). In the 1920s and 1930s the Gandhian-nationalist rejection of colonialism combined with socialist and communist critiques of British imperialism to create a "split" among Indian writers and intellectuals. One group, consisting of writers in languages like Bengali and Hindi, protested against Indian writing in English on nationalistic grounds, mainly because it was the language of British domination. The other group, consisting of Indian writers in English, continued to write in the language of the colonizer, but now used the alien medium to produce poems, novels, stories, and essays along overtly *indigenous* lines. When independence from Britain became imminent, the first group hoped that English language itself would disappear from India along with the imperial agent. But the second group, already expanding to include the first generation of postcolonial Indian English writers, found that English was not a language it could give up easily or at will. These, then, are the polarities at the end of the colonial period which generate an extended debate after independence and lead to long-term consequences, both for Indian writing in English and for Indian-language literatures.

THE POSTINDEPENDENCE CRITIQUE OF ENGLISH

Throughout the 1950s and 1960s Indian-English writers and their counterparts in the Indian languages fought out a national, even nationalistic, battle in the postcolonial public sphere over the place of the English language and Indian-English writing in the contemporary Indian literary and cultural worlds. Surveying *Indian Writers of English Verse* in 1933, Latika Basu had drawn the nationalistic conclusion "As long as the vernaculars in India are . . . alive it should be the aim of Indians to develop them, for writing in a foreign tongue can serve no useful purpose," and "English is not alive in India. . . . That is why Anglo-Indian verse is of such poor quality" (qtd. in McCutchion 7). More than twenty-five years later the Indian English poet P. Lal, who established the Writers Workshop in Calcutta in 1958, attributed a very different cultural power to English in India: "The real writer in English not only thinks, but makes love in English. English is at the tips of his senses" (Lal, "Indian Writing" 300–301). In fact, Lal went further to suggest provocatively that "only in English can the real Indian poetry be written; any other poetry is likely to be Bengali-slanted or Gujarati-based, and so on. Only Indian writing in English can hope to attain the 'Indian' flavour, which is a cosmopolitan flavour" (qtd. in Hess 25).

Reacting to Lal in 1960 and echoing Basu from the previous generation, the Bengali writer Jyotirmoy Datta elaborated half a dozen major points against the postcolonial Indian English writer's conscious decision to write in English. From Datta's viewpoint, English was not close to any of the social and regional groups or populations in India; its literary function in modern India was not similar to that of Sanskrit in ancient India; and even though it is more "developed" than the Indian languages, this does not mean that works written in it are automatically superior to those in the Indian languages. Moreover, Datta continued, English in India is a "dead" language, especially after independence; it is used to convey information and not to explore feelings or new ideas; and so it deprives the Indian English writers' imaginations of "the stimulus of living speech." Instead, in a "nightmare of sterility," English writers produce "novels feeding on past novels, poems springing from other poems." If an Indian English writer were marooned on a desert island, Datta concluded, he would almost certainly write in his mother tongue, "the true language of his soul" (289–96).

The sharp differences between Lal and Datta shaped much of the discussion of Indian English writing during the 1960s and well into the 1970s (see, for example, Rajan 2–3; McCutchion 5–10; Hess 23–26; Iyengar 4–21; Parthasarathy 3–9). Around the mid-1970s, however, the two polarized groups entered a fresh symbiotic relationship. Saleem Peeradina's anthology, *Contemporary Indian Poetry in English* (1972), demonstrated the high quality of the latest Indian English verse, while Adil Jussawalla's anthology, *New Writing in India* (1974), using exciting new English translations, pointed to the excellence of postindependence writing in about a dozen Indian languages. Such books, along with periodicals like *Poetry India*, *Quest*, *Opinion Literary Quarterly*, *Dialogue India*, *Indian Literature*, *Soliloquy*, *Vagartha*, *Chandrabhaga*, and *The Illustrated Weekly of India*, generated the discursive space for a phenomenon that had been unduly marginalized in the heated debates of the preceding two or more decades: the presence of a strong bilingualism or multilingualism among modern Indian writers, and the concomitant practice of literary translation.

During the 1970s it became evident once more that several of the best postcolonial Indian-English writers, along with a number of talented writers committed to writing in their mother tongues, were first-rate translators from the Indian languages into English. Among the former were A. K. Ramanujan (Tamil, Kannada), Arun Kolatkar and Dilip Chitre (Marathi), Arvind Krishna Mehrotra (Hindi), Jayanta Mahapatra (Oriya), and R. Parthasarathy (Tamil), while among the latter were Jyotirmoy Datta (Bengali), Vinda Karandikar (Marathi), Kishori Charan Das (Oriya), and K. Ayyappa Paniker and O. V. Vijayan (Malayalam), to name a few obvious examples (see Jussawalla, *New Writing*). These writers articulated a complex continuum between English and the various modern Indo-Aryan and Dravidian languages, all of them related to each other through translation mainly into the "common" medium of English. This renewed symbiosis maintained the complicated tensions between English and the Indian languages, but it also helped to "rehabilitate" English as a culturally necessary and historically inescapable component of the national literary system, and to "domesticate" it in a network of linguistic interdependences.

In the late 1970s and early 1980s, however, the status of Indian English writing in relation to writing in the regional languages changed drastically because of two publication events. The first was the appearance in 1976, almost simultaneously, of ten excellent books of Indian English poetry: six from Oxford University Press (New Delhi) and four from The Clearing House, Bombay (see Paniker). The second event was the appearance in 1980 of Salman Rushdie's *Midnight's Children*, a book that catapulted its author into the front rank of contemporary fiction writers from around the world. The literary and commercial success of these publications made the position of Indian writing in English as a whole virtually unassailable fact: it could no longer be attacked, as it had been until the 1960s, for lack of linguistic and technical competence, literary quality, imaginative force, public impact, or cultural significance.

A new generation of Indian English writers—the second since independence—emerged in print in the mid- to late 1980s, directly reaching large international audiences and achieving more or less instant fame. This generation includes Amitav Ghosh, Vikram Seth, I. Allan Sealy, Shashi Tharoor, Rohinton Mistry, Agha Shahid Ali, and Sujata Bhatt, and, together with slightly older writers like Anita Desai and Bharati Mukherjee, Indian-English texts have become an accepted part not only as Indian literature, but also as British or Commonwealth literature, third world and postcolonial literature, and contemporary international literature. The success of the Indian-English writers of the 1970s and 1980s, in fact, has turned them into models for Indian-language writers. Thus magical realism, postmodernism, and minimalism, for example, have become commonplace in languages like Hindi, Marathi, Bengali, and Urdu since the 1980s, at least partly because of their successful use a little earlier by the Indian English writers. In the 1990s, therefore, there is rarely any questioning of the "authenticity" or "relevance" of Indian-English writing.

As the foregoing discussion should indicate, the cultural situation in India—especially with the numerous languages, the literatures with long histories and classical origins, and the extensive interrelations among them—makes it virtually impossible for Indian English literature to remain a homogeneous or unified phenomenon. Moreover, in the last four or five decades Indian writing in English has changed so rapidly and in such unexpected ways that it cannot manifest or represent either nationalistic pride or postcolonial resistance unequivocally. In fact, throughout the postindependence period, there is a complexly interconnected yet continuously changing set of attitudes in the literature toward nation, national identity, nationalism, colonialism, postcolonialism, anticolonialism, resistance, subversion, and conservation. In the following accounts of representative and notable texts and authors in the genres of prose fiction and lyric poetry, we will focus on the significant continuities and changes in those attitudes between the 1940s and the present.

INDIAN ENGLISH LYRIC POETRY

As suggested, two distinct generations of men and women have shaped Indian English poetry since Independence. The poets of the first postcolonial generation—more than 130 of whom, including 30 women, were represented in P. Lal's large anthology, *Modern Indian Poetry in English* (1969)—began to publish their work between the late 1940s and the end of the 1960s and became dominant or influential in the 1970s. With the exception of a dozen distinguished figures, such as Nissim Ezekiel, A. K. Ramanujan, Dom Moraes, Adil Jussawalla, R. Parthasarathy, A. K. Mehrotra, Shiv K. Kumar, Keki Daruwalla, and Jayanta Mahapatra, the members of this generation usually did not succeed in publishing their work abroad. The poets of the second postcolonial generation started appearing in print in India and in Great Britain, America, Europe, and the British Commonwealth countries (especially Canada and Australia) primarily in the 1970s and 1980s. With its international success, this generation—which includes Vikram Seth, Agha Shahid Ali, Meena Alexander, Sujata Bhatt, and Chitra Divakaruni—has significantly helped Indian English poetry as a whole to reach a large readership scattered around the globe (for poems, see Parthasarathy; Daruwalla; for criticism, see McCutchion; Hess; Kulshreshtha; Shahane and Sivaramkrishna). The cultural politics of both these generations can be analyzed under three convenient thematic headings: (a) Indianness, (b) a postcolonial anticolonialism, and (c) a new cosmopolitanism.

Indianness

During the 1950s and 1960s most of the new postindependence Indian English poets developed a depoliticized aesthetics of poetry, focusing strategically on self-expression or self-exploration and thematically on self, sensibility, and individual or personal experience (see King 1–19; Kulshreshtha 175–86). However, the attacks by Indian-language writers, as chauvinists and nationalists, on the foreignness, colonial complicity, inauthenticity, and irrelevance of English writing in India forced many prominent Indian English poets to reconsider the question of what constitutes their "Indianness" or their national-literary identity as a group. Between about 1960 and 1990, this reconsideration has generated three important types of Indian English poetry based on three distinct orientations toward "India" and "Indian" materials and themes, interlinking the poets of the two postcolonial generations across their literary differences in different ways.

A certain construction of Indianness appears in the poetry of Nissim Ezekiel, which has affinities with that of Dom Moraes, Adil Jussawalla, Keki Daruwalla, Meena Alexander, and Vikram Seth. Like the other poets just mentioned, Ezekiel is practically monolingual in English and therefore has not been in a position to choose to write (or even read) in an alternative Indian literary language. As a result, since the late 1950s Ezekiel has tried to discover and invent ways of poetically representing India and Indians—characters, situations, motives, desires, beliefs, behavior patterns, and even speech—that are firmly "rooted" in actual individual and collective experience or everyday "reality" and, at the same time, accessible entirely and transparently through the medium of English (see, for instance, "Night of the Scorpion," "The Visitor," "Background, Casually," "Goodbye Party for Miss Pushpa T. S." and "Poem of the Separation" in Parthasarathy 31–39). Such representations, however, cannot be simply positive toward India and things Indian, since Ezekiel's monolingualism as well as his ethnic and social background tend to "alienate" him from his immediate environment, whether in Bombay or in other parts of India (he was born into a middle- to upper-class secular Bene–Israeli Jewish family in Bombay and received his higher education in philosophy and literature in England). Ezekiel therefore almost always views India from a cultural and philosophical distance, which is troped as irony and ambiguity in his poetic constructions of Indianness. The same is true, with the appropriate adjustments, of Dom Moraes and Meena Alexander, who come from English-speaking Christian communities on the Indian west coast, and of Adil Jussawalla and Keki Daruwalla, who are monolingual Parsis, at least as far as their literary reading and writing are concerned. Taken together, these poets appear to have limited access to the Indian-language worlds around them and therefore have to construct ironic, ambiguous, even alienated visions of the subcontinent through the filters of their own monolingual-English sensibilities.

Another type of construction of Indianness surfaces in the work of those post-independence poets who actively read and/or write in English as well as at least one Indian mother tongue, but who choose to write poetry in English mainly while living outside India. This paradigmatic position is best represented by the poetry of A. K. Ramanujan, who lived in the United States since 1959 but cultivated a complex of literary languages: he writes poetry and prose in English and Kannada and translates extensively from Tamil and Kannada into English as well as from English into Kannada. Other bilingual or multilingual postcolonial Indian English poets living abroad include R. Parthasarathy (Tamil), Agha Shahid Ali (Urdu), Sujata Bhatt (Gujarati), and Chitra Divakaruni (Bengali) and others, most of whom practice their bilingualism mainly in the form of translation. Ramanujan's literary multilingualism gives him remarkable access to Indian-language sensibilities and experiences, enabling him to construct a poetic "Indianness" that is in much closer contact with Indian "realities" than, say, the Indianness of Ezekiel or Moraes (King 1–19, 60–103). However, like the poets of the first paradigm, Ramanujan also does not merely praise or celebrate an authentic, unmediated India, "Indianness," or Indian national identity: instead, his interest in and representation of Indianness are constantly modified by his long exile abroad, which introduces a critical distance between his feelings, emotions, or responses and his objects of poetic representation. This critical distance again manifests itself in the trope of irony, which ambiguates any attitudes Ramanujan might hold toward Indian history, culture, and society (see especially "Looking for a Cousin on a Swing," "Love Poem for a Wife I," "Small-Scale Reflections on a Great House," and "Obituary" in Parthasarathy 97–107). In short, any nationalistic pride expatriate bilingual Indian poets may wish to express is consistently mediated by doubt, skepticism, and even aversion toward specific aspects of life in modern India.

The third type of construction of Indianness in postcolonial Indian English poetry is closely related to the second, since it also is articulated by bilingual writers. Unlike Ramanujan, Parthasarathy, and others who live abroad, however, these bilingual writers—such as Arivind Krishna Mehrotra (Hindi), Gieve Patel (Gujarati), Kamala Das (Malayalam), Jayanta Mahapatra (Oriya), and Dilip Chitre and Arun Kolatkar (both Marathi)—have spent most of their lives in India. They resemble the poets of the first paradigm sketched out earlier, since their immediate commitments are to local situations on the subcontinent, but they also resemble the poets of the second paradigm because of their literary bilingualism or multilingualism. At the same time, however, their linguistic ambivalence differentiates them significantly from the monolingual poets living in India, and their residence on the subcontinent separates them from the poets living abroad. Nevertheless, the bilingual Indian English poets living in India also adopt an ambiguous stance toward India and things Indian, developing a complex, multifaceted poetic tenor that is at once deeply critical of the nation, national identity, and national culture, as well as knowledgeably appreciative of local, regional, and subcontinental traditions (see, for instance, the poems by Das, Kolatkar, Mahapatra, Mehrotra, and Patel included in Parthasarathy).

Anticolonialism

Most of the postcolonial Indian English poets articulate a depoliticized aesthetic vision of modern or contemporary India, treating any version of Indianness (including their own) with skepticism and ambivalence. However, there are a few important exceptions who reveal postcolonial critiques of their British-colonial heritage. The exceptions include satirical poems about the Company and Raj periods of English rule in India, and about postindependence "wog" culture in India or about the postcolonials' "mimicry" of their departed colonial masters, such as Keki Daruwalla's "Routine," Nissim Ezekiel's "Background, Casually," Shiv K. Kumar's "Days in New York," and Parthasarathy's "Exile." Poems of this kind mock and reject social attitudes, behavioral norms, or class politics of colonial India, implicitly valorizing "indigenous" Indian cultural values and social codes.

Among the Indian English poets of the two postcolonial generations, only Adil Jussawalla goes substantially further than the others in articulating a strong concern with the colonial and postcolonial subjection of Indians. His representative work—influenced particularly by the ideas of Frantz Fanon—is *Missing Person* (1976). In this book-length sequence of political-psychological poems, mostly short and dramatic-lyric or discursive in themselves, Jussawalla attempts to dismantle the conventional (modernist and New Critical) aestheticism of his contemporaries to such an extent that he seems sometimes to have lost sight altogether of poetry and the poetic. Risking an extreme form of political anti-poetry, Jussawalla constructs the postcolonial Indian citizen and intellectual as a "missing person," who is "missing" precisely because his subjectivity and agency have been annihilated by the colonial past and the postcolonial present on the subcontinent. Jussawalla's antiheroic protagonist in the sequence represents himself, as well as his overall social or cultural situation, as a series of unrelatable, unrecoverable fragments. His "mind," or the zone of postcolonial consciousness he represents as a type, has been reduced to schizophrenia, incoherence, and possibly even madness. If this character is to restore himself to health, sanity, and wholeness, then he can do so only by erasing the colonial and postcolonial conflicts and contradictions which have produced him and which he still embodies. In hinting at this strategy of hypothetical recovery, Jussawalla comes closest among the Indian English poets to representing a full-fledged anticolonial postcolonialism of the kind familiar from African and Caribbean literature and theory (especially in Fanon and Aime Cesaire). In contrast to Jussawalla, most of the other Indian English poets of the two postindependence generations view English and Indian English writing as phenomena that cannot (and perhaps should not) be erased or reversed. For them, English in India has had a devastating and destructive effect on Indian culture but, at the same time, has also proved to be an undeniably stimulating and productive influence.

Cosmopolitanism

Most of the Indian English poets who appeared after the late 1940s have resolved the acute tensions within and around themselves between modernity and tradition, or colonial and postcolonial Westernization and Indianness, by adopting a manifold cosmopolitanism. This cosmopolitanism, which is not just a European attitude but also has indigenous origins in Indian Islamic and classical Hindu cultures, opposes both nonironic forms of nationalistic pride as well as unilateral, unequivocal anticolonialism.

Among the poets of the second generation, however, this cosmopolitanism is rarefied and aestheticized into a new "postmodernist" internationalism from which national identities, nationalistic concerns, and Indianness sometimes vanish altogether. Thus Vikram Seth, Agha Shahid Ali, Meena Alexander, Sujata Bhatt, and Chitra Divakaruni write poems that do not reflect in any way—except in their authors' obviously Indian names—on India or things Indian. Seth's self-styled pure poetry in *The Humble Administrator's Garden* (1985), Ali's longing for a lover in *A Nostalgist's Map of America* (1991), and Bhatt's aesthetic exoticization of Europe (Ireland, Germany, Russia) in *Brunizem* (1988) and *The Monkey Shadows* (1992), for instance, make no reference to their authors' national identities. In contrast to the first-generation Indian English poets who sought to "Indianize" themselves or to develop an anticolonial postcolonial stance, several of the second-generation poets simply ignore the themes of colonialism, postcolonialism, and anticolonialism and seem to accept (and even celebrate) the new world order that has emerged in the neocolonial global economy.

INDIAN ENGLISH PROSE FICTION

In the preceding discussion of Indian English poetry, the self-fashioning strategies of two generations of poets have been highlighted. In discussing the Indian English novel, two influential frameworks formulated by recent theories of postcoloniality to study of narrative fiction will be discussed. One is Homi K. Bhabha's contention that "narration" plays a constitutive role in the formation of a "nation" (Bhabha 3). The other is Fredric Jameson's argument that all third-world narratives are by their very nature "national allegories" (Jameson 69). These theoretical positions point to antithetical movements in late-colonial and postcolonial Indian English fiction that emphasize not the formal or aesthetic features of fiction but its role in the evolving cultural and political life of the nation. The first frame characterizes the novels of Mulk Raj Anand, Raja Rao, and R. K. Narayan, inasmuch as they offer "discourses of the nation" (Bhabha's term) in narrative form, and also appears in parodic form in G. V. Desani's best-known work. The novelistic careers of these writers began in the 1930s and have continued beyond independence, intersecting in different ways with the nationalistic upheaval that ended colonial rule in India. The second frame opposes the first and appears in its strongest form in the antinational and transnational allegories of Salman Rushdie's fiction. Although an expatriate writer, Rushdie has made a distinctive contribution to the story of Indian nationhood that needs to be discussed here at least briefly. Aside from this dialectic, a third significant frame in Indian English fiction generates what critics call the "East-West theme," and this can be explicated with reference to the fiction of Ruth Prawer Jhabvala, Anita Desai, and Amitava Ghosh.

The cultural and political ambivalence of the Indian response to colonization and nationhood is best represented in the prose fiction of the late-colonial period by two Indian-English novels written in the last ten years of British rule: Raja Rao's *Kanthapura* (1938) and G. V. Desani's *All About H. Hatterr* (1948). Rao's novel is a local, oral, folksy narrativized history of colonialism and nationalism as it manifested itself in "village India." It deals explicitly with the concrete particulars of economic exploitation, cultural power, racism, and political domination in the Raj (in a coffee-plantation region in South India), followed by the Gandhian "awakening" of the villagers' consciousness, their resistance to and confrontation with British power, and finally the destruction of the village named in the title of the book. In contrast, Desani's self-consciously Joycean novel is a stylized, allusive, erudite, highly schematic allegory of the psychology of the colonial subject and his experience in British India. His narrative is cast in the double form of a quest story and a kunstlerroman, with the action representing little or no overtly political resistance to the British presence on the subcontinent. As

M. K. Naik has observed, "*All About H. Hatterr* is probably the most complete exploration of colonial experience in Indo-English fiction. Employing the strategies of both realism and symbolism, it illuminates several aspects of the phenomenon" ("Colonial Experience" 250). In Naik's reading of the novel, Hatterr's dog, Jenkins, represents the lowest human-animal level of colonial-cultural subjection; Yeti Beliram represents the Indian "native" who cunningly exploits the colonial order for his own petty purposes; Nath C. Banerrji represents the Bengali *babu*, who comically and pathetically aspires to become an "Englishman"; and Hatterr himself represents the "half-breed Eurasian" who is cast out by Indians as well as Englishmen and wanders all over India in search of a metaphysics of identity and spiritual salvation. In a sense, both texts serve as examples of nationalistic and anticolonial novels.

Rao's and Desani's novels define "prototypical" moments in the ambivalent treatment of colonialism, nationalism, and the theme of the east-west encounter in Indian English prose fiction, against which subsequent works play out other variations. For example, in his second major novel, *The Serpent and the Rope* (1960), Raja Rao himself was to move away from the political concerns of *Kanthapura* toward the more cultural concerns explored in Desani's novel, viewing "the east-west encounter mainly from a metaphysical stand-point and free of a colonial context" (Naik, "Colonial Experience" 250). However, Rao's and Desani's respective explorations of an adequate "Indian spiritualism" to counteract "European materialism" do not exhaust the colonial prototypes of Indian English fiction written after independence. A third major model had appeared a little before them, in the work of Mulk Raj Anand, whose long series of novels and short stories began with *Untouchable* (1935) and *Coolie* (1936). Anand developed a mixed Progressive and Gandhian style of "social realism" which enabled him to deal with the Indian political situation in the late colonial and early postcolonial periods from a primarily "subaltern" perspective (see Iyengar 331–57).

R. K. Narayan views the politicization of fiction as an aberrant effect of nationalist politics, which for a time suppressed the comic, psychological, and individualistic possibilities of the novel. In Narayan's opinion, however, after independence the Indian novelist was free to present "the way of life of the group of people with whose psychology and background he is most familiar," and to hope that national and international audiences would find this more "novelistic" subject matter interesting (qtd. in Iyengar 360). Narayan's evident disengagement with politics may be the best authorial strategy for him, because his one overtly political "Gandhi-novel," *Waiting for the Mahatma* (1955), is perhaps his weakest work. But his fiction is not apolitical: it merely expresses its politics differently. It is very much a part of the discourse of the nation because Malgudi, the small South Indian town where the novels are set, is "the perfect comic product or by-product of the colonial situation" (Kaul 51). Unlike Kanthapura, Malgudi undergoes no violent anticolonial catharsis and is rarely visited by Western characters. But as A. N. Kaul argues, there is in Narayan's work "a remarkable East-West comedy and, underneath the still more remarkable fact of a static traditional Indian life which the West touches at all points but without real penetration anywhere" (50). With its river and forest, trains and buses, schools and schoolboys, shopkeepers and householders Malgudi represents, microcosmically, a type of provincial Indian experience that may have encountered colonialism as a political and administrative structure, but not as a transformative cultural force. Narayan offers, in short, the most extensive record in modern Indian fiction of ordinary life which has no need to resist colonialism strongly because it was never appropriated by colonialism.

Fredric Jameson argued in "Third World Literature in the Era of Multinational Capitalism" (1986) that "All third-world texts are necessarily . . . allegorical, and in a very specific way: they are to be read as . . . *national allegories.*" In fact, he claimed, "Third-world texts, even those which are seemingly private and invested with a properly libidinal dynamic, necessarily project a political dimension in the form of a national allegory: *the story of the private individual destiny is always an allegory of the embattled situation of the public third-world culture and society*." (Jameson 69; emphasis in original). Various critics have taken Jameson to task for this imperial and uncritical categorization of third world texts. Modifying Jameson's reductive essentialization of "all third-world texts," and developing his undifferentiated conception of a national allegory into several subtypes, Vinay Dharwadker has argued that

> a national allegory articulates its concern with nationhood and nationality through fairly determinate thematic orientations. For instance, in the colonial period, many Third World and Commonwealth writers constructed elaborate *nationalistic*, even patriotic allegories of a particular land and its people, contributing frequently to an anti-colonial nationalist movement and a future nationalist state ideology. In contrast, in the postcolonial period we find a proliferation of nationalistic as well as *antinationalistic* allegories of the same land and people, but now with a far more variable conception of nation, national unity and identity, national history, and so forth. (Dharwadker, "National Allegories" 4–5)

And, "the protagonist of a Third World national allegory is not merely an abstraction translated into a functional simulacrum of consciousness, but often a realistically portrayed character with psychological depth, whose personality and situation are *typical* of those of a large number of people in his country, and whose personal story mimics or parallels the history or situation of his nation through a variety of correspondences, coincidences, and connections" (7). Salman Rushdie's *Midnight's Children* (1980) is the most explicitly, and in some ways conventionally, allegorical novel when compared to Rao's and Desani's fictions. Rushdie's protagonist, Saleem Sinai, is an intricate personification of subcontinental India, with his body composed of nearly six hundred million parts corresponding to the region's population, his face mirroring its map, and his atrociously sized nose iconically representing the dangling peninsula. Saleem's birth at midnight on August 15, 1947, coincides with the birth of independent India, and his subsequent life story, as also more generally his family history going back to his adamic grandfather, parallels in an extensively fantastical form the modern political history of the nation. Cast in the mode of magical realism, the dense allegory provides an alternative history of modern Indian nationhood and national identity. The important question that arises in this context is whether Third World and Commonwealth writers have found ways of breaking out of the ultimately closed circle (or vertiginous spiral) of conservative or reactionary nationalism. The most interesting answer lies in Rushdie's *The Satanic Verses* (1988), which attempts to break out into a genuinely *transnational* allegory. As the antithesis of a national allegory, a transnational allegory attempts to translate the problem of personal and cultural identity onto a frame larger or other than the nation in its various senses. *The Satanic Verses* is hence an explicitly allegorical, sometimes partial account of several nations, their histories, and their present situations—India, Britain, Iran, Arabia, the Muslim nation, the Hindu nation, the Sikh nation, and so on. It is peopled almost exclusively by characters who are personifications, "metaphorical beings" caught in multiple migrations and translations between antithetical places, none of which they occupy exclusively and most of which they inhabit at once. As an allegory especially of the postcolonial condition, it is ambiguously antinationalistic in the extreme, since it dismantles the whole emotional framework of national identity erected on concepts like "home," "self," "land," and "belonging," and apparently accepts the radical disruptions of migrancy and metropolitan cosmopolitanism. However, as the controversy over this novel reveals all too clearly, a transnational allegory of this sort only deepens the contradiction between internationalization and nationalism which it attempts to break down.

While the differences between the preceding group of male novelists and the final category of "cross-cultural" writers need not be exaggerated, some sort of distinction is necessary here, because Ruth Prawer Jhabvala, Anita Desai, and Amitav Ghosh, among others, simply are not writers of the same *kind* as Anand, Rao, Narayan, and Rushdie, although Ghosh's two novels are counted among the "children of *Midnight's Children*." One major factor that sets these novelists apart is their uniquely complex relationship with their material. Jhabvala is a novelist of Polish-Jewish descent who left her adopted country, Germany, for England in 1939; left England for India in 1951, when she married the Parsi architect Cyrus Jhabvala; and has now left India for the United States because, in her words, India is a country "for which I was not born" ("Myself" 14). She prefers to be described not as an "Indian novelist" but as a "European novelist of India" in the tradition of Kipling and Forster, although she lived in Delhi for about twenty-five years and launched her career as a writer there. Anita Desai is half-German but has lived mainly in India: her bicultural sensibility negotiates the pluralities of Indian experience in her fiction without creating a bicultural milieu. However, in her *Bye, Bye, Blackbird* (1971) and *Baumgartner's Bombay* (1991) she addresses the cross-fertilization of cultures directly by dealing respectively with immigrant Indians in Britain and a mid–twentieth-century German-Jewish immigrant in Bombay. Amitav Ghosh is fully Indian by birth, education, and upbringing, but in both *The Circle of Reason* (1986) and *The Shadow Lines* (1988) he creates such singular variations on the East-West theme as to transform it altogether. Even this brief description should indicate how, like the poets, second- and third-generation Indian English novelists problematize the categories of neonationalism and anticolonialism. Because of the complex geography of her triple passage across the globe (her latest novel is aptly titled *Three Continents*, 1987), Jhabvala's fiction displays a unique pattern of engagement and disengagement with India-as-material. The two early novels, *To Whom She Will* (1955) and *The Nature of Passion* (1956), deal almost exclusively with the lives of middle, and lower-class Indian (specifically Panjabi) characters in Delhi. *Esmond in India* (1958) initiates the detailed portrayal of Western characters in India, and *The Householder* (1960) in part follows this lead. The East-West dialectic develops fully in Jhabvala's most celebrated novel, *Heat and Dust* (1975), where through a double narrative, an unnamed female narrator arrives in India in the 1970s to recreate the life of her grandmother Olivia Rivers, who was the wife of a British civil servant, and had left her husband for a Nawab in the 1920s. This is Jhabvala's most Forsterian novel, one in which she takes on the period of the British Raj fully and conflates colonial with postcolonial India; it is also the last of her novels to be set entirely in India. In Ralph J. Crane's words, her last two novels, *In Search of Love and Beauty* (1983) and *Three Continents*, attempt "to combine her triple European, Indian, and American heritage," giving relatively minor roles to Indian characters (105).

Anita Desai, geographically more rooted in comparison, has earned in various ways her title as the foremost contemporary Indian woman novelist in English. Her novels are regarded as lyrical, existentialist, Woolfian studies of individual selves that only incidentally belong in middle-class, postindependence India. But *Bye-Bye, Blackbird* (1971) breaks away from this apoliticality by portraying the lives of "Macaulay's bastards" in postimperial Britain, and by reversing the themes of colonization and "postcolonial revenge" before these issues become central in the work of writers like Salman Rushdie and Hanif Kureishi. Her protagonist Dev, the Anglophobe turned Anglophile, rationalizes his decision to stay on in England by assuming the role of an ambassador who must "interpret my country to them, to conquer England as they once conquered India, to show them," because history may well "turn the tables now" (*Blackbird* 140, 68). Her more recent novels are again concerned with the appropriation of individual human destiny by larger political circumstances. *In Custody* (1984), for instance, focuses on Deven, a professor of Hindi in a small town college, who becomes embroiled in the linguistic and cultural politics of Hindi versus Urdu in postindependence India when he becomes the "custodian" of Nur, the genius of an Urdu poet.

Amitav Ghosh's novels have so far provided two very different versions of the "clash of cultures." *The Circle of Reason* (1986) alternates at first between Calcutta and the small Bengali village of Lalpukur, creating in sharp, evocative detail the kind of localized urban and rural communities that are usually associated with

Indian-language fiction. Halfway through the novel, when the protagonist, Alu (a master-weaver with a "potato-head"), flees India to escape charges of terrorism, he arrives not in England or the United States but in the imaginary Middle Eastern Islamic principality of al-Ghazira, where he joins a multiethnic ragbag community of similarly displaced and freakish individuals. The cultural other in this case is not the imperialistic and Christian West but the Islamic Orient, and there is an Arabian Nights quality about the second half of the novel. More importantly, Ghosh's narrative radically revises the usual connotations of displacement, exile, and alienation in cross-cultural fiction, besides unsettling the urban, upper-class, English-oriented milieu of most Indian English novels. *The Shadow Lines* (1989) returns to more conventional subject matter by portraying the friendship (and antipathy) between various branches of an upper-class Bengali family and an English family over three generations. The England of this novel does not arouse fantasies of domination and revenge in the mind of the narrator; it is simply the partial setting for his own experiences of love, discovery, and loss. Sex between the characters is also not a metaphor for empire. Ghosh displays, in other words, the same cosmopolitanism in treating postimperial England and postcolonial India that characterizes the current generation of Indian English poets.

CONCLUSION

At the end of this discussion, it would be appropriate to stress that Indian literature in English is among the most disorderly of contemporary Indian literatures, and certainly the one most resistant to generalizations. Given the high incidence of bilingualism and the high quality of translations from the Indian languages into English, the rubric of "Indian English literature" can also now include literature in translation. At the same time, it is becoming increasingly difficult to determine who the "Indian" writer is, because some of the best Indian poets and novelists in English live and work abroad—some are no longer even Indian citizens. Salman Rushdie, Bharati Mukherjee, and Ruth Prawer Jhabvala have been claimed by their expatriate or foreign status, but India is central to their work and Indian literature ought to be able to claim them in turn. The domain of Indian English literature increasingly shifts its boundaries to accommodate global mobility, which has already rendered the 1960s questions about authenticity and relevance rather archaic.

WORKS CITED

Ali, Agha Shahid. *A Nostalgist's Map of America*. New York: Norton, 1991.

Amur, G. S., and S. K. Desai, eds. *Colonial Consciousness in Commonwealth Literature*. Bombay: Somaiya Publications, 1984.

Anand, Mulk Raj. *Coolie*. 1936. Bombay: Kutub-Popular.

———. *Untouchable*. 1935. Bombay: Kutub-Popular.

Ayyub, Abu Sayeed, and Amlan Datta, eds. *Ten Years of Quest*. Bombay: Manaktalas, 1966.

Bhabha, Homi K. "Introduction: Narrating the Nation." *Nation and Narration*. Ed. Homi K. Bhabha. London: Routledge, 1990. 1–7.
Bhatt, Sujata. *Brunizem*. Manchester: Carcanet, 1988.
———. *The Monkey Shadows*. Manchester: Carcanet, 1992.
Crane, Ralph J. *Ruth Prawer Jhabvala*. New York: Twayne, 1992.
Daruwalla, Keki. *Two Decades of Indian Poetry, 1960–1980*. New Delhi: Vikas, 1980.
Datta, Jyotirmoy. "On Caged Chaffinches and Polyglot Parrots." Ayyub and Datta. Bombay: Manaktalus, 1966. 286–96.
Desai, Anita. *Baumgartner's Bombay*. New York: Knopf, 1989.
———. *Bye-Bye, Blackbird*. 1971. New Delhi: Orient Paperbacks, 1991.
———. *In Custody*. New York: Harper & Row, 1984.
Desani, G. V. *All About H. Hatterr*. Harmondsworth, England: Penguin, 1972.
Dharwadker, Vinay. "National and Transnational Allegories in Recent Commonwealth Fiction." Division of English Literature Other than British and American, MLA Convention, Chicago, 29 Dec. 1990.
———. "Some Contexts of Modern Indian Poetry." *Chicago Review* 38.1–38.2 (1992): 218–231.
———. "The Poems of Sujata Bhatt Are Such." *Arc* 25 (1990): 78–82.
Ghosh, Amitav. *The Circle of Reason*. New York: Penguin, 1986.
———. *The Shadow Lines*. New York: Penguin, 1988.
Hess, Linda. "Post-Independence Indian Poetry in English." In *Considerations*. Ed. Mukherjee. New Delhi: Allied, 1978. 23–42.
Iyengar, K. R. Srinivasa. *Indian Writing in English*, 2nd ed. New York: Asia Publishing House, 1973.
Jameson, Fredric. "Third-World Literature in the Era of Multinational Capitalism." *Social Text* 15 (1986): 65–88.
Jhabvala, Ruth Prawer. *Esmond in India*. 1958. Harmondsworth, England: Penguin, 1980.
———. *Heat and Dust*. New York: Harper & Row, 1976.
———. *The Householder*. Harmondsworth, England: Penquin, 1980.
———. *In Search of Love and Beauty*. New York: William Morrow, 1983.
———. "Myself in India." In *How I Became a Holy Mother and Other Stories*. Harmondsworth, England: Penguin, 1981.
———. *The Nature of Passion*. Harmondsworth, England: Penguin, 1986.
———. *Three Continents*. Harmondsworth, England: Penguin, 1988.
———. *To Whom She Will*. Harmondsworth, England: Penguin, 1985.
Jussawalla, Adil. *Missing Person*. Bombay: Clearing House, 1976.
———, ed. *New Writing in India*. Harmondsworth, England: Penguin, 1974.
Kaul, A. N. "R. K. Narayan and the East-West Theme." In *Considerations*. Ed. Mukherjee. New Delhi: Allied, 1978. 43–65.
King, Bruce. *Three Indian Poets: Nissim Ezekiel, A. K. Ramanujan, Dom Moraes*. Madras: Oxford University Press, 1991.
Kulshrestha, Chirantan, ed. *Contemporary Indian English Verse: An Evaluation*. New Delhi: Arnold-Heinemann, 1980.
Lal, P. "Indian Writing in English: A Reply to Mr Jyotirmoy Datta." Ayyub and Datta. Bombay, Manaktalus, 1966. 297–303.
———, ed. *Modern Indian Poetry in English*. Calcutta: Writers Workshop, 1969.
Macaulay, Thomas Babington. "Minute on Indian Education." *Thomas Babington Macau-*

lay: Selected Writings. Ed. John Clive and Thomas Pinney. Chicago: University of Chicago Press, 1972. 237–51.

McCutchion, David. "Indian Poetry in English." In *Considerations,* Ed. Mukherjee. New Delhi: Allied, 1978. 5–22.

Mukherjee, Meenakshi. "Macaulay's Imperishable Empire." *The Literary Criterion* 17.1 (1982): 30–39.

———. *The Twice Born Fiction: Themes and Techniques of the Indian Novel in English.* New Delhi: Heinemann, 1971.

———, ed. *Considerations.* New Delhi: Allied Publishers, 1978.

Nabar, Vrinda. "Keki N. Daruwalla: Poetry and a National Culture." *Kulshreshtha* 272–85.

Naik, M. K. *A History of Indian English Literature.* New Delhi: Sahitya Akademi, 1982.

———. "Colonial Experience in *All About H. Hatterr.*" In *Colonial Consciousness in Commonwealth Literature.* Ed. Amur and Desai. Bombay: Somiya Publications. 25–58.

Naik, M. K., and S. Mokashi-Punekar, eds. *Perspectives on Indian Drama in English.* Madras: Oxford University Press, 1977.

Narayan, R.K. *Waiting for the Mahatma.* 1955. Rpt. Chicago: University of Chicago Press, 1981.

Paniker, K. Ayyappa. "Peacocks among Patriarchs." In *Contemporary Indian English Verse: An Evaluation.* Ed. Kulshreshtha, 98. Chirantan. New Delhi: Arnold-Heinemann, 1980. 98–121.

Parthasarathy, R. ed. *Ten Twentieth Century Indian Poets.* New Delhi: Oxford University Press, 1976.

Peeradina, Saleem, ed. *Contemporary Indian Poetry in English: An Assessment and Selection.* Bombay: Macmillan, 1972.

Rajan, Balachandra. "Identity and Nationality." In *Considerations.* Ed. Mukherjee. New Delhi: Allied, 1978. 1–4.

Rao, K. Raghavendra. "Communication and Content in Gandhiji's Hind Swaraj." *Perspectives on Indian Prose in English.* Ed. M. K. Naik. Atlantic Highlands, N.J.: Humanities Press, 1982.

Rao, Raja. *Kanthapura.* New York: New Directions, 1963.

———. *The Serpent and the Rope.* London: John Murray, 1960.

Roy, Rammohun. "A Letter on Education." In *Sources of Indian Tradition,* vol. 2, 2nd ed. Ed. Stephen Hay. New York: Columbia University Press, 1988. 31–33.

Rushdie, Salman. *Midnight's Children.* (1980) New York: Avon, 1982.

———. *The Satanic Verses.* (1988) New York: Viking, 1989.

Seth, Vikram. *The Humble Administrator's Garden.* Manchester: Carcanet, 1985.

Shahane, Vasant A., and M. Sivaramkrishna, eds. *Indian Poetry in English: A Critical Assessment.* New Delhi: Macmillan, 1980.

Suleri, Sara. *The Rhetoric of English India.* Chicago: University of Chicago Press, 1992.

Vishwanathan, Gauri. *Masks of Conquest: Literary Study and British Rule in India.* New York: Columbia University Press, 1989.

Wilson, H. H. "Education of the Natives of India." *Asiatic Journal* 29 (1836): 14.

Prolegomena to the Study of Pakistani English and Pakistani Literature in English

Alamgir Hashmi

English in Pakistan has found both utility and authenticity in the process of other-language incorporation and a growing linguistic symbiosis.[1] The statement is silent about the kind of English spoken, its textures and its qualities. English in Pakistan—particularly during the last two decades—has become domesticated and emerged as endogenous in both Pakistani dress and speech, vocabulary and indigenous linguistic structures. This blending together is seen in the Islamic ritual, code, and ethos, so that it has become equally a Pakistani version of the English language, since "Pakistan remains a congeries of linguistic communities bound together by two tongues (namely English and Urdu) of differing degrees of foreignness" (Hands 117–18). English is subordinated in that Urdu has become increasingly a trans-regional lingua franca in the entire country. Though Urdu might not yet be the language of modern knowledge as is English, it is not like "that vegetarian monster Hindi," "the language of peasants," "the language that is raised on radishes and potatoes" in India, as described by a character in Anita Desai's novel *In Custody*. This character, a magazine editor, glories in "Urdu—language of the court in days of royalty" (15). Urdu in Pakistan has begun to connect agricultural farms, the playgrounds and the government while parrying or pairing with English in the office, the factory and the home.

Historically, English did not sprout from the subcontinental fields but rather came to South Asia by appointment to the King of England during imperial times as the language of the colonizer. But, over time, it was adapted by Indians and Pakistanis acquired local traits, a local habitation, and a name, and would happily pass for an idigenized Pakistani language of the South Asian region. Pakistani scholarship has taken note of this important transition of English, or for that matter of Pakistan's composite culture, which English partakes of it in good measure. Yet while some educational and literary cartography has been practiced and accomplished, linguistic explanations of the English phenomenon have not been forthcoming. For example, Braj Kachru correctly states that "language planning and the role and status of English in Bangladesh, Pakistan, Nepal, and Sri Lanka has not been much different from India." But he also notes that "the literature on this topic for these countries, however, is not as profuse as that in India, but a number of studies are available to help in making a comparable study." Small help for Pakistan since the latest (and the only) work he cites is "Dil, 1966" (54), since its publication a good deal of antithetical planning has determined the role and status of English in this country even if it has not amounted to much.[2] For two decades now, English linguistic studies and Pakistani linguistic circles have not had the benefit of membership of such scholars as Anwar S. Dil, Shahidullah and Hameed Ahmad Khan. Only the rare article in a journal or newspaper has cared to look at Pakistani English as English and as Pakistani; mostly abiding by an exclusivist linguistic strategy, the writers have been dismissive of the general English language practice here either as non-Pakistani English (British, American, or another variety) or as non-English Pakistani (a language other than English).

As linguistic recognitions are themselves language-forming, they are a complementary exercise in the general cultural process of encoding and stabilizing both language and letters. Next only to the holy book, the dictionary is deemed central to a language culture or the composite culture. The *Supplement* (1972–86) to the *Oxford English Dictionary*, incorporated later in the second edition (1989) of the *OED*, did finally come to the recognition that English is not for England only; that it is a *world* language—contributed to by a horde of diverse language cultures and employed in scores of different regions and societies of the world; and that South Asia as a whole is one of the first half-dozen regions which in that respect has primacy. That is why, with reference to the tradition of English lexicography, the editor of the *Supplement*, Robert Burchfield, admits to having "made bold forays into the written English of regions outside the British Isles, particularly into that of North America, Australia, New Zealand, (the West Indies), South Africa, India, and Pakistan" (Introduction *OEDS*, 1, xiv). Burchfield further claims that the "written English of [these] regions has been accorded the kind of treatment that lexicographers of a former generation might have reserved for the English of Britain alone." Burchfield feels quite satisfied with the policy of the *Supplement*, by which "equality of attention has been given to the sprawling vocabulary of all English speaking countries" (Preface *OEDS* 4, ix).

There is as yet no regular Pakistani English, and the subject is not taught anywhere even if it is clear as Robert Baumgardner (1988) states "that in spite of the vast majority of shared features with other world varieties of English, Pakistani English manifests differences from other native and non-native [contexts]." The trouble with the concepts of "native" and "non-native" is that they rely more on ethnic, innate, or mystical than empirical or actual data. Baumgardner remarks that English at the "linguistic level" shows that "these differences are attributable to the 'new' context in which the language is used in Pakistan by a relatively small but articulate segment of Pakistani society" (85). However, a case can be made recently for why a "discriminatory" treatment should indeed not be meted out to this Pakistani language by teachers in the West and in South Asia. Messrs. Nihalani, Tongue, and Hosalie seem to have been motivated to compile their *Handbook of Usage and Pronunciation* on recognizing and noting the necessity "to provide aids for keeping Indian English in touch with British and American English, and *enabling Indians to recognize peculiarities in their usage*" (vii; emphasis added). Given the rate, range, and depth of change (semantic, phonetic, and in levels of usage) that we are witnessing in Pakistan, one supposes that a similar handbook will soon be required for keeping British and American English in touch with Pakistani English, and enabling the British and Americans and other English speakers to recognize peculiarities in *their* usage.

With its 3 percent relatively privileged anglophone population, Pakistan is an English-speaking country just as it is an Urdu- or Arabic- or Persian-speaking area. One cannot dwell too long on the origins or the whys of the existence of many ingredients of any given culture without the risk of wasting time and sorely straining the rational limits of the subject. *Why* the emphasis on Pakistan or Arabic, for example, in what truly was a Hindu-Jain-Buddhist India divided broadly in its northern and southern terrains or into Aryan and Dravidian sets of languages? Or, why Sanskrit or Gurmukhi embeddings appear in our midst, in the languages spoken today in the Islamic Republic of Pakistan? These queries have obvious answers. The more reasonable and useful occupation is to attend to the present uses of English, and to investigate the relationship it has come to have with Pakistani languages and literatures.

As the grammar of culture here is still most tolerantly pluralistic, the modern Islamic culture of Pakistan presents a choice of literary expression in several languages, whose development through the centuries has yielded a literary harvest of the highest order. The names of Mir, Ghalib, Iqbal Faiz, Rashed, Abdullah Hussain, and Manto, for example, evoke some of the best of world literature which is in Urdu. Nevertheless, one cannot but recognize that Pakistan is heir to a rich, polyglot, multivalent, and progressive literary tradition in all its major contemporary languages such as Urdu, English, Punjabi, Sindhi, Balcuhi, Pashto, as well as Kashmiri, Arabic, Persian, and so on. But particularly in Urdu and English, which are of central importance to the national cultural spectrum, English has played an important role in education, law and government for over a century. More recently, it has become the language of trade, science and technology. What is perhaps equally important is the fact that the language has been used ordinarily in South Asia for almost two centuries, and its uses have not been limited to the practical and pragmatic spheres alone; it has also been the literary vehicle for some of the best that has been written in these parts. Literature in English is the youngest of the major literatures and oral texts of Pakistan, but its achievement is a vital part of our literary heritage.

Therefore, it should surprise no one in Pakistan that today Pakistan has a vibrant and fine body of writing in English, whose generic and formal traditions go far back into the nineteenth century. What may, however, appear incredible is the fact that the writings *about* it have been preciously few and far between, and criticism has largely existed in coffeehouses, private living rooms or academic campuses, as was the situation before independence in 1947. Prior to 1947 in united India and Pakistan, the quantity of creative writing in English by Muslims was minimal, though by no means negligible. The colonial arguments against English—linguistic, pragmatic, national or ideological—are all too familiar. What is borne out of nearly all latter-day cultural developments is the fact that the reformist Sir Syed Ahmad Khan and his like-minded colleagues and followers have definitively redirected the course of our cultural and literary history—perhaps far more than had Lord Macaulay—in convincing Pakistanis of the worth of this new learning. Despite the sometimes indifferent attitudes during the colonial period, South Asian Muslims in the eighteenth and nineteenth centuries had taken to English, and some of them were making an effective use of the language even before Lord Macaulay or Sir Syed Ahmad Khan. In fact, it was an Indian Muslim, Sake Deen Mohammed, who wrote the very first book to be published in English by a South Asian: his *Travels*, which appeared before the end of the eighteenth century, in 1794, established India and Pakistan as one of the first regions outside the United Kingdom and the United States to use English for literary purposes. Also instructive is the fact that nearly a half-century before the last Mughal emperor and noted Urdu and Persian poet, Bahdur Shah Zafar, succeeded to the throne in Delhi (in 1837), *Travels* was being written in English by a South Asian Muslim. During the nineteenth century, there were a few Muslim writers who wrote well in English in their chosen literary forms, and who made a name for themselves: Syed Amir Ali, Hamid Ali Khan, Lutfullah. Some notable works by South Asian Muslim writers were published in India as well as in Britain in the first half of the twentieth century. These writers included Sir Mohammed Iqbal, Shahid Suhrawady and Ahmed Ali. The works of all these nineteenth-century and twentieth-century writers have spanned such forms as nonfiction, fiction, and poetry, as well as general, cultural, and scholarly writing, which has attained the status of literature.

With independence and decolonization in 1947, the momentum continued and increased, as English was still the official language in Pakistan. Shifts in the official language structure have been witnessed in the subsequent decades, but creative writing in English has flourished. An account of the writing by subcontinental Muslims is a necessary antecedent to literary characterization and historiography in an ideological state, insofar as the place and functions of postcolonial Pakistani writing in English are to address the notion of a widely accepted cultural form. It is important to realize that Pakistani literature in English is not an ethnic or religious minority literature because it has been enriched by the contributions of Pakistani writers from non-Muslim background as well. In a fundamental sense, thus, it is national. Furthermore, apart from communicating personal visions and fulfilling individual needs of writer and reader, Pakistani literature in English has been responsive, increasingly and almost inevitably as a national literature, to the society in which it is created, and to the sensitivities that the society engenders. The quality of writing has definitely improved in the passage from colonial subservience to an era of national self-definition, providing more room for literary experiment and innovation. A balance, so to speak, is being restored and the results cannot be ignored or contradicted. The quality of the writing in Pakistan is best described by a literature which has outstripped its colonial origins and developed a new personal identity of its own.

To take poetry first, it can be safely said, in general, the South Asian epic tradition and other metaphysical poetics joined to the Romanticism learned in English by nineteenth-century South Asian English writers which made them excessively imitative of both the main traditions without the individual excellence of either, and made them, at best, the experimental go-betweens, or "pioneers," in a new area. Much of that kind of writing lacked the precision, conciseness and enhanced subjectivity of the *ghazal.* The present day work of the Pakistani poets, as of the writers in other genres, finds its beginnings in the 1930s in the modern and witty, if austere, compositions of Shahid Suhrawady. Suhrawady's *Essays in Verse* (1937), drawing on the fine precision of Muslim art and often on English neoclassical taste, is a high watermark of South Asian poetry in the first half of the twentieth century.

Poetry since 1947 has achieved its distinctive voice—modern, at times modernist, but contemporary, relevant, and genuinely of the place, it is a voice that carries both the responsibility and the authority of an ancient civilization recomposed part by part in its newer settings. Indeed some of the best English poetry written in Pakistan was a substantial topic of literary discussion in the 1960s and 1970s, in such cities as Lahore, Karachi, Dhaka, Chittagong, Rajshahi and Peshawar. The focus narrowed relatively in 1970s, and proponents such as Syed Ali Ashraf, Syed Sajjad Husain, and Taufiq Rafat saw historical forces transform the cultural continuum that was built in Pakistani English. The post-1971 situation in Pakistan (without the former East Pakistan) changed the priorities of literary discussion in Pakistani literary societies, which was always ancillary to actual literary practice anyway; for a Pakistani (or Northwestern) English idiom did exist in these parts of South Asia even before it was proffered somewhat officially and earnestly in the 1960s. What remains to be examined critically is to what extent the poets achieved their objective as well as what techniques they employed to *arrive* there. Indeed, there has been more sloganizing in this regard than actual probing. When a prominent writer was asked to comment on the subject as to what constituted a "Pakistani idiom in English" besides the local-colorist techniques and translation from other Pakistani languages, the answer came in the form of a stony silence. Another relevant inquiry would be to see whether the "Pakistani idiom" in English was not better achieved in work originating in quarters where it has been least talked about. It may be noted that the best English poetry in Pakistan was being written in the 1970s, when the talk about "Pakistani idiom" was already dying. Poets whose work has been established in both literature and the criticism of it are mainly those anthologized in *Pakistani Literature: The Contemporary English Writers* (1987). Particularly worth citing are the works of Taufiq Rafat's and Daud Kamal's of the period 1970–85; Shahid Hossain's work of the 1960s and 1970s; Ahmad Ali's and G. Alana's poetry of several decades, which will require elaborate periodization; and Zulfikar Ghose's work published during 1964–91. Kaleem Omar was a prolific poet during the 1970s. Then and during the early 1980s he produced work of considerable gusto. Maki Kureishi, also a fine poet, wrote during the 1970s and early 1980s. Her work, like Kaleem Omar's, has been anthologized (by both these poets and Rafat) and has elided more into poetic silence or into the salon-side seduction of *vers de sociêté* since the early 1980s. Yet it is essentially these poets who did the groundwork for Pakistani English poetry.

The novel as a genre has done extremely well, despite the commercial constraints that this particular category puts on the writer of Pakistani English. Some outstanding work has been published—mostly abroad—though there has been a steady stream of short stories also published within the country. It is Ahmed Ali's work that has generated much of Pakistani literature in English, for without him any account of South Asian English letters would not be complete. And the novel, among the various forms of his creative enterprise, is his major achievement. He has produced a substantial amount of original English poetry, nonfictional prose, and literary criticism, and an enormous body of translations from Urdu, Indonesian, Chinese and Arabic. Of Ali's three novels, two, *Twilight in Delhi* and *Ocean of Night*, were written, he notes, to "depict a phase of our national life and the decay of a whole culture, a particular mode of thought and living, values now dead and gone," as he studied the matter in colonial India. Accordingly, *Twilight in Delhi* is set in the great Indian center of Muslim civilization, Delhi, and the plot revolves around a simple love story of a boy and a girl, of Mughal and noble Arabic extractions, respectively, who go through ecstacies and agonies to have their love accepted, formalized and renewed despite social barriers or death. Around it is built a whole way of life, filled with customs and ceremonies that sustain a colorful though declining feudal culture, including the father's (Mir Nihal) pigeon-flying pastime, the *zenana* (female quarters), and the wedding rituals. In the outer circle, round the old house in a by-lane of Old Delhi *history* is seen at work in the Great Durbar held by the King-Emperor in 1911, the public reactions to the First World War, the influenza epidemic of 1919 and the political turmoil of 1920 in Northern India. *Ocean of Night* is set in the other great Muslim center, Lucknow. The mood is somewhat subdued; the atmosphere is one of repose amid a celebration dance and Muslim ideas of love, peace and friendship. The Nawab's mistress is a fine courtesan, and the young lawyer in love with her cannot overcome the class barrier to find fulfillment. The intellectual and mystical elements in the Muslim tradition are related to the political degeneration of Muslim civilization, and both ordinary feelings and the more delicate emotions are seen as atrophied or sacrificed to the remaining oligarchy's reckless life-style and idle, indiscriminate social pursuits.

These early novels by Ahmed Ali were concerned with the last of Muslim civilization in British India, of which little was left in that form after the British left. Both novels are in the realistic-poet tradition and actually use verse quotations as explicating, moralizing, and foreshadowing frames within the straightforward prose narrative. The device is also used by other Pakistani novelists, who either quote other language verse in translation or invent English jingles and Edward Lear–like rhymes. But Ali's more recent concerns in *Rats and Diplomats* are with general decay in the world, in which representatives of the "newly-freed fourth world" find analogues of decay and depravity matched to their own and prevalent on a universal scale. Consequently, the poetry disappears completely and so does realism. In *Rats and Diplomats*, a dismissed general named Sourirada Soutanna is appointed "Minister Plenipotentiary and Ambassador Extra-ordinary" of the People's Presidency of Bachusan and posted to the Ratusanian capital of Micea. Thus he finds himself catapulted headlong into quasi diplomacy—after suffering humiliation in a lost war, some dubious decoration and dishonor—in a country he had earlier found difficult to locate on a map or by compass. His handling of actual life and affairs in the territory proves no better than his theoretical grasp of the place, and after a clumsy and rather public escapade he is peremptorily recalled by the president of Bachusan. There ends the novel, as well as the hero's short and not-too-happy career in diplomacy. But what is more important is that, before the very end, he wakes up one morning with a tail grown at his back and transformed into a rat. Hardly anything in Ali's earlier longer fiction could have suggested the development of his present style. The historical imagination was always there; but such verve and humor had never been to the forefront in his English. It is a narrative which constantly alludes to signs, objects, and institutions of the familiar natural and social world, and it aspires to the moral status of a fable. General Soutanna relates all in his vigorous and sometimes self-parodic language, and what he relates is bleak though humorous, in a style now grave, now brisk, and in a novel that takes Ali's fiction into the postcolonial era and into a postcolonial mode.

This development, though individual in performance, has not taken place in isolation from the South Asian and international literary milieu, wherein the magical realism of a Marquez, Grass, Borges, Fowles, Fuentes, or Kundera has held the attention of a large readership and even pepped up the vogue for magic realism. This in turn ironically plays off the fantastic and comic against realistic social settings. Evidently an ironic instrument of discourse, the "scalpel"[3] had to replace the idealistic and reconstructive fictions of the colonial period which insufficiently grasped the historical forces at work and the tremendous flux that they had caused in the fundamental structure of colonial societies. The sheer proportion of change and cultural transmutation invoked gargantuan analogies and a comprehension of the overall absurdity of the situation.[4] Salman Rushdie's Saleem Sinai in *Midnight's Children* through his riotous imagination demolishes the distinction between the internal and external experience, and private and public history. Rushdie's *Shame*, likewise, uses the fairy-tale/nightmare technique to structure a fabulistic roman à clef that satirizes well-known referents picked from the contemporary common life which first pretend to a mock-history. The choppy text is made to mimic the discontinuity of good sense and harmony in the subject itself.[5]

But the fact that fiction need not mimic what it shows or deal with is succinctly brought home by Zulfikkar Ghose. Since the publication of his first novel, *Contradictions* (1966), Ghose's writings have displayed a consistent concern with language as the stuff of fictive life, which transcends both time and the material reality of which history is constituted. His last major work in the realistic/reconstructive tradition was *The Murder of Aziz Khan* (1967). Then followed the trilogy *The Incredible Brazilian* (1972–78) and *Crump's Terms* (1975), the latter in the stream-of-consciousness style with metafictional commentaries. Although *The Incredible Brazilian* is effective as historical romance, its major concern is with the "poetry of language . . . a mystical breathlessness" (*A Different World* 1978) and with "life [as] a constant process of elaborating a language" (*The Beautiful Empire* 1975). Further, Ghose's *Hulme's Investigations into the Bogart Script* (1981) asserts language as the only tangible reality, and the fiction to be an ironic history of self and society. *Figures of Enchantment* (1986), a superb postcolonial novel, which in its dislocations of both time and reality leaves only language as a textual figuration of survival amid all other human matter "decomposing . . . on the beach" at the end of the book. His latest novel, *The Triple Mirror of the Self* (1992), accentuates issues of marginalization against the deceptive mirrors of a repetitive, solipsistic reality and a self-constructing self. Cast as a spell over several continents, the narrative itself is the redemption sought for the "shadow man" of his hermetic imperial drama, which could as well mark the progress of a spiritual quest.

While the publication of such major novels by Zulfikar Ghose and Salman Rushdie, in the meantime, has swayed postcolonial fictional modes from realism to fantasy and metafictional language myths, Ali's work exemplifies a development different from any other writer. The reductio ad absurdum devices, including hyperbole, entailed in "wielding the scalpel" are, in fact, an enlargement of perception based on a new assessment of the historical moment. The new postcolonial modes have also arisen from new philosophical and literary interests. Two of Bapsi Sidhwa's three novels, *The Crow Eaters* (1978) and *Ice-Candy-Man* (1988), have introduced a farcical strain on another plane of performance into the Pakistani novel in English, a strain in which "sacred facts" appear laughable, and family and communal reserves and loyalties are put to a severe comic or eccentric test, even if it is only to explain, rationalize or accept those very facts. Desire is mixed with horror, astrology and mysticism with history, in Adam Zameenzad's *The Thirteenth House* (1987), to connect the past with the present and regain the child's freshness of perception. Tariq Ali's most recent novel, *Shadows of the Pomegranate Tree* (1992), seeks the source of strength in the great syncretic civilization of Muslim Andalusia but in the years just before the end of Muslim supremacy and the final collapse of its social structures. The family saga as a national or cultural narrative, in the vein of Ahmed Ali, is effective; and the colorful ambience of the medieval Muslim-European world is evoked to rejoin certain contraries which history, in spite of its explanations, does not seem able to justify. The novel is thus a ratiocinative instrument at a particular stage of our sociohistorical development. From poetic elegies to a dying civilization in colonial India, the move and the mood are not of regenerative celebration after Independence (1947); nor do the poetry and realism cleave any longer to history. Rather it is a pathetic humor and sad farce in the service of satire that appears to be the apposite instrument of a new postcolonial fiction.

There is little space to discuss short fiction, all of which indicates differing interests and stylistic strains as well as a fair level of accomplishment, in the work of such new writers as Aamer Hussein, Muneeza Shamsie, Rukhsana Ahmad, and Javaid Qazi. But judging from work done unto the end of the 1980s, we can definitely conclude that in fiction a new beginning has been made, no less than in poetry; and in this sense, although the styles and language textures vary,[6] there has been little formal distance between the writers working inside and outside the country. Temporally structured novels, episodic and talelike narratives and the realistic short story are all widely practiced alongside some experimental fiction.

It is, however, nonfiction that has been the most prolific genre. The writing and reading of biography, memoir, reportage and the sketch are still popular. Khalid Hasan and Anwer Mooraj are noted for the sureness and varieties of humor in their short-length, crisp journalism, while Shuaib bin Hasan has also been writing a popular newspaper column in his quirky if sententious style, proving that newspaper language in Pakistan is not the characterless and flat English practiced as a second (or second-rate) language, but that it has literary worth. Some of the outstanding writers of fictional work have been Allama Mohammed Iqbal, Quaid-e-Azam Mohammed Ali Jinnah, M. R. Kayani, A. K. Brohi and Zulfikar Ghose.

Critical forums in the country are few, but scholarly and literary journals more or less regularly publish creative and critical writing. Only a handful of books of literary worth appear every year, but the tradition is strong and continuous. Several academic institutions within the country and abroad now include Pakistani authors in their literature offerings. The interaction between English and other languages in the country has increased and intensified. English thus can now be an aware *local* catalyst for change. In fact, it has already begun to fulfill the new demands made upon it. No doubt, RP and the British Standard have increasingly gone out of use while remaining an academic reference point. Actually, during the last few decades, we have been going through one of the best creative periods in our linguistic and literary history. English writing is likely to receive further impetus from the country's rejoining of the Commonwealth. In time it should affect the creation of pertinent correspondences and complementarities in the literary culture. Indeed, from our sometimes separate paths it is largely English that brings us all together. The Pakistan Academy of Letters in Islamabad, which, among works in other Pakistani languages, awards the best book-length original English works as its national literature prize, is called the Patras Bokhari Award.

The recipients of this award so far have included A. R. Tabassum, Alamgir Hashmi, Bapsi Sidhwa, and Muhammed Musa. The demand for the removal of English by the constitutional deadline of 1988 has been met with further recognition and institutionalization of both Pakistani English and Pakistani literature in English; and what was least desired or at best doubtful until yesterday, or the day before, is now honored throughout the land. Academia is also a little more attentive, and Pakistani literature has been the focus of some master's theses at Government College, Lahore. Thus official ambivalence and systematic divergence have consistently found a solution within the larger framework of a strong educational tradition, whose scientific substance, Islamic complexion, and English medium will further contribute to sustaining and revivifying the resistance to colonial gestures.

NOTES

1. This chapter is a revised version of a paper presented at the First International Conference on English in South Asia, held at Islamabad, Pakistan, January 4–9, 1989.
2. An account of the planning and development of English and English studies in Pakistan pertaining to the 1978–88 period is to be found in my annual reports in *The Journal of Commonwealth Literature* (particularly in the "Introduction" and the "Research Aids" sections and in *Kunapipi*).
3. In a recent statement, Ali speaks about "Wielding the scalpel" (18) in *Contemporary Novelists*. 4th edition. Ed. D. L. Kirkpatrick (London and Chicago: St. James Press, 1986).
4. My earlier statements on Salman Rushdie (in "New Literature vs. Old Criticism: What Can You Do with a Text Like This?" *The Nation* October 17, 1986, p. iv) are not meant to be altered or qualified by the present statement; only a definition of his quality of humor and its occasion are here elaborated.
5. I am unable to discuss *The Satanic Verses* by Salman Rushdie as I have not read it, as a result of its proscription and unavailability in Pakistan. This is a case of censorship that needs to be addressed.
6. See Rahman 1990b.

WORKS CITED

Ali, Ahmed. *Twilight in Delhi*. London: Hogarth Press, 1940.

———. *Purple Gold Mountain*. London: Keepsake Press, 1960.

———. *Ocean of Night*. London: Peter Owen, 1964.

———. *Rats and Diplomats*. Karachi: Arkash Publishers, 1986.

Ali, Tariq. *Shadows of the Promegranate Tree*. London: Chatto and Windus, 1992.

Allana, G. *Hills of Heaven: Selected Poems*. Karachi: Royal Books, 1980.

Amir, Ali, et al. *The Life and Teachings of Mohammad: Or The Spirit of Islam*. London: W. H. Allen, 1891.

———. *A Short History of the Saracens*. London: Macmillan, 1899.

Baumgardner, Robert J. "The Pakistanization of English." *Higher Education News* (Islamabad) 8:12 (1988).

———. "The Indigenization of English in Pakistan." *English Today* 21 (1990) 59–65.

Burchfield, Robert, ed. *Supplement to The Oxford English Dictionary*. Oxford: Oxford University Press, 1972–1986.
Desai, Anita. *In Custody*. London: Heinemann. 1984.
Dil, Anwar S. *The Position of Teaching English in Pakistan*. Lahore, 1966.
———. *Pakistani Linguistics: Shahidullah Presentation Volume*. Lahore: Linguistics Research Group of Pakistan, 1966.
Foreign Area Studies, Several Hands Group for the U.S. Government. *Pakistan: A Country Study*. Washington D.C.: The American University Press, 1983.
Ghose, Zulfikar. *Contradictions*. London: Macmillan, 1966.
———. *The Murder of Aziz Khan*. London: Macmillan, 1967.
———. *The Incredible Brazilian: The Native*. London: Macmillan, 1972.
———. *The Beautiful Empire*. London: Macmillan, 1975a.
———. *Crump's Terms*. London: Macmillan, 1975b.
———. *A Different World*. London: Macmillan, 1978.
———. *Hulme's Investigation into the Bogart Script*. Austin, Tex.: Curbstone, 1981.
———. *Figures of Enchantment*. London: Hutchinson, 1986.
———. *A Triple Mirror of Self*. London: Bloomsbury, 1992.
Hamid Ali Khan. *A Farewell to London*. London: Whiteley, 1885.
Hashmi, Alamgir. *Commonwealth Literature: An Essay towards the Redefinition of Popular/Counter Culture*. London and Lahore: Vision Press, 1983.
———, ed. *The Worlds of Muslim Imagination*. Islamabad: Gulmohar Press, 1986.
———, ed. *Pakistani Literature: The Contemporary English Writers*. Islamabad: Gulmohar Press, 1987.
Kachru, Braj B. *The Alchemy of English: The Spread, Functions, and Models of Non-Native Englishes*. Oxford: Pergamon Press, 1986.
Kamal, Daud. *Recognitions*. Budleigh Salterton, England: Interim Press, 1979.
———. *A Remote Beginning*. Budleigh Salterton, England: Interim Press, 1985.
Lutfullah. *Autobiography of Lutfullah*. London: 1857.
Rafat, Taufiq. *Arrival of the Monsoon*. London: Vanguard, 1985.
Rahman Tariq. *Pakistani English: The Linguistic Description of a Non-Native Variety of English*. Islamabad: National Institute of Pakistani Studies, Quaid-i-Azam University, 1990.
Rushdie, Salman. *Midnight's Children*. London: Jonathan Cape, 1981.
———. *Shame*. London: Jonathan Cape, 1983.
Sake Deen Mohamed. *Travels*. Cork: Ireland, 1974.
Sidhwa, Bapsi. *The Crow Eaters*. London: Jonathan Cape, 1978.
———. *The Bride*. London: Jonathan Cape, 1983.
———. *Ice-Candy-Man*. London: Heinemann, 1988.
Singh, Rahul, ed. "Art and Literature." In *Khushwant Singh's View of India: Lectures on India's People, Religious History and Contemporary Affairs*. Bombay: India Book House, 1974.
Sirajuddin, Shaista Sonnu. "Three Contemporary Poets: A Study of Their Use of Language." *Explorations* 14: 1(1991), 51–63.
———. "Holding Language to Feeling," *The Nation Friday Review Explorations* 14:1 (1991), 51–63. (Oct. 30 1992), 20.
Suhrawardy, Shahid. *Essays in Verse*. Cambridge: Cambridge University Press, 1937.
Zameenzad, Adam. *The Thirteenth House*. London: Fourth Estate, 1987.

Canadian Writing in English and Multiculturalism

Leon Litvack

> Canada is an unknown territory for the people who live in it, and I'm not talking about the fact that you may not have taken a trip to the Arctic or to Newfoundland, you may not have explored—as the travel folders have it—This Great Land of Ours. I'm talking about Canada as a state of mind, as the space you inhabit not just with your body but with your head. It's that kind of space in which we find ourselves lost.
>
> What a lost person needs is a map of the territory, with his own position marked on it so he can see where he is in relation to everything else. Literature is not only a mirror; it is also a map, a geography of the mind. Our literature is one such map, if we can learn to read it as *our* literature, as the product of who and where we have been. We need such a map desperately, we need to know about here, because here is where we live. For the members of a country or culture, shared knowledge of their place, their here, is not a luxury but a necessity. Without that knowledge we will not survive.
>
> Margaret Atwood, *Survival*[1]

In terms of finding a voice for itself within postcolonial discourse, Canada presents interesting challenges. As Atwood's statement demonstrates, Canadian literary theory and practice are concerned with place and displacement, and with the development of an effective identifying relationship between self and environs. Canada is a unique, diverse country, stretching three-thousand miles from east to west, and also north to south. It has two official languages (English and French), and many unofficial, colloquial tongues. It shares its vast east-west border with the United States, an English-speaking, culturally aggressive nation-state boasting almost ten times its population. Its aboriginal peoples now constitute less than 2 percent of its inhabitants. While it covers almost four million square miles in area, three-quarters of the population live in towns or cities, and most of those are within two-hundred miles of the American border. Although Canada came together as a stable political unit in 1867, its present boundaries were only established in 1949.[2]

As a colony, Canada was difficult to sustain, yet the colonizers clearly perceived of it as worth having. The extensiveness and ruggedness of the landscape accounted for its gradual settlement by the European imperial powers. At first, white communities consisted of isolated trading posts and military garrisons, with scattered settlements (French and English) in the eastern part of the country. Increasing imperial ambitions inevitably led to a clash between the two main powers interested in the control of North America. The defeat of the French by the English in 1759 resulted in a brief period when most of settled North America was British. However the American Revolution soon followed, and it left Canada in a curiously anomalous position. At that time it largely consisted of a series of loyal communities which preferred to align themselves with Britain rather than with the United States, and which, from the beginning, sought to establish a viable society that assumed British social and political customs without hurrying into the extreme experiment of immediate independence. Within English Canada this loyalist community, unwilling to sever connections with the mother country, formed the nucleus of what eventually cohered as the Canadian nation. Thus there existed in the country/colony a firmly entrenched culture which was profoundly affected by the imperial process and carried reverberations and ramifications which extend from the moment of colonization to the present day.

While Canada's written history stretches back 500 years,[3] its English literary tradition is comparatively recent. The settlers who came (the euphemistic hewers of wood and drawers of water) looked back to Britain for literary sustenance, and because Canada had not severed political ties with the mother country, there was little reason to break literary connections. There were also practical barriers to indigenous literary productivity, such as the absence of a leisured class, the economies of printing and distributing, and the ready availability of cheap books from British and American publishers. In light of the persistence (for practical, political and cultural purposes) of the settler mentality, it is understandable that the incentive to produce an independent national literature, that might stand as both a foundation and a symbol, was comparatively weak.

It may almost seem quixotic to speak of a Canadian literary tradition. Early works, such as Susanna Moodie's *Roughing It in the Bush* (1852) and Catherine Parr Traill's *The Canadian Crusoes* (1852), both published in London and addressed to English audiences, concentrate on the "otherness" and "foreignness" of Canada for a European sensibility, and thus emphasize the privilege of "home" over "native," or "metropolitan" over "provincial." Even after the formation of the Dominion of Canada in 1867, it was not unseemly or unusual to equate pride in the new country with pride in the empire, thereby perpetuating sentiments and models derived from the colonizer. This is borne out in the work of Canada's "Confederation Poets," Charles G. D. Roberts, Bliss Carman, Archibald Lampman, and Duncan Campbell Scott. It is interesting to note that Roberts (1860–1943), the acknowledged "father" of Canadian literature, was simultaneously an imperialist and a Canadian, with no sense of conflicting loyalties. The models these poets used were largely derived from the English Romantic poets, particularly Wordsworth and Keats, and so there developed a poetry in which detailed reportages of the Canadian landscape were conveyed to readers in a domesticated form which, while eloquent and technically commendable, betrayed a sense of having been produced under imperial license. The Keatsian rhythms and the hauntingly elusive sense of loss and melancholy are unmistakable in the opening lines of Carman's "Low Tide on Grand Pré" (New York, 1893):

> Was it a year or lives ago
> We took the grasses in our hands,
> And caught the summer flying low
> Over the waving meadow lands
> And held it there between our hands?[4]

Carman (1861–1929) was widely read in his own time because he produced poems that conformed to popular preconceptions concerning what poetry—that is, English poetry—ought to be and do. He wrote of love and life and loss; his imagery was drawn from conventionally poetic subjects—flowers, sunsets, the sea, seasons (especially autumn)—with frequent references to dream and enchantment. He and his contemporaries confirmed the then dominant conviction that the colonizer's description of the relationship between self and place could be artfully translated across the Atlantic, with little need for alteration or even paraphrase. Promoters of the conservative colonial culture insisted on highly idealized literary forms, with appropriately unattainable moral implications.

The Canadian imagination was trapped by its colonial heritage until at least 1945, suffering from what the acclaimed Canadian critic Northrop Frye has termed Canada's "garrison mentality." Communities, surrounded by physical or psychological "frontiers," established cultural forts, which catered to closely knit, beleaguered societies, providing bastions against a huge, unthinking, menacing and formidable physical setting.[5] Given this situation, which emphasized the "victim position" and engendered survival strategies, it is understandable that Canadian communities not only encouraged shared human values and a great respect for law and order in the quest for social cohesion and protection of a fragile way of life, but also refused to engage with concepts of cultural difference, place and displacement. Until this debate could be initiated, Canada would not become a *bona fide* participant in the search for that key constituent of any postcolonial society: a distinctive identity.

The development of an independent Canadian literature depended upon the abrogation of this constraining power of a garrison mentality, and the appropriation of language and writing for new and distinctive usages. This movement away from sentimental filial gratitude to an older culture had its roots in the so-called McGill movement of the 1920s and 1930s, when F. R. Scott, in his poem "The Canadian Authors Meet,"[6] satirized the genteel tradition of a pious British

Canadianism, equating their "zeal for God and King" with their delight in nibbling on "sweet" cakes. Further, the Canadian National Anthem too is mocked, when the poet asks: "O Canada . . . Oh can a day go by" without the blind adoration of its colonized poets? As early as 1927, then the literati recognized that the perpetuation of "Little Englandism" was at best undesirable, and at worst degrading. Canadians were consistently portrayed as having to use the language of others, rather than one of their own creation, in order to give voice to the Canadian imagination.

The quest for and a definition of a Canadian identity became a national obsession, particularly after the Second World War. Paradoxically, Canada's participation in the conflict strengthened imperial sentiment and loyalty to Britain and resulted in a steady flow of writers, including Mordecai Richler and Margaret Laurence, to the imperial metropolis in order to undergo an extended literary apprenticeship. Yet there was an opposing trend, which forced on Canadians a rapid consideration and formulation of their identity and autonomy: the encroaching influence of the United States. This exercise of power was not confined to economic control of industry and natural resources, but manifested itself as the pervasive presence of American television, film, book and magazine publishing, and the ubiquitous manifestations of "pop" culture. Canadians have always felt ambivalent toward their southern neighbor. In the first half of this century the country experienced a brain-drain which took thousands across the border to university positions, journalism, publishing, films, radio, and music, as well as to American industry. Cultural enterprises, including publishing, filmmaking and broadcasting, all suffered as a result of American competition. Canada was in danger of becoming a cultural branch-plant satellite of the United States. This fear has not been allayed—and may have become intensified—in the wake of the North American Free Trade Agreement of 1992; Canada continues to run the risk of anonymity, concealed by the shadow of a society which unashamedly asserts its efficient consumerism, its superior technological inventiveness, and its status as world's only enduring superpower.

Canadian resentment of and resistance to the American "invasion," coupled with the dissipation of cultural obeisance to Britain, resulted in the development of a Canadian critical school which specialized in what may be termed "denial response" discourse. The academics and literati at the center of the debate wished to establish that the texts constituting a Canadian literature were separate from the metropolitan canon. This they tried to do in three ways: (1) by attempting to define the relationship between social and literary practices in the old world and the new (in this case complicated by the omnipresence of the United States); (2) by analyzing the association between the imported language and the new place; and (3) by giving expression to some numinous idea of national identity, which emphasized the distinctive features of the particular national or regional culture and landscape. In each case the response focused on what other countries were, and what Canada was not. In literature this position may be seen in Margaret Atwood's poem "Backdrop Addresses Cowboy":

Then what about me

what about the I
confronting you on that border
you are always trying to cross?

I am the horizon
you ride towards, the thing you never can lasso

I am also what surrounds you:
my brain
scattered with you
tincans, bones, empty shells,
the litter of your invasions.

I am the space you desecrate
as you pass through.[7]

Canada, seen here addressing the United States, is a horizon, a space, something which cannot be captured, but by the same token, something unattainable, something denied.

Also unattainable in Canada was a truly independent literary world, either a Bohemia or an establishment. As a result, many Canadian writers have been forced into institutional settings—an exceptionally high proportion of them are linked to universities, and literature and criticism have become almost inseparable as a result.[8] So close is the correspondence that George Woodcock was able to formulate an "identikit" for the average Canadian writer: living near a campus, teaching at least part time at university level, mingling too much for his work's good with academics, doing as much writing as he can for the Canadian Broadcasting Corporation (CBC), and always hoping for a Canada Council Fellowship that will take him away for a year in Mento or the Greek Islands.[9] This common experience caused English Canadian writing to become institutionalized, protectionist, middle-class, monocultural, and blinkered in its concerns. There was little awareness shown of the vast physical reach in the country, or of the diversity of cultural origins. The prospect of finding a monolithic national or nationalist culture was nonexistent; the vacuum created by the absence of an independent national literature remained.

By a strange twist of fate, however, the control/support which the government offered to writers proved to be the impetus required to lift literature from its anomalous position, and it sparked an explosion in the arts in Canada. The transformation began with Vincent Massey, who presided over a Royal Commission on the State of the Arts (1949–51), which arose out of a sensitivity to (or fear of) the dangers of foreign influence and foreign control of the arts in Canada. The recommendations he made to government, including the provision of funds to stimulate creative and scholarly activity, resulted in the formation of the Canada Council (1957). From the beginning the Canada Council was allowed an "arm's length" relationship with government: grants to artists, publishers and performers were awarded by independent juries selected from the artistic community and representative of all regions. The result has been an incredible (though politically induced) upsurge in artistic activity in every part of the country and has helped to collectivize—and thus unify—creative potential. The Massey Commission was aided by a feeling of cultural nationalism surrounding Canada's centennial year (1967), and this encouraged the establishment of national reading venues (such as the Harbourfront Festival in Toronto), the opening of new theaters (particularly in regional centers such as Halifax, Edmonton and Regina), the founding of organizations such as the League of Canadian Poets and the Writers' Union of Canada, and, significantly, the introduction of Canadian literature into schools in the 1970s. Bookstores began to stock Canadian books in ever increasing numbers, and people read them.[10]

On a university level the effect was even more striking. A Royal Commission headed by T.H.B. Symons was formed at the request of the Association of Universities and Colleges in Canada, and its report, *To Know Ourselves* (1975), led to a doubling of the number of undergraduate Canadian literature courses across the country. This development in turn encouraged the Department of External Affairs to embark on a deliberate policy of raising Canada's cultural profile abroad—and (as part of an unstated agenda) producing an impression of national unity. This self-promotion, aided by financial incentives, has led to the foundation of Canadian studies programs throughout the United States and Europe, and also in India, Russia and the Far East, as well as to the formation of an umbrella organization, the International Council for Canadian Studies.[11] At home, developments were encouraged in publication; grants in aid of research led to several new critical publications, including *Journal of Canadian Studies, Essays on Canadian Writing, Studies in Canadian Literature,* and *Canadian Poetry.* Thus, as the result of government incentives, Canada was beginning to assert its literary and cultural independence. Gone were the days of Northrop Frye's model of literary discussions in Canada as a shopper's dialogue: "Have you any Canadian literature today?" "Well, we're expecting something in very shortly."[12] However artificially or incongruously, Canadian literature had arrived.

The injection of capital did not, however, dispel the disillusionment caused by the unquantifiable nature of "Canadianness" and the impossibility of affirming distinctive features of national culture. This meant that Canadian critics tended to use thematic models as a means of discovering order at the base of social and cultural trends, and hence as a basis for discourse. Seminal works such as Atwood's *Survival* (1972) concentrated on the "victim position," and on the presence of a central unifying and informing symbol at the core of society.[13] Survival as a symbol is multifaceted and adaptable, stretching from survival in the face of "hostile" elements or natives, to survival of crisis or natural disaster, to cultural survival, to survival of a vanished order which has managed to persist after its time is past. Northrop Frye's *The Bush Garden: Essays on the Canadian Imagination* (1971) has been extremely influential, forming the basis for much critical discussion, even today. His Jungian analysis (combined with his own training in theology) lodged

Canadian criticism in the wilderness by advocating that the question which should be asked is not "Who am I?" but rather "Where is here?" The query promulgates others: Where is this place in relation to other places? How do I find my way around? and even How did I get "here" in the first place? Frye's psychological exploration derived from Christian metaphor, and from the belief that literature is not about life but about other literature; that is, it recodes cultural heritage by reenacting the patterns of previous writing. This version of cultural expression was clearly colonial, because it accepted European culture as the ideological frame of reference for interpreting Canada and anticipated "mythic" patterns of recurrence.

However outdated or alienating this thesis might seem as the basis for an assertive, postcolonial Canadian literary criticism, and as a politics of culture, Frye's study does have lasting value. His work was pioneering and provided Canadian literary theory with extraliterary functions. Extraordinarily perceptive in gauging national moods and trends, he was aware that the problem of Canadian identity needed to be regionalized, localized, even individualized, in order to be understood properly; he therefore distinguished between two concepts which were often seen as synonymous: Canadian identity and unity. Identity, he believed, was local and regional, rooted in the imagination and in works of culture; unity, on the other hand, was national in reference, international in perspective, and rooted in political feeling.[14] *The Bush Garden*, then, pointed to the effectiveness of Canadian criticism as a social instrument, serving as a vehicle of political comment and social awareness.

The centrally funded cultural nationalism of the 1960s and 1970s, which had helped to foster so much creative energy and had inspired literary and pedagogical commitment, had, by the early 1980s, become diluted by economic depression, constitutional difficulties, and cultural disillusionment. The then prime minister, Pierre Trudeau, worked toward the repatriation of the Canadian Constitution; the process ended in 1982 with the Canadian Constitution Act, which removed the last remnant of British government authority over Canadian law.[15] The new Act was, however, problematic: because of insufficient recognition of Québec's special cultural status within the Canadian federation, the province did not sign the agreement. Most importantly, clauses dealing with Indian aboriginal rights were left for later discussion. Such issues, which are as yet unresolved, led to a multiplying of social tensions within the country.

Paradoxically, the political disappointments of the 1980s, and the consequent erosion of national unity, have resulted in increased opportunities for individual expression. The concept of identity, which Frye had shown to be more localized than at first believed, was redefined, focusing on regional consciousnesses in Canada, through the work of such writers as Alistair MacLeod, Margaret Laurence, Rudy Wiebe and Robert Kroetsch. On a critical level, the denial of national coherence was aided by developments in poststructuralism, which abandoned unity, continuity and homogeneity for diversity, discontinuity and otherness. The promotion of regionalism was complemented by a chorus of voices from communities that had previously been silenced as a result of the distinctly academic character of literary practice, and the consequent authority exercised by a confident middle-class literary establishment.[16] These new voices, many from minority and immigrant cultures (whose ethnic distribution in Canada is largely regional in character),[17] were not burdened by the persistent quest for national unity; they celebrated personal pasts and a range of futures. Once again, however, the agenda was being set by central government: the literary map of Canada was being redrawn through the adoption of an official policy of multiculturalism. In light of rising social tension, trends in immigration and the changing ethnic makeup of the country, the institution of multiculturalism could be seen as Canada's attempt to defuse the Anglophone-Francophone dualism; to forge a national image unlike that of the American ideology of the melting pot; to make an outstanding contribution to the field of race and community relations; and to function as a political springboard from which to achieve the ever-elusive goal of national cohesion. This sentiment, of course, is the distilled idealization of both political and cultural leaders who envision a new Canada that is unique, yet is a participant in the global forum.

The word "multiculturalism" emerged in Canada during the 1960s to counter the word "biculturalism" as used in the terms of reference of the Royal Commission on Bilingualism and Biculturalism.[18] By 1971, when the term was officially adopted by the federal government to describe a policy enclosed within a bilingual (English and French) framework, it enshrined three distinct meanings. It was (1) the social policy of encouraging retention of group heritages and full participation in Canadian society; (2) the philosophy or ideology of cultural pluralism; and (3) a measure of ethnic diversity within a society.

Multiculturalism has been embraced on a political level in a number of ways. In the new Canadian Constitution of 1982, clause 27 stated that the *Charter of Rights and Freedoms* shall be interpreted in a manner consistent with the preservation and enhancement of the multicultural heritage of Canadians. In 1985 a House of Commons Standing Committee on Multiculturalism was established. In 1988, as part of a plan to strengthen the multicultural provisions of the constitution, Parliament passed the *Canadian Multiculturalism Act*, which was committed to four distinct areas: (1) Race Relations and Cross-Cultural Understanding; (2) Heritage Cultures and Languages; (3) Community Support and Participation; and (4) Cross-Governmental Commitment. In the same year the Prime Minister announced the creation of a new Department of Multiculturalism and Citizenship, devoted to promoting Canadian pluralism and encouraging an active and informed citizenry. More specifically, the Minister of Multiculturalism and Citizenship is mandated to promote among all members of Canadian society an understanding of the values inherent in Canadian citizenship, and to encourage participation in the social, cultural, political and economic life of Canada, as well as to promote a greater awareness and understanding of human rights, fundamental freedoms and related values.

Multicultural writing in Canada treats these issues with great insight and draws immense strength from looking to cultural roots for inspiration. Despite the sometimes "other-worldly" nature of their experience, these writers also consider themselves "Canadian," and their writing provides an arena for dialogue about reconciling different aspects of their identities. Recent trends in immigration prove that ethnocultural diversity is now an integral part of the Canadian experience: at present the majority of Canadians can trace their roots back to origins which are non-British or non-French.[19] Generalizations cannot be made without the experience of "hyphenated" Canadians: questions of gender, class, religion, race, and education affect the lived experience and literary productions of writers in fundamental ways. At the core of many literary productions which can be grouped under the multicultural heading is the development of a sense of individual identity and self-worth. Although the novelist Frank Paci, for example, cannot be said to speak for a monolithic Italian-Canadian experience, his writing about this duality (which he says played a "large role" in shaping him) casts some light upon the attempt to come to terms with two—or more—identities. As Paci admits, writing "seemed the only way to find out who I was and why I was on earth."[20]

In the past, it might have been possible to designate Canada as a country of "two solitudes," a phrase taken from the title of Hugh MacLennan's novel. In 1945 when the work was published, perhaps French and English were still the dominant ethnocultural groups in Canada; certainly the only people who could contest their historical claim to founding status were the indigenous native populations. Almost half a century later, however, the multiracial, pluriethnic nature of Canada is an undeniable reality. And one of the consequences of this change is that MacLennan's idealistic optimism has to be reconsidered, for his title alluded to a poem by Rainer Maria Rilke: where the lovers "touch, and greet each other."[21] With the cultural diversity that twentieth-century immigration has brought to Canada have come both cultural riches and social tensions that move far beyond those of bilingualism and biculturalism. When, on 12 July 1988, the House of Commons passed Bill C-93, "An Act for the Preservation and Enhancement of Multiculturalism in Canada," it enshrined both an ideal and an ideology.

It is clear that the degree of government support of national literature emphasizes how broadly political the cultural affairs of Canada have become. While the new voices are not visibly frozen into a hierarchical relationship with the dominant group, the writers are deeply conscious of the potential of immigration and ethnic diversity for emphasizing difference and division, rather than any social ideal. There are various questions which must be asked in considering how literary critics should align themselves in the multicultural debate: (1) How do we construct a federation that will accommodate racial and ethnic diversity without infringing on individual rights, group rights, and state rights to govern? (2) How do we approach a concept that simultaneously liberates yet confines, enhances yet detracts, unites yet divides, and provokes yet reconciles? (3) Does multiculturalism increase the risk of ethnic conflict, or do multicultural policies enhance social peace by fostering the equality of all races and cultures? (4) To what extent is multiculturalism a preservative policy with respect to culture, as opposed to a transformative doctrine with the potential to restructure Canada along pluralist lines?[22]

As Ashcroft, Griffiths and Tiffin have realized, multiculturalism has nationalist liberationist potential. However, the result of adopting an official multicultural policy could be political quietism, ineffectiveness, and even a reactionary stance. Postcolonial discourse in Canada, with the special emphasis given to it by multiculturalism, runs the risk of adopting colonizing tendencies itself, and thus serving as a device for the reintroduction and reincorporation of difference, leading to cultural neocolonialism among politicians and theorists alike.[23] The dangers are obvious: multiculturalism has been cultivated as part of a political agenda and has been employed by sociologists as describing "a formal instrument for *managing diversity*" (emphasis added).[24] While Canada has experienced a radical destabilization of national unity, multiculturalism, as a response, runs the risk of being hijacked in order to function as a new model to describe the power relations between "center" and "margin."

Multicultural writing in Canada is at an early stage of development. Many of the writers are concerned with declaring the experience of a particular ethnic group. The literature is in many ways consistent with postmodern conceptions of literary discourse, fostering a critical reconsideration of the relationship between fact and fiction, and consequently the deconstruction of previous treatments of historical data.[25] Joy Kogawa, for example, in her novels *Obasan* (1981) and *Itsuka* (1992), documents the history of the Japanese-Canadians, from the time of their forced evacuation from the Pacific coast into internment camps during World War II, through the period of the postwar government dispersion policy, to the eventual achievement of financial redress in 1988. Such works are often semi-documentary, taking the form of the bildungsroman. One typical premise results in integration and success. Another common motif, such as that found in Frank Paci's *Black Madonna* (1982) and *Black Blood* (1991), involves a child of immigrant parents adapting to the new land more readily than the parents, but never quite seeming to belong. The impulse to reject old values (or the desire to retain them) recurrently stands between the individual and the majority. The nationalities involved are various: Jan Drabek (*The Exotic Canadians*, 1990) traces the plight of the Czech refugee; Austin Clarke (*Nine Men Who Laughed*, 1986) that of the West Indian in urban Canada; Myrna Kostash (*All of Baba's Children*, 1977) of the Ukrainians; and Katherine Vlassie (*Children of Byzantium*, 1987) of the Greeks. In each case the writer explores the resistance to the label of "immigrant," probing instead the representative life of workers, mothers and other individuals whose "otherness" in Canada tends to obscure fundamental estimations of their quality, character, social role, or options for the future.

The increased output of multicultural literature over the last ten or fifteen years has interrupted the nationalist search for—and canonization of—a Canadian literary mainstream. In achieving postcolonial status, Canada has benefited from multiculturalism, because the various cultures represented have produced a quasi hybridization. As Ashcroft et al. have pointed out, whereas in much European thinking, history, ancestry, and the past form a powerful reference point for epistemology, in postcolonial thought, temporal lineality is replaced with a spatial plurality: time broadens into space.[26] Canadian literary theory has, in breaking away from European domination, generally retained a nationalist stance; yet, in the wake of regionalism and multiculturalism, theories of literary hybridity have not yet replaced the nationalistic approach. Instead many critics, including Frank Davey, W. H. New, W. J. Keith, and George Bowering, have strived for outside recognition by retreating from the dynamics of difference into the neouniversalist internationalist stance. Canadian scholars have found it difficult to accommodate the multicultural or ethnic factor into their aesthetic approaches.[27] There have been exceptions, such as Eli Mandel ("Ethnic Voice in Canadian Writing"), E. D. Blodgett (*Configurations*), Francesco Loriggio ("The Question and the Corpus"), and Linda Hutcheon (introduction to *Other Solitudes*); however these do not yet seem to have been incorporated, to a significant degree, into mainstream Canadian literary theory.

This confrontational stance, and reluctance to acknowledge hybridization as part of Canadian critical discourse, points to a fundamental difficulty shared by many postcolonial theorists: the problematic transmuting of time into space. For many postcolonial societies, including Canada, the present is struggling out of a past heavily laden with cultural baggage and is attempting to construct a future. The cultural encounter between the center and the margin must function on a level where difference is accepted on an egalitarian basis. The initiation of cross-cultural dialogue has the potential to put an end to the apparently endless human history of conquest and annihilation justified by the myth of group "purity," and thus serve as the basis on which the postcolonial world can be creatively stabilized.[28] This view, advocated by Ashcroft et al., provides a framework of "difference on equal terms," within which multicultural theories, both within and between societies, may continue to be fruitfully explored.

A prominent feature of most postcolonial writing is the part played by aboriginal people in the finding of their own voice, and the staking of a claim for themselves in the literary canon. In Canada the status of Native Canadians is a sensitive issue (particularly in light of the recent negotiations with the federal government over land claims), and while it may be helpful to consider their imaginative productions in the light of postcolonial theory and practice, they must not be shunted into the category of multicultural writers. If this is done, then it amounts to another denial response of literary critics, who refuse to recognize the difference between Canadian *writing* in English, and the tradition of *orature* which lies at the heart of Native Canadian culture and narrative construction. When in 1973 W. H. New identified a "historical absence of an Indian presence in Canadian literature,"[29] it was filled first by non-native writers, including George Ryga (*The Ecstasy of Rita Joe*, 1967), W. O. Mitchell (*The Vanishing Point*, 1973), Rudy Wiebe (*The Temptations of Big Bear*, 1973, and *The Scorched-Wood People*,

1977) and Robert Kroetsch (*Gone Indian*, 1973). While these works were sympathetic to the Native Canadian cause, they nevertheless betrayed a patronizing attitude, by denying Native Canadian writers a much-needed autonomy. Orature tends towards the anecdotal and episodic, and to readers schooled in the English literary tradition, the rambling conversational manner and exaggerated action of Indian myths can seem tedious, and their subject matter and hermetic meanings frustrating.[30] When texts stemming from the oral tradition first appeared in the 1960s, they were usually collected, translated, and often heavily edited by non-native missionaries, anthropologists, and hobbyists. Moreover, they tended to represent Native "tales" from the igloo, the smokehouse, or the campfire as "quaint" or "exotic," fit for ethnological inquiry perhaps, but not for serious literary study.[31] Native authors are now speaking out against the abuses of their cultural heritage by non-natives, who claim varying degrees of authority and initiation and who produce books for a growing market that is increasingly hungry for specific aspects of Native cultures. In the process, the appropriators acquire money, fame, and prestige, while simultaneously perpetuating colonial oppression by obliterating those in whose voices they speak or claim to speak.

Many Native writers were outraged by the effective control exercised over the means of communication. After centuries of material dispossession, relocation, and genocide, the colonizers were now engaged in plundering Native spirituality, the essence of their identity. In Canada today, authors who produce books about Natives, and especially those whose narrators or personae assume Native voices, are being asked to halt their appropriation of Native stories, and to give the Native authors a chance to gain autonomy over their imaginative expressions. Non-native authors in Canada have reacted widely and publicly to such demands, and their reactions have ranged from compliance (Anne Cameron stopped writing in the Native voice), to defiance (Lynn Andrews continues her writing), to outraged cries against "censorship" (George Bowering and Betty Jane Wylie).[32]

An important aim of Native Canadian writing is the assertion of social and cultural difference. The conversational manner, the fragmentariness, the nonlinear narrative structures in the work of such writers as Harry Robinson ("An Okanagan Indian Becomes a Captive Circus Showpiece in England") and Thomas King ("The One about Coyote Going West") have radically questioned assumptions made by about the characteristics of genres usually employed by Canadian literary critics as structuring and categorizing definitives (novel, lyric, epic, etc.). The sense of that which ought to be given the name "literature" has been altered by writers such as Lenore Keeshig-Tobias, Lee Maracle, Ruby Slipperjack, Jeannette Armstrong, and others, incorporating and adapting traditional forms of imaginative expression to the exigencies of an inherited English language.[33]

In making pronouncements about culture, politics and literature (concepts which are inextricably linked in Canada as elsewhere), it must be recognized that all but 2 percent of the country's present inhabitants are descended from immigrants. Margaret Atwood reminds us that "We are all immigrants to this place even if we were born here."[34] Today's English Canadian writing, which has been identified by Malcolm Ross as "the impossible sum of our traditions," is closely allied to the growing pains of Canadian nationhood.[35] While multiculturalism as a political construct may be seen by its critics as a sign of the collective historical guilt (or even hypocrisy) resulting from Canada's earlier immigration policies; as a sophisticated form of assimilation; or a stratagem to divert attention from questions about identity, it is undeniable that as a result of profound changes in the country's ethnic makeup, there is an explicit commitment, on all levels, to diversity. From the point of view of literature, the postcolonial stance of an increasing number of writers privileges usage and syncreticity and hopes to amend individual and community assumptions about the acts of reading and writing, currently entrenched in institutional structures which are still obsessed by nationalist ideologies. Some writers are wrestling with a new language to describe a new place; others are seeking to alter the unprivileged position into which their experiences, narratives and languages have been placed by the colonizing power. The forces which threaten to relegate Canadian postcolonial discourse to the margin must be opposed for the sake of those whose voices are not being heard for the first time. "Center" and "margin" now have the potential to reach a state of equilibrium, revealing a treasure trove of creative energy. A course must be set for a critical position where Canadian experience may be confidently viewed as uncentered, pluralistic, and multifarious, and where a postcolonial model of indigeneity may be firmly established.

NOTES

1. Margaret Atwood, *Survival: A Thematic Guide to Canadian Literature* (Toronto: Anansi, 1972) 18–19.

2. In 1867, when the Dominion of Canada was created ("Confederation"), the country consisted of New Brunswick, Nova Scotia, Ontario and Québec. In 1870 these provinces were joined by Manitoba, in 1871 (on the understanding that there would be a transcontinental railway) by British Columbia, and in 1873 by Prince Edward Island. Alberta and Saskatchewan joined in 1905, and in 1949 the province of Newfoundland joined Confederation to complete the nation's current boundaries.

3. The explorer John Cabot entered the Gulf of St. Lawrence in 1497.

4. Bliss Carman, "Low Tide on Grand Pré," *Poets of the Confederation*, ed. Malcolm Ross (Toronto: McClelland and Stewart, 1960) 26, lines 16–20.

5. Northrop Frye, "Conclusion to a Literary History of Canada," *The Bush Garden: Essays on the Canadian Imagination* (Toronto: Anansi, 1971), 225.

6. See F. R. Scott, "The Canadian Authors Meet," *The New Oxford Book of Canadian Verse in English*, ed. Margaret Atwood (Toronto: Oxford University Press, 1982), 91, lines 9–24.

7. Margaret Atwood, "Backdrop Addresses Cowboy," *Poets of Contemporary Canada 1960–1970*, ed. Eli Mandel (Toronto: McClelland and Stewart, 1972), 98–99, lines 25–37.

8. These institutionalized literary figures have included Earle Birney, George Bowering, Robertson Davies, Louis Dudek, Northrop Frye, Graeme Gibson, Hugh Hood,

Robert Kroetsch, Michael Ondaatje, Hugh MacLennan, Eli Mandel, Jay Macpherson, E. J. Pratt, James Reaney, and Rudy Wiebe.

9. George Woodcock, "*Away From Lost Worlds*: Notes on the Development of a Canadian Literature," *Odysseus Ever Returning: Essays on Canadian Writers and Writings* (Toronto: McClelland and Stewart, 1970), 3. It should be noted that part of the government mandate to the CBC is that it should, through its broadcasts, encourage the promotion of Canadian identity and unity.

10. In the late 1970s the incentive to read Canadiana was increased by such incentives as the "half-back" scheme, instituted by the government of Ontario: readers could exchange provincial lottery tickets for discounts of up to 50 percent on Canadian books.

11. Organizations like the British Association for Canadian Studies, founded in 1974, owe their existence and scholarly output to generous annual grants from the Academic Relations Division of the External Affairs Department.

12. Northrop Frye, conclusion, *Literary History of Canada*, 2nd ed. (Toronto: University of Toronto Press, 1976), 3: 319.

13. See Bill Ashcroft, Gareth Griffiths, and Helen Tiffin, *The Empire Writes Back* (London: Routledge, 1989), 141–142, where Atwood's *Survival*, advocating the Canadian "victim position," is seen (by these Australian critics) as being at the center of contemporary critical discourse in Canada.

14. Frye, *The Bush Garden*, ii.

15. Until the Canadian Constitution Act was passed, relations between the provincial and federal governments were subject to review in London, and the British Judicial Committee of the Privy Council functioned as Canada's highest court.

16. Consider Ann Diamond's recent assessment of a reading sponsored by the Canadian branch of PEN: " 'Canadian Literature' is a private club, surrounded by an empty wilderness. And we, the people Outside, are the animals. As well as the audience. There is room for only a few in the garrison culture, and those few will never budge. Many are called in Canada, but all the positions are taken. They were filled before you got here. For life. Here's where the *Survival* formula gets a bit threadbare. Just what exactly is surviving here, these days?" ("The Animals in That Country: A Look at the Toronto-Centric Universe," *Books in Canada*, April 1993, 28).

17. Ethnic is understood here as a terminological market characterizing both the racially and culturally distinctive features of a certain group. This definition allows for an application of the term to indigenous peoples such as the aboriginals (Indians and Inuit), confessional denominations such as the Mennonites, as well as groups like the Ukrainians and Italians, who have preserved a unique cultural heritage in their adopted country.

18. For this summary on the development of Canadian multiculturalism I am indebted to the Minister's Message in *Together* 1.1 (Winter 1990): 2–3.

19. See the chapter on "Multiculturalism: A Fact of Canadian Life" in Augie Fleras and Jean Leonard Elliott, *Multiculturalism in Canada: The Challenge of Diversity* (Toronto: Nelson, 1992), 25–52.

20. Frank Paci, interview with Joseph Pivato, *Other Solitudes: Canadian Multicultural Fictions*, ed. Linda Hutcheon and Marion Richmond (Toronto: Oxford University Press, 1990), 231.

21. Epigraph to Hugh MacLennan, *Two Solitudes* (1945; Toronto: Macmillan, 1991).

22. For a full debate on these questions see Fleras and Elliott.

23. *The Empire Writes Back*, 179.

24. Fleras and Elliott, 2.

25. See Linda Hutcheon, "Canadian Historiographic Metafiction," *Essays on Canadian Writing* 30 (1984–85), 228–239.

26. *The Empire Writes Back*, 34.

27. See Barry Cameron's survey, "Theory and Criticism: Trends in Canadian Literature," in *Literary History of Canada*, ed. W. H. New, 2nd ed. (Toronto: University of Toronto Press, 1990), 4: 108–132.

28. See Enoch Padolsky, "Cultural Diversity and Canadian Literature: A Pluralistic Approach to Majority and Minority Writing in Canada," *International Journal of Canadian Studies* 3 (1991): 110–128.

29. W. H. New, "Fiction," *Literary History of Canada: Canadian Literature in English* (Toronto: University of Toronto Press, 1973), 3: 248.

30. See, for example, the patronizing assessment by Penny Petrone in the entry "Indian Legends and Tales," in *The Oxford Companion to Canadian Literature* (Toronto: Oxford University Press, 1983), 377–83.

31. See Hartmut Lutz's preface to his *Contemporary Challenges: Conversations with Canadian Native Authors* (Saskatoon: Fifth House, 1991), 1–11.

32. For an interesting consideration of the partnership between a Native writer and a white academic in the compilation of an anthology of Canadian aboriginal writing see "Preface: Two Voices" in *An Anthology of Canadian Native Literature in English*, ed. Daniel David Moses and Terry Goldie (Toronto: Oxford University Press, 1992), xii–xxii.

33. Two useful anthologies, which give some idea of the panorama of native writing, are Moses and Goldie, and Thomas King (ed.), *All My Relations* (Toronto: McClelland and Stewart, 1990).

34. Margaret Atwood, afterword, *The Journals of Susanna Moodie* (Toronto: Oxford University Press, 1970) 62.

35. See Malcolm Ross, "The Impossible Sum of our Traditions," *The Impossible Sum of our Traditions: Reflections on Canadian Literature* (Toronto: McClelland and Stewart, 1986), 184–202.

WORKS CITED

Ashcroft, Bill, Gareth Griffiths, and Helen Tiffin. *The Empire Writes Back: Theory and Practice in Post-Colonial Literatures.* London: Routledge, 1989.

Atwood, Margaret. "Backdrop Addresses Cowboy." In *Poets of Contemporary Canada 1960–1970.* Ed. Eli Mandel. Toronto: McClelland and Stewart, 1972. 98–99.

———. *The Journals of Susanna Moodie.* Toronto: Oxford University Press, 1970.

———. *Survival: A Thematic Guide to Canadian Literature.* Toronto: Anansi, 1972.

Blodgett, E. D. *Configurations: Essays on the Canadian Literatures.* Toronto: ECW, 1982.

Cameron, Barry. "Theory and Criticism: Trends in Canadian Literature." In *Literary History of Canada: Canadian Literature in English*, 2nd ed. Ed. W. H. New. University of Toronto Press, 1990. 4:108–32.

Carman, Bliss. "Low Tide on Grand Pré." In *Poets of the Confederation.* Ed. Malcolm Ross. Toronto: McClelland and Stewart, 1960. 26–27.

Clarke, Austin. *Nine Men Who Laughed.* Markham, Canada: Penguin, 1986.

Diamond, Anne. "The Animals in That Country: A Look at the Toronto-Centric Universe." *Books in Canada* (April 1993): 27–28.

Drabek, Jan. *The Exotic Canadians.* Ottawa: Borealis, 1990.

Fleras, Augie, and Jean Leonard Elliott. *Multiculturalism in Canada: The Challenge of Diversity.* Toronto: Nelson, 1992.

Frye, Northrop. *The Bush Garden: Essays on the Canadian Imagination.* Toronto: Anansi, 1971.

Hutcheon, Linda. "Canadian Historiographic Metafiction." *Essays on Canadian Writing* 30 (1984–85): 228–39.

Hutcheon, Linda, and Marion Richmond, eds. *Other Solitudes: Canadian Multicultural Fictions.* Toronto: Oxford University Press, 1990.

King, Thomas, ed. *All My Relations: An Anthology of Contemporary Canadian Native Fiction.* Toronto: McClelland and Stewart, 1990.

Kogawa, Joy. *Itsuka.* Toronto: Viking, 1992.

———. *Obasan.* 1981. Toronto: Penguin, 1983.

Kostash, Myrna. *All of Baba's Children.* Edmonton: Hurtig, 1977.

Loriggio, Francesco. "The Question and the Corpus: Ethnicity and Canadian Literature." In *Future Indicative: Literary Theory and Canadian Literature.* Ed. John Moss. Ottawa: University of Ottawa Press, 53–69.

Lutz, Hartmut. *Contemporary Challenges: Conversations with Canadian Native Authors.* Saskatoon: Fifth House, 1991.

MacLennan, Hugh. *Two Solitudes.* Toronto: Macmillan, 1991.

Mandel, Eli. "Ethnic Voice in Canadian Writing." In *Another Time,* Erin, Canada: Press Porcepic, 1977. 91–102.

Moses, Daniel David, and Terry Goldie, eds. *An Anthology of Native Canadian Literature in English.* Toronto: Oxford University Press, 1992.

New, W. H. "Fiction." In *Literary History of Canada: Canadian Literature in English.* Toronto: University of Toronto Press, 1973: 3: 233–83.

Paci, Frank G. *Black Blood.* Ottawa: Oberon, 1991.

———. *Black Madonna.* Ottawa: Oberon, 1982.

Padolsky, Enoch. "Cultural Diversity and Canadian Literature: A Pluralistic Approach to Majority and Minority Writing in Canada." *International Journal of Canadian Studies* 3 (1991): 110–28.

Petrone, Penny. "Indian Legends and Tales." In *The Oxford Companion to Canadian Literature.* Toronto: Oxford University Press, 1983. 377–83.

Ross, Malcolm, "The Impossible Sum of our Traditions." *The Impossible Sum of Our Traditions: Reflections on Canadian Literature.* Toronto: McClelland and Stewart, 1986. 184–202.

Scott, F. R. "The Canadian Authors Meet." *The New Oxford Book of Canadian Verse in English.* Ed. Margaret Atwood. Toronto: Oxford University Press, 1982. 91.

Vlassie, Katherine. *Children of Byzantium.* Dunvegan: Cormorant, 1987.

Weiner, Gerry. "Minister's Message." *Together* 1.1 (1991): 2–3.

Woodcock, George. "*Away from Lost Worlds*: Notes on the Development of a Canadian Literature." In *Odysseus Ever Returning: Essays on Canadian Writers and Writings.* Toronto: McClelland and Stewart, 1970. 1–11.

Historical Review of African-American Literature

Christopher Wise and Cora Agatucci

While the term "postcoloniality" suggests a relatively recent development in contemporary literary theory, there is also a sense in which African-American literature has always been a postcolonial literature, even in its least political manifestations. In other words, "postcoloniality" implies that colonization is already behind us, and not an ongoing historical dilemma or process: a situation which aptly describes the conditions of emergence for African-American literature. Thus, while we must be careful about collapsing necessary distinctions between African-American and other postcolonial literatures, especially those that threaten to efface the historical integrity of any unique body of writings, there can be no question that African-American literature constitutes but one local response to the much larger global process of colonization itself, specifically imperial capitalism. However, African-American literature differs from most postcolonial literatures in that it is written by members of a minority community who reside within a nation of vast wealth and military power. Crudely put, the level of the economic therefore provides the most coherent means of clarifying both the universal and distinctive features of African-American literature through history.

But any number of mystifications have tended to obscure a fact appalling to acknowledge: that African-Americans were introduced into the United States as goods to be traded, another result of capitalism's global ascendancy, following geographical discoveries made by Christopher Columbus, Vasco De Gama, and others. Like the novel form itself, which arises as a historical response to the situation of mercantile capitalism, the various forms of African-American literature are finally inconceivable outside of their basis in the process of imperial capitalism. For example, that written works of literature are even necessary as a form of cultural expression for former Africans is often passed over in silence by writers of anthologies and literary histories. Besides the fact of brute oppression, the primacy of the written (versus the oral) text in white American culture may also explain why no real African-American literature was produced during the first 250 years of the African's existence in the United States. The formal contradictions entailed by the imposition of an alien medium, such as the novel, the autobiography, or even the poem, may all speak to the formidable ideological and cultural differences which separated Europeans and Africans. Understandably, most surveys of African-American literature begin with a discussion of African music, especially its impact upon the language, songs, and folklore of African-Americans through history.

More complicated appropriations of alien media, like Phillis Wheatley's neoclassical poetry or Olaudhau Equiano's spiritual autobiography, tend to reveal the inherent contradictions resulting from the ideology of form itself, often undercutting even the most revolutionary criticisms of white European culture. The slave narrative, for example, which shares an uneasy alliance with the confessional, does not simply demonstrate the barbarism of the antebellum South, but reinscribes many of the conditions of that society's existence. Similarly, literacy created the basic conditions for the slave's ultimate freedom while interpellating him/her into a bewilderingly complex and hostile signifying order; in this sense, literacy also ensured the bondage of the slave for decades to come.

In the case of Equiano's *The Interesting Narrative of the Life of Olaudah Equiano* (1789), which Henry Louis Gates, Jr., has called "the prototype of the nineteenth century slave narrative," it is not incidental that Equiano's autobiography is accompanied by a signed engraving of the author holding an open Bible in his lap (*The Classic Slave Narratives* xiv). The clearly marked verse in this engraving of Equiano reads as follows: "Salvation is found in no one else, for there is no other name under heaven given to men by which we must be saved" (Acts 4:12). Equiano's scriptural citation operates on at least two different levels of meaning: Literally, Equiano suggests that belief in Jesus Christ will lead to spiritual and material "salvation" for the African; however, Equiano may also be suggesting that it is not Christ who will save the African, but the *name* (or language) of Christians. Similar appropriations of Christian ideology, especially evident in the deployment of the genre of the Augustinian confessional, both permeate the slave narrative tradition (from Equiano through Malcolm X and Maya Angelou) and demonstrate the bewildering extent of African-American literature's postcoloniality.

Nonliterary modes of visual and oral expression were more powerful vehicles for the spiritual and political message of Sojourner Truth, probably the most highly regarded African-American woman of the nineteenth century. The former Isabella Van Wagenen changed her name at the prompting of mystical voices in 1843 and proclaimed her mission: to "sojourn" in the land and speak God's "truth" (Washington, introd. xv), although her version of that "truth"—including unflinching exposure of the sexual politics of slavery and outspoken advocacy of rights for black as well as white women—often discomfited even her supporters. This bold and brilliant orator, who never learned to read or write, dictated her *Narrative of Sojourner Truth* to her amanuensis Olive Gilbert in 1850, and some of Truth's speeches were later recorded in Elizabeth Cady Stanton's *The History of Woman Suffrage* (1881–1886). But the uneasy relationship between Truth and Cady Stanton cannot be explored here, even though it bears noting.

Acquisition of literacy was the key to freedom for self-taught Frederick Douglass. In his classic work, *Narrative of the Life of Frederick Douglass* (1845), the genre of the slave narrative reaches its apex, partly through Douglass' great skill as a writer and partly through the historical circumstances surrounding his life. Not only was Douglass effective as a writer and orator, but he is often studied today for his contributions to African-American and United States political history as well as his extensive contributions to literature. The most striking aspect of Douglass' prose style consists in its easy readability, which enabled him to appeal to a wide readership and hence contributed to his tremendous popularity, while the context of his writings paradoxically focused upon the most complex issues of his day. The deceptive simplicity of Douglass' approach also contributed to the plainly allegorical features of his writing: the (often unarticulated) implication that the brutality he suffered was representative of the experiences of *all* black slaves. In this sense, his three great narratives, *Narrative of the Life of Frederick Douglass, My Bondage and My Freedom* (1855), and *The Life and Times of Frederick Douglass* (1881), may be understood as "ur-forms" (or structural precedents) of the postcolonial testimonial, especially insofar as they deliberately subvert the narcissism of the Christian confessional in favor of a more "collective" concept of the individual.[1]

Perhaps the most significant African-American writer of all, W.E.B. Du Bois began his career as a social scientist and historian with few literary pretensions. However, after earning his Ph.D. at Harvard in 1896, followed by the publication of two major scholarly studies on African-Americans, Du Bois became increasingly disenchanted with the limitations of academic discourse. Although he continued to produce scholarly publications throughout his career, Du Bois's *The Souls of Black Folks* (1903) signaled a major break from his previous "disinterested" methodology toward a more deliberate and politicized writing style. Today, *The Souls of Black Folks* remains the prototype of postcolonial approaches to historiography. While Du Bois originally advocated a more conciliatory position with the United States government (yet firmly opposing the capitulationist philosophy of Booker T. Washington), his views radically changed as he began to recognize the connection between economics and politics. Later, Du Bois would state

> The history of our day . . . may be summed up in one word—Empire; the domination of white Europe over black Africa and yellow Asia, through political power built on the economic control of labor, income and ideas. The echo of this industrial imperialism in America was the expulsion of black men from American democracy, their subjection to caste control and wage slavery. (*Autobiography* 255)

Like that of many following him, Du Bois's disillusionment with the United States's political system was transformed into social activism, culminating in his membership in the Communist party of the United States in 1961, his renunciation of American citizenship, and his becoming a citizen of Ghana, where he died in 1963. As a social scientist, historian, novelist, poet, pamphleteer, and editor, Du Bois demonstrated that a multitude of literary genres may be pressed into service for the liberation of Africans across the globe. Additionally, Du Bois's illustrious career, which included founding the National Association for the Advancement of Colored People (NAACP) in 1909, as well as the Pan-African Congress in 1919, continues to serve as an activist model for African-American and other postcolonial intellectuals throughout the world.

Besides Du Bois, many writers of the Harlem Renaissance were also influenced by Marxist and pan-African thought, especially Langston Hughes and Claude McKay. Richard Wright, who was the best-known African-American writer of the 1930s and 1940s, also belonged to the Communist Party of the United States of America (CPUSA) and was deeply influenced by the writings of Marx and Lenin. However, like Hughes, Wright faced political persecution from McCarthyism and eventually went into exile in Paris, where he turned toward existentialism. Wright's most significant contributions to African-American literature consist in his development of a socially engaged writing style and his appropriation of realistic and naturalistic modes of writing for African-American deployment. With Wright, and his contemporary Zora Neale Hurston, the African-American novel reaches full maturity. Other novelists, like Ralph Ellison and James Baldwin, while critical of Wright's overtly politicized approach, nevertheless acknowledge their indebtedness to him in shaping their own themes and concerns.

In the 1960s, the Black Arts Movement reflected the rise of militancy in the black masses and the rise of a new generation of writers who valued "self-determination, self-respect, and self-defense" (Baraka, "The Revolutionary Tradition in Afro-American Literature" 321). In this regard, Malcolm X played the most pivotal role in shaping the agenda and themes of an entire generation of writers, especially in opposition to the nonviolent strategies of Martin Luther King, Jr., and the Southern Christian Leadership Conference (SCLC). Coauthored with Alex Haley, *The Autobiography of Malcolm X* (1964) remains a central text for African-American and other postcolonial intellectuals, and many of Malcolm X's speeches continue to have an impact upon contemporary political issues. Specifically, *The Autobiography of Malcolm X* both introduces and legitimates Islam for many African-Americans, as well as for many other (non-Islamic) Americans. At a moment when Islam on a global basis is increasingly seen as a viable means of resisting western imperialism, the influence of Malcolm X in this regard may not be overemphasized. Second, Malcolm X's turning away from a more narrowly conceptualized black nationalism toward a global critique of western imperialism signals for many the inauguration of postcolonial practice and politics within the African-American community.

However, it is not until the early 1970s and the advent of black feminism that African-American literature assumes key qualities closely associated with contemporary postcolonial theory. More specifically, the collapse of the black nationalist paradigm with its separatist logic gives way to increasing dialogue among various theories of oppression based upon class, gender, and race. Black women writers benefited from many of the crucial insights of the mainstream feminist movement of the 1960s, became more aware of their own particularity, and began to open up possibilities for more inclusive and unified theories of both gender and racial oppression.

A stellar year, 1970 marked the publication of Toni Morrison's *The Bluest Eye*, Alice Walker's *The Third Life of Grange Copeland*, and Maya Angelou's *I Know Why the Caged Bird Sings*. The two decades since have seen an unprecedented growth in the popularity and critical celebration of African-American women writers, eclipsing that of their male counterparts not least because these works have crossed separatist lines, as Henry Louis Gates, Jr., points out, and attracted an international "doubled readership" both black and female (*Reading Black, Reading Feminist* 4). Black feminists have not responded to their own exclusion from representational authority with a "counter-politics of exclusion" by insisting upon a monolithic construction of black woman's experience, by "legislating who may or may not speak on the subject," or by "policing boundaries between 'us' and 'them'" (8). Rather, African-American women writers have emerged as a synthesizing force among fragmented and specialized subaltern groups. Postcolonial theorists may name their affinities in black feminists' will to invent, as much as reclaim, common creative traditions; in their desire to chart enabling sororial models and construct alliances on an inclusive map of multiple context-specific subject positions; and in black women writers' extraordinary success in appropriating existing literary and cultural forms and in creating expressive discourses for self-invention and emancipation. Indeed, African-American women have produced inherently politicized and lyrical testimonies for their experience that locate new sites of oppression and internal colonization and that necessarily work toward decolonizing imaginations previously incapable, for example, of picturing "the questing figure, the powerful articulate voice" as a Maud Martha, "plain, dark-skinned housewife living in a kitchenette apartment on the south side of Chicago" (Washington 32).

Now stories of the pain of displacement and quests for identity like Maya Angelou's, traced through six autobiographical volumes since 1970, have moved from the margins into the centers of mainstream American literary institutions. Angelou's autobiographical statements resonate so compellingly because the Augustinian paradigm has been turned against itself, re-visioned in the last two centuries as a potent ideological tool to bear public witness to racial and gender oppression by those who want control of their own lives, who seek political and social representational authority. Continuing the tradition transfigured by Frederick Douglass and Harriet Jacobs, *I Know Why the Caged Bird Sings* describes a process of cultural displacement, violation, and loss so complete that the first place Angelou acknowledged that she ever felt at home was Ghana, visited much later in her life.

To be sure, using the Master's tools to dismantle the Master's house is a perilous, contradictory venture, as Audre Lorde has warned us. Yet Lillian Robinson expresses the survival strategy impelling such postcolonial endeavors: "Of *course* you use the Master's tools if those are the only ones you can lay hands on" (35). The act of taking up the tools, of entering the site of contestation, constitutes a transformative experience reopening representational closure. "All my work, my life, everything is about survival," Angelou explains. "All my work is meant to say, 'You may encounter many defeats, but you must not be defeated.' In fact, the encountering may be the very experience which creates the vitality and the power to endure" (7).

Angelou also speaks of the process of inventing positive images of black women, of teaching herself to see, not only "whites and males in dominant roles," but "our mothers, aunts, our sisters, and grandmothers," when looking out at the world around her (1–2). Central to the postcolonial project of multitalented African-American women writers like Maya Angelou and Alice Walker is the conscious process of self-invention, model discovery, and tradition creation. Walker, in particular, has argued eloquently for the primacy of all three as prerequisites for bringing the black woman as artist into existence. In the opening of her collection *In Search of Our Mothers' Gardens* (1983), Walker particularizes black women's prose as "womanist," rather than "feminist," a necessary redefinition completed by the title essay: a room of one's own and money to support oneself are hardly enough for an ancestress like Phillis Wheatley, imprisoned by "contrary instincts'" predicated on her colonized situation, a slave "who owned not even herself" (235). To nontraditional, unrecognized art forms like her mothers' gardens and quilts Walker credits the survival of black women's spirituality and creativity. She recovered her foremother Zora Neale Hurston from a footnote and praises Toni Morrison for writing the kinds of books she wanted to read. Beside conventional models of social activism, Walker posits the important alternatives of personal transformation and strategies of silence in works like *Meridian* (1976), her second novel. In *The Color Purple*, a 1982 best-seller and Pulitzer Prize winner, she appropriates western narrative forms, blending epistolary, sentimental novel and spiritual-sexual confessional as vehicles for subverting oppressive social structures and awakening to power Celie, a protagonist who begins without words even to name the parts of her own violated body.

The literature of African-American female writers is unapologetically about black women, their "thoughts, words, feelings, and deeds, . . . experiences that make the realities of being black in America look very different from what men have written" (Washington 35): this is an inherently politicized situation for those traditionally denied subject positions even by their black male counterparts. Yet the subject matter of black female writing has been misinterpreted as nonpolitical or wrongly dismissed as inconsequential, because it does not consistently project its dilemmas in confrontations between the black and white worlds or in male-centered experiences, but often in terms of sexual politics and female-centered perspectives that, nevertheless, engage, contest, then renegotiate racist, sexist, and class formulations.

As the senior editor at Random House for two decades, Toni Morrison promoted African-American writing and drew black female writers like Toni Cade Bambara and Gayl Jones to national attention. Morrison's own fine body of fiction moves readers through the alienation, power and danger of growing up black and female in America, recounted in works like *The Bluest Eye* (1970) and *Sula* (1973); to novels like *Song of Solomon* (1977) and *Tar Baby* (1981), more overt treatments of class, race, and gender oppression produced by the historical processes of post-coloniality. Morrison's *Beloved*, Pulitzer Prize winner in 1987, enacts the legacy of slavery in post–Civil War Ohio in a mother's story of blood chilling and loving infanticide. Morrison returns us to a pivotal moment in African-American history to "rememory" the female slave Sethe's defiance, bringing to bear all Morrison's considerable affective representational skills to explain the inexplicable, to bring both Sethe and her readers to the moment of Paul D's affirmation: " 'You your best thing, Sethe. You are' " (273).

"This is not a story to pass on," *Beloved*'s narrator warns at the end of the novel. Yet Morrison understands that such stories must be passed on: "You have to be willing to think the unthinkable" (qtd. in Lanker 32). Thus many African-American women create for themselves subject positions within an expanded literary-historical landscape. Rita Dove, an influential new poetic voice, recognizes those like Langston Hughes, Toni Morrison, James Baldwin, and Gwendolyn Brooks whose work has spoken to her and made her poetry possible. But she is also conscious of the necessity of self-invention: "the fact that, when I was growing up, I could not find anything written about what it was like to grow up as a black woman, or woman-child, was important—I wanted to read that book so I try to write those poems. . . . It's a hole I'm trying to fill" (Vendler 488). Such African-American women writers position themselves within an expansive map of inter-related subject positions, each filling holes left by others even as they (re)write each other's stories.

Definitions of self can be illuminated in the silences of others. In her first book of poetry *The Yellow House on the Corner* (1980), Dove recreates past languages and personas in poems like "David Walker (1785–1830)," "The Transport of Slaves from Maryland to Mississippi," and "The Slave's Critique of Practical Reason." Dove recounts her intention to explore the edges between what language can say and what it withholds, for in the silences at the edges of the "so-called 'civilized' language" of the slave narratives the full horror of enslavement may be felt (Vendler 483). In *Thomas and Beulah*, winner of the 1986 Pulitzer Prize, Dove rewrites her family's more recent past. This, Dove's third book of poems, is based on her grandparents' lives and is structured as two parallel but fragmented narratives of the title personae, expressing lost love and unfulfilled longing in a marriage of missed connection. While writing *Thomas and Beulah*, Dove faced her own silence regarding motherhood and children: "an unspoken notion . . . [that] you just don't write about those things" (Vendler 489–490) propelled her to uncover a very important part of her life through poems included in her next book, *Grace Notes* (1989).

In the last decade, "nation politics" has been increasingly replaced by antiseparatist "identity politics" among postcolonial writers. This emphasis may be seen in the works of Michele Wallace, bell hooks, and Terry McMillan. Initial steps toward building community and dialogue across class, race, and gender divisions have been taken in controversial black feminist critiques like Wallace's *Black Macho and the Myth of the Superwoman* (1981). As Sherley Anne Williams persuasively argues, black women like Wallace should confront "what black men have said about us," as well as "what they have said about themselves," if separatist tendencies in African-American criticism are to be challenged (74). The way for gifted new writers like Terry McMillan has now been prepared, and novels such as McMillan's *Disappearing Acts* (1989) can honestly and passionately address the barriers and inequities constantly threatening black male-female relationships at complex intersections of classism, racism, and sexism in our society.

Moreover, identity creation is a crucial project for black women if they are to counter the invisibility long imposed on them. In her successive critical works *Ain't I a Woman: Black Women and Feminism* (1981), *Feminist Theory from Margin to Center* (1984), *Talking Back: Thinking Feminist, Thinking Black* (1989), and *Yearning: Race, Gender and Cultural Politics* (1990), bell hooks (Gloria Watkins) has developed forceful challenges to divisive paradigms of black and white feminist thought that ultimately act to reinscribe western patriarchal discourses. In a 1989 *Talking Back* interview, hooks describes the unifying and liberatory potential in choosing to be "woman-identified," in exercising powers of self-invention, and in nurturing an inclusive "womanist" imagination—for she believes that "what we can't imagine, can't come to be" (174, 176). In "Variations on Negation and the Heresy of Black Feminist Creativity," Michele Wallace has astutely analyzed the forms black female invisibility continues to take, in spite of the popularity of African-American female writing. She calls for radical new modes of black feminist creativity that self-consciously reject "archetypal choices available to black women (except lesbians) in this culture," and that deliberately "choose and take responsibility for what we will emphasize in ourselves and others" (66).

The liberating agency of black feminism has made it possible for Dove, McMillan, and many other new writers to transcend the multifarious forms gender, race, and class oppression may take in the postcolonial context. While the vast majority of African-Americans continue to experience both economic and social oppression, the efforts of writers from Equiano through Wallace have provided a garden within which a fully mature postcolonial culture has taken root and flourished on hostile soil. However, in the context of a largely bankrupt consumerist society, where mainstream literature (all white) has become less socially central or interesting, African-American writers and their postcolonial counterparts in Native American, Asian-American, and Latin American communities have generated a broad base of enthusiasm and support from many sectors of American society who can no longer ignore both the vitality and the beauty of these traditions.

NOTES

1. For more in this regard, see Fredric Jameson's often-cited essay "Third World Literature in the Era of Multi-national Capitalism" (*Social Text* 15: Fall 1986: 65–88). Here, Jameson argues that texts such as the Latin American testimonial and the third world novel "necessarily project a political dimension in the form of national allegory: *the story of the private individual destiny is always an allegory of the embattled situation of the public third-world culture and society*" (69; Jameson's emphasis). Jameson emphasizes the purely allegorical dimensions of third world texts in opposition to the realist and modernist novel of the West, which is instead characterized by "a radical split between the private and the public, between the poetic and the political" (69).

WORKS CITED

Angelou, Maya. Interview. *Black Women Writers at Work.* Ed. Claudia Tate. New York: Continuum, 1983. 1–11.

Baraka, Amiri. "The Revolutionary Tradition in African-American Literature." In *The LeRoi Jones/Amiri Baraka Reader.* New York: Thunder's Mouth Press, 1991.

Du Bois, W.E.B. *The Autobiography of W.E.B. Du Bois.* New York: International Publishers, 1968.

Gates, Henry Louis, Jr. *The Classic Slave Narratives.* New York: Mentor Books, 1987.

———. "Introduction." In *Reading Black, Reading Feminist.* New York: Meridian-Penguin, 1990. 1–17.

hooks, bell. *Talking Back: Thinking Feminist, Thinking Black.* Boston: South End, 1989.

Jameson, Fredric. "Third World Literature in the Era of Multi-national Capitalism." *Social Text,* 15, (1986) 65–88.

Lanker, Brian. "Toni Morrison." In *I Dream a World.* New York: Stewart, Tabori and Chang, 1989. 32–33.

Lorde, Audre. "The Master's Tools Will Never Dismantle the Master's House." In *This Bridge Called My Back.* Ed. Cherrie Moraga and Gloria Anzaldua. Watertown, Mass.: Persephone, 1981. 98–101.

Morrison, Toni. *Beloved.* New York: Plume–New American Library, 1987.

Robinson, Lillian S. "Canon Fathers and Myth Universe." In *Decolonizing Tradition.* Ed. Karen R. Lawrence. Urbana: University of Illinois Press 1992. 23–36.

Vendler, Helen. "Interview with Rita Dove." In *Reading Black, Reading Feminist.* Ed. Henry Louis Gates, Jr. New York: Meridian-Penguin, 1990. 481–91.

Wallace, Michele. "Variations on Negation and the Heresy of Black Feminist Creativity." In *Reading Black, Reading Feminist.* Ed. Henry Louis Gates, Jr. New York: Meridian-Penguin, 1990. 52–67.

Washington, Margaret. "Introduction." In *Narrative of Sojourner Truth.* New York: Vintage-Random, 1993. ix–xxxiii.

Washington, Mary Helen. " 'The Darkened Eye Restored': Notes toward a Literary History of Black Women." In *Reading Black, Reading Feminist.* Ed. Henry Louis Gates, Jr. New York: Meridian-Penguin, 1990. 30–43.

Williams, Sherley Anne. "Some Implications of Womanist Theory." In *Reading Black, Reading Feminist.* Ed. Henry Louis Gates, Jr. New York: Meridian-Penguin, 1990. 68–75.

III

INDIGENOUS LITERATURES

Margin or Center? "Let me tell you! In the Land of my Ancestors I am the Centre": Indigenous Writing in Aotearoa

Powhiri Wharemarama Rika-Heke

E nga iwi o te ao, tena koutou.
E kui ma, e hine ma, e koro ma, e tama ma
titiro ki te takiri o te haeata ko te wa tenei o te puawaitanga.

INTRODUCTORY REMARKS

This paper is presented in two parts. The first part deals with the historical origins of Maori literature, white images of the indigenous other and an overview of how we, as Maori, have portrayed ourselves, our lives, in literature. The second part deals specifically with selected excerpts from Maori women's literature, in English, which shows our diversity, our concerns, our struggles and our aspirations as women in and of Aotearoa.

In studies of this nature it is fairly commonplace to include a discussion of the indigene writers' literary image of themselves or their culture. It is also expected that there may be comments on the debates associated with indigenous literature. I have some statements to make with reference to these points.

First, the recognition of my own center leaves me reluctant, though not necessarily unable, to provide any "mainstream" comment on these issues. My reluctance comes from the fact that I am not identified with the "mainstream" because of my self-placement within the "other" as well as the "mainstream's" own notions about where I belong. However, I recognize that I am still able to provide "mainstream" comment on these issues because I have lived within the "mainstream" and gained from the "mainstream."

Second, I question the right of anyone to "judge" another's presentation of his or her own culture. I believe that if "outsiders" feel the need to "criticize" indigenes' literary presentation of themselves then they need to be fully cognizant of the historical, political, and cultural influences upon the indigene—from the perspective of the indigene. The attempt by indigenous people to seek sovereignty within white-dominated federal states includes the refusal to accept the definition of themselves put forward by the culture in power.

As a privileged member of the "powerless" culture—I have a regular income and the time to indulge myself in writing such essays—I intend simply to include in this work, ideally without prejudice, a brief presentation of the historical beginnings of Maori literature; an overview of some of the issues that some Maori writers refer to in our literature, especially some of the issues of self-definition; as well as some of the topics of debate for Maori readers and writers surrounding Maori literature. Finally, this essay also contains a selection of excerpts from stories and poetry, written by Maori, which shows that we are not a homogeneous group, that we all claim identities which are not necessarily constant, that we are as complex, as multifaceted and as diverse as any race or culture of peoples anywhere. The writings chosen highlight some of the places we fill in society, some of our concerns, our struggles and our aspirations. I will also attempt to place Maori literature within a context of oral literature. It is, by no means, definitive or comprehensive but merely an announcement to both the national and international literary community that Maori writers exist and have something to share which reaches beyond local or regional readership.

HISTORICAL ORIGINS: ORAL LITERATURE

Before the invasion of Aotearoa (New Zealand) by Britain, with consequences both negative and positive upon the indigenous people of this country, there existed a rich world of oral literature founded in the ancient histories of the Maori ancestral homeland, Hawaiiki. The tradition of oral literature has continued as an integral and vital component of Maori life, albeit with modifications, adaptations, and a marked decrease in usage and occasion due to the incipient processes of colonization.[1]

The oral literature of the Maori was, and still is, both rich and complex, concerning all aspects of life—comments upon local events and scandals, taunts and insults to enemies, relationships between people, emotions of love, sorrow, joy, *iwi* (local/tribal) histories, *whakapapa* (genealogy) links, sacred and secular etiquette, common and esoteric lore about customary skills and practices. The main genres of Maori oral literature I have identified are *whakapapa*, *whakatauki* (sayings/proverbs), *whaikoreo* (narratives), *waiata* (sung poetry), and *karakia* (incantations). The language used in the oral texts is often elaborate and poetic, with much use of imagery and formulaic expressions. Respect for the words of various forms of oral literature has resulted in word perfect recitation of much of the literature since the texts were first composed. Some of the oral literature, especially waiata, has been changed; for example, a waiata composed of extolling the virtues of one specific person has undergone a simple name change to fit yet another specific person and occasion, though the initial sentiments remain.[2]

Despite the decline, in the 1830s and 1840s, of the great classic tradition of Maori poetry due, in some respects, to the Christianization of Maori, and the resultant decline in the significance of the traditional myths and images, new subjects began, to some extent, to replace the old ones.[3] Christianity, at first a subject to be celebrated, later became a stimulus, along with the tragedy of the land wars; land confiscations; protests at Pakeha (white settler) greed, colonization and appropriations; and the prophetic leaders of the nineteenth century for further compositions. Although much of the oral literature remains and is, indeed, being added to regularly, it is, nevertheless, not as powerful a force in Maori society as it once was as it is usually only on occasions of large family, tribal or other formalized gatherings that the real beauty of the oral literature is given voice.

WHITE IMAGES: THE INDIGENOUS "OTHER"

During the imperial period, writing in the language of the imperial center was produced by literate settlers, travelers, and explorers whose primary identification was with the colonizing power, Britain. Thus, the texts produced in the colony emphasized the "home" over the "native," the "metropolitan" over the "colonial" or "provincial." Accordingly, nonfictional and fictional texts inevitably privileged the center, as a large number of British publishers shared the opinion that no colonial could write anything worth reading. Nevertheless, the colonials wrote anyway, and immigrant literature was seen as a variant of the British tradition as they perceived it. Fiction and poetry exploiting the "exotic" landscapes, the savage Maori, and the trials of pioneers for the delectation of a British audience were concerned with "nature," domestic sentiment and abstract ideals of the Pastoral Paradise and the Just City. The conformity of the works and the truths about the indigenous people they claimed to depict is striking. The reality of these texts and their ideology is clearly due to the ideology of the authors and their white culture. Behind this reality of an ideology lies another reality, a reality of a history of invasion and oppression. The indigenous people were forced to succumb to the needs of British imperial expansion. The Maori, because of our attitude toward the land and economics, seemed of limited "use" for the colonials at the beginning and remained so. The overwhelming factor of oppression gave semiotic control to the invaders and, since then, the image of "us" has been "theirs."[4]

The relationship with Britain—economically and culturally—remained an underlying yet dominant factor in most nineteenth and even twentieth century attempts to predict what the settlers might become. National character was regarded as a sentiment that colonial New Zealand lacked but would need to be cultivated if New Zealand were to achieve full nationhood. One major source of a distinctive national character was the presentation of the indigenous culture, its legends, and the landscapes of rural New Zealand. The emerging cities—as well as life on the farms—were likely to be dismissed as poor copies of British cities and provincial life. Urbanization had come to represent a mode of living and a pattern of economic organization imposed upon a land in which cities were considered inappropriate and in which the settlers hoped for a better Britain in the south.

In their need to become "native," to belong here, for many writers, the only chance for indigenization seemed to be through writing about the people who were indigenous (Goldie 13). But the indigenous "Other" was of interest only to the extent that it commented on the white self; in addition, the image of the "Other" was within the one field of discourse, that of British imperialism. Still, today, the signifying process, as it applies to indigenous people, is formed by a certain semiotic field, a field that provides the boundaries within which the images of the indigene function. Most of the literary texts by Pakeha writers paved the way to appropriation, that is, through various attempts to capture the subjectivity of the indigene. The commodities—sex, violence, oral tradition, mysticism, the prehistoric—can be seen as part of a circular economy within and without the semiotic field of the indigene (Said 190). They are poles of attraction and repulsion and serve to define the "Other." During the nineteenth century the indigene thus became, for example, a sign of oracular, malevolent power, whereas contemporary white literature usually emphasizes the beneficent character. But still, today, terms such as "backward," "cruel," "barbaric," "cannibalistic," "primitive" are immediately suggestive, everywhere, of the indigene and based on the dominant model of power—and interest—between the supposed inferiority of the native and the putative superiority of white society.[5] To date, literary texts show clearly that we, the Maori, remain part of the tension of an indigenous consciousness for the Pakeha. But it is neither the contemporary Maori nor a truly historical one which remains, but rather a romanticized historical artefact. Thus, the white culture attempted to incorporate the "Other," rather superficially, through referring to Maori place names, to Maori legends, ceremonies; putting *kowhai*, *puarangitoto*, *manuka*, *rata*, *tarapunga* (native flora) on postage stamps; or selling Maori carvings, fake or genuine (Frame 44). For the Pakeha—mostly the displaced Britons—the use of untranslated words had an important function in inscribing difference from the center. They signified a cultural experience which the white settlers could certainly not hope to reproduce: the difference, however, was validated by the new situation. Moreover, the justification for this appropriation was to save the culture of a dying race. The Maori was a nonparticipant; our absence was at the same time a negative presence. It is the white image of us that serves the nevertheless impossible necessity of the Pakeha in becoming indigenous.

The image of the Maori also serves the psychological needs of the Pakeha. The embrace of the indigene is presented, in many texts, as a return to a whole, before the abstraction and splitting of civilized life. The natural indigene is an explanation of the holistic indigene, the human who has not ceased to be part of an integrated planet. The image of a "simple" society conveys a sense of the balance of mind and body and the integration of mind, body, nature, unlike the White technological society, which attempts to situate mind over body and its larger self, nature. Most images in indigenous sexuality, oral tradition, and mysticism are viewed as an affirmation of "undomesticated" wholeness. This white image of Maori society as an anarchic,[6] disordered, contemporary society is shown as an extension of the "natural" freedom of the imagined indigene of the past. Thus, naturalness is opposed to a tightly restrictive system. It is the imperialist view that defines the colonized according to its own needs for reflection.[7] The image of the indigene, which is created, reveals very little about us or our culture. It reveals, however, a great deal about the whites and their culture. The Maori as cultural item is the result of hegemonic textualization: we are described and defined in order to preserve our position as a unified symbol of national essence. That is, this textualization incorporates an indigenization which excludes the indigene. It is this textualization which gives rise to the need for Maori writers to begin the process of self-definition, to create ourselves in literary texts, to "right" ourselves.

ORAL LITERATURE: THE FOUNDATION

For nearly one hundred and fifty years Maori voices, and in particular Maori women's voices, have for the most part been silenced, and others have written about us. The strangers' voices were either strident with denigration of no-good "horis"—the women to be had "on the mat" for booze, a blanket, some trinkets—or else romantic with various versions of the noble savage. A common thread of Maori experiences is that we've all been defined, in one way or another, by outsiders.

Although I referred, earlier, to the invasion of Aotearoa by Britain, I should, in all fairness, point out that the defining of us and our land, by outsiders, began in 1642, when the Dutchman Abel Tasman came to my country and named it Staten Landt, which Dutch geographers later changed to Nieuw Zeeland or New Zealand. The international community has associated that name with my country ever since. But it is not the name of my country. We had a name before Abel Tasman came, a name we still use—it is Aotearoa, the land of the long white cloud, though I sometimes call it the land of the wrong white crowd. We, as the tangata whenua (people who belong to the land), have been redefined, by a post-contact generic term, as Maori. I am not Maori. I belong to a group of people which comprises iwi or tribes, each tribe an independent sovereign nation. I am Ngati Hine—that is my iwi. Our founding ancestor is Hineamaru, a strong and noble woman. Her blood flows in my veins and the veins of my iwi—we are one. I, and my people, are only Maori to outsiders or to ourselves when we can't be bothered explaining. For convenience, I will, however, use the generic term "Maori" when referring to our writings.

Although Maori oral literature is of a lesser significance in postcolonial Aotearoa, it is, nevertheless, an essential entry to both literature in Maori and Maori literature in English because it complements both literatures. It is not simply the forerunner to a written Maori literature but exists within it and alongside it (Sturm 3).

Rosemary Kohu, or as she calls herself now Hinewirangi Kohu, writes about where she has come from, in terms of her whakapapa. The recitation of whakapapa is one of the main genres of Maori oral tradition. She has taken this ancient oral tradition and used it as the basis for a modern rendition of whakapapa.

Hinewirangi

I, Hinewirangi, was born.
With me came the blood of my mother,
the blood of my father
the blood of the ancients
—blood pulsating through my veins,
giving me life.
I was born.
I carried proudly the heritage,
Kahungunu,
the mighty warrior,
handsome and free.
I inherited from Rongomaiwahine
a strong spirit.
She, the beauty of the tribe,
the ariki, the puhi,
the strength,
the mana.
I, Hinewirangi, was born
strong and free
to share that birthright. (Hinewirangi 11)

A number of Maori writers oppose any monocentric view of human experience. We do so by maintaining distance and "otherness" while appropriating the colonial language. Thus, our texts create the reality of the "Other" and at the same time show the potential of alternative values: we replace language in a specific cultural location and refer to the integrity of the "Otherness," which historically has been employed to keep us at the margins of power, of "authenticity," and even of reality itself. By doing so, we simply refuse to allow a separation between experience and language—both for so long controlled by the colonials (themselves marginalized by the center which produced them). We clearly refer to a tradition which for us is the center, in the land of our *tupana* (ancestors), whereby the aim of writing is, whether consciously or not, at least fourfold: first to alert Maori to what we are in danger of losing and to foster pride in Maori identity by placing positive self-defined and self-created images of Maori "out there"; second, to show respect for a way of life that is essentially Maori, giving "some insight into what it is to be a Maori"[8] by expressing some of the pain and joy of being Maori in an alien world; third, to educate Pakeha about Maori tradition and current Maori issues in a nonthreatening, though sometimes provocative, way; and fourth, there is a distinct Maori view of life, a perspective unable to be replicated by Pakeha writers, no matter how empathetic they are with things Maori, which is worth sharing with a discerning literary community.

Although much of the early writing which emerged in the cultural movement termed the Maori Renaissance, from the 1970s to the present, is seen by some as a romantic passion for the pastoral, the rural, the idyllic,[9] the various works are, more often than not, subtle but powerful critiques of the effects of colonization and the colonizing culture, as well as a defense of the indigenous one, embodying a specifically Maori sense of being (Williams 111).

In the bush
there were plenty
of fat juicy pigeons
the river
was full of eels
dinner swam past
all we had to do
was catch it

The bush
got chopped down
the river dammed
and the lake polluted

It seems to me
the closer
the Pakeha got to us
the more difficult
he made it for us to live.[10]

From the early sixties, an increased number of stories and poems by Maori writers began to appear in Te Ao Hou.[11] Almost universally, we spoke of the experience of leaving our rural land and, inherent in this, our culture, for the cities. They were invocations of loss, filled with regret, nostalgia, and resignation which did not threaten anybody.

Hemi couldn't quite forget the old valley and the bay. On some nights he thought he heard the waves breaking out on the reef and for a while he worried about his mother. He spoke Maori as often as he could just for her sake. (Johns 215)

In the seventies many Maori writers used a more aggressive, conscious approach to the expression of Maori identity.[12] Writings from this period included topics such as sit-ins, racial discrimination, and the construction of aluminum companies, or the like, on Maori land. The uncompromising and often bitter writing, fed by the growing awareness of double standards in New Zealand, in which, unofficially at least, there were one set of rules for Pakeha and another set for Maori, as well as the pain and anger of injustices resulting from colonization, was beginning to appear alongside the nostalgic, "safe" writing of "paradise lost." In an imagined landscape of pastoral splendor where the "(descendents of the old chief)" are assembled and bear witness to the fact and the speech that all the land was once theirs, but now all that remains is the irony and poignancy of a nation wrenched from the natives is evident in the whole poem (Habib, "Memorial Day" 108).

The activism that grew as effects of an economic recession hit the urbanized Maori, as well as a continued loss of Maori land, was also fertile ground for a more critical Maori literature. The 1975 Land March, the reoccupation, by Maori, of traditional Maori land such as the Raglan Golf course and Bastion Point during 1977–78, the protest against the 1981 Springbok Rugby tour of New Zealand became part of this new literary expression and this new self-determination. What the text spoke about was the "here and now," and the anger that came from violations felt and seen.[13] They thus closed the gap between writing and reality, between past and present. In "Moment of Truth" Habib writes of brutal beatings of the Maoris. (106)

By rewriting the past many Maori writers have adjusted the novel form to accommodate a Maori view, mythology and history and allow the entry of our perspectives, our experiences, and our values into literature.[14] Fiction thus enacts the process of challenging the hegemony of the "authorized" version of the dominant group, by merging fact and fiction to a degree which challenges the Pakeha need to establish a single view of the truth. Novels, as well as poems and short stories, write and rewrite history in the sense that they continually rework the past into narratives whose perspectives and emphases are determined by the contingencies of the present.

What characterizes this kind of writing is not simply the introducing of the history of colonial oppression, but the struggle for control of the word. Writing retains the seeds of self-regeneration and the power to create and recreate the world. By inscribing meaning, writing releases it to a dense proliferation of possibilities. As Maori authors we show ourselves to be writers who reject simple binary oppositions by reveling in multiplicities, and the unnaming power of ambiguity. This is to say that we determine the "self-other" dichotomy by proposing possibilities which do not fit simply at the poles of experience. The logical extension of constituting no clear "other" is the absence of a "self" position which arrogates to itself all power to name individuals, groups, and events in its own interests.

> They know what grandmother's like. Honest to goodness, if only she knew what people really think of her. Even her rich Khandallah friends find her upper-crust ways a bit much. I want you to understand that it's not pretence with Grandmother. Her family are well heeled and titled too, in jolly old England, but she's got to realise that this is Aotearoa and her ways are out of place here. (Rika-Heke, "Grandmother" 160)

MAORI LITERATURE IN ENGLISH: SELF-DEFINITION

Questions of definition and struggle find their way into our texts, our language, our discursive strategies, and our modes. In Aotearoa the relations between dominating and dominated language find their expression in, for example, the struggle of Maori against, such things as education policies which hinder the process of Maori self-determination and real access to our own language, and in our own literature. Maori writers writing in the dominant language English use literary strategies which ensure that our texts are transmitted in the way we want them to be. Many Maori poets and fiction writers, writing in English, incorporate aspects of oral literature into our texts or use the various genre of oral literature as a foundation for contemporary texts. More often than not, Maori words and phrases, often without translations for monolingual anglophones, are used, and stand for the latent presence of Maori culture. The reader is then forced into an active engagement with the other culture in which these words/terms have meaning. Cultural difference is, therefore, not inherent in the text but is inserted by the use of such strategies.[15]

There are a profusion of patterns, of shapes, used by Maori writers as a whole, that cluster together according to style and cultural concepts. At one end of the continuum are writings in Maori, while at the other end are those in English. Spanning these diversities are the bilingual texts which endeavor to present the same body of knowledge, of experience, of thought, in each language. Characters express themselves in their first language, Maori, and then follow their statements with a comment in English. I believe that the inclusion of an "explanation," in English, as part of the text of the story occurs because the author is aware of the ignorance of the Pakeha reading audience with regard to the Maori language.

The inclusion of Maori language emphasizes the coexistence of that language with English, as a living language. Moreover, the interplay of Maori and the dominating language in such texts allows for a complex expression of cultural conflicts in the narrator's or fictional character's speech or mind. Code switching constitutes a literary strategy which expresses cultural conflicts through linguistic tensions. Another strategy, used more often, is to overcode the central meaning with ritual, spiritual or mythological references to Maori culture. For example, novels such as Patricia Grace's *Potiki* can be read and enjoyed simply as is or, if prior knowledge of Maori mythology is part of the reader's background, can be read at another, deeper level.

Fundamental to the texts is the idea that change and renewal do not mean a rejection of the past. The need to recover and preserve Maoritanga is a strong theme in Maori literature. It is the basis from which an opposition to the dominant construction of New Zealand reality by Pakeha culture can be taken. Many Maori writers actively re-present the world in terms of alternative kinds of truth. One means of doing so is by the use of continual movement in writing: mixing modes and genres and moving between poetry and prose, drama and myth, realism and dialogue and transcription of characters' thoughts.[16] Many Maori authors make extensive and innovative use of our "native" traditions; this allows for a "dual vision," a different form of perception that questions cultural, political and social boundaries and explores new territories in between. Both the spiritual perception of a different reality and the blending of myth and history mark a transgression of realistic and fantastic modes, more recently, in the direction of magic realism.

Another underlying theme of much Maori writing is the concept of land as home and place of one's origin.[17] To be deprived of this place is a painful and emotionally shattering experience. Land is sacred, essential to tribal histories and the peoples' sense of "belonging." Our identity is linked to the land: we are tangata whenua. In contrast to the dominant culture, the quest for the "self" in Maori literature almost always poses the problem of the individual's return to one's group, the family, the tribe, the *marae* (the center for ceremonies and gatherings), the land. The imposed alienation, through colonization, and the desire to return to one's origins, underlies a large part of Maori literature. The destructive impact of the power culture upon Maori accounts for much of the alienation from our culture. In addition, the intersections of class, gender and race make for a more complex description of hegemony. Many Maori writers understand our writing as a political act of solidarity and collective self-definition. Much of our writing is concerned with securing Maori values, but also looks at the ways in which bicultural Maori tread the middle ground between our culture and the dominant culture while maintaining our essential Maoriness.

I am a descendant of the tribes of Ngati Porou, Ngati Kahungunu, Rongowhakaata, Te Aitanga-a-Mahaki. I was born in Rangitukia on the east coast, ten miles from the East Cape. I enjoy words that speak, whether they be Maori, my mother tongue, or English. What a privilege it is to inherit and to appreciate a language and to enjoy another equally. I hope that Pakeha New Zealanders avail their children of the opportunity to explore the indigenous language of this wonderful country.[18]

Whose History?

Contemporary Maori literature is inextricably linked with the politics of being "black" in Aotearoa. We examine a New Zealand history and a New Zealand identity from a Maori perspective—reviewing the historical "facts" which have been provided by the dominant Pakeha culture, reselecting and re-presenting the information which has hitherto been made available to the people of Aotearoa. In the main, the literature produced by Maori writers draws on Maori social context, Maori experiences and Maori history. It is, as a result, an entirely different view from that produced in the heroic Pakeha view.

The Treaty of Waitangi, the 1840 pact which formalized the relationship between some of the sovereign nations of Aotearoa and the British Crown, as well as the resultant negative consequences for the tangata whenua, are either alluded to or directly referred to in many writings.

Neighbours

Been neighbour for years; longer than we care to remember. You moved in some time after we did. Heck, it's part of the history of the place the day you officially took up residence. Some even celebrate it—never could understand that. Lots of your mates decided to pack up and come here too. We played host—treated you like honoured guests; gave you food when you were short; looked after your kids; cleaned your house; even gave you some of Granpa's land across the way—at the time your need seemed greater than ours.

Yep! We remember those early days. Funny how things change though. You and your mates kept 'til we lost count. Nowadays we come to you for our food because we're always short. You look after our kids—apparently we're not capable of doing for them what we'd done for years before you came. We still clean your house—if we're lucky—that hasn't changed. We never did get Granpa's land back. In fact, you've even got our place now. Funny people, neighbours. (Rika-Heke, "Neighbours" 165)

we all know the news
150 years of oppression
150 years of losin' more each day
150 years of feelin' sick
150 years of survival
we all want more than that

I'm taking my life back
back before the whalers the missionaries
the white settlers settling on us and serving their own interests
with money earned off our oppression figure-headed by the queen
i'm takin' anything i can
i have no more left to give you
nor do i want to give you anything
you who abuse every gift
and wear us out with your destructive wanting
and then complain we have no patience
no more—(Potiki 35–36)

Some writers express anger and anguish over the loss of our culture, our language, our land, over the past 150 years. We write of the impact of Christian missionaries, of land alienation, of land, language and cultural colonization, of racial discrimination, of power and powerlessness, about personal and cultural dignity.

"God it was hot. We ran out of water once, but luckily we had tankers full of beer. The hories loved it."

Everyone in our class roared except me. I knew my face was red, and I was kind of numb when I stood.

"You are always going on about Maoris, Mr. Bull," I said quietly.

Everyone stopped laughing. I could feel them staring at me. Some of them were whispering. Mr. Bull's face went white and he took a while to answer.

"Sit down, Simpson. I'm afraid you're over-reacting, though it's understandable in the circumstances. I'd like you to know, Simpson, that one of my aunties married a Maori."

But I wouldn't sit down. It was like I was standing up for myself and much more, or something, it felt good. My face was still red, I was still numb as I stomped down the aisle, stood in front of Mr. Bull's desk. (Stewart 122)

Social change in Maori society has occurred as a direct result of Pakeha colonization, institutionalization and socialization processes. A significant impact of these has been in the area of male/female roles in Maori society. Within traditional Maori society, the roles of men and women were seen as complementary rather than as being inferior or superior to the other. European contact presented a different role for men, a role in which men were superior, "their" women subservient. Many Maori men were seduced by this new notion, embracing it with a passion, and proceeded to relegate Maori women to a position of lesser significance. Although these attitudes are now being challenged, there are still Maori men who hold the view that women exist only to serve them, rather than as people to be honored and respected as "nga whare tangata."

to all the smug men
who think that speaking the reo is going to save them
who think that the language makes them one better than
someone else
particularly women

to all the men who think that just being born
and speaking our own language
is enough

I'm telling you it's not
no it's not enough
though it may win you a job in the new corporation
it may mean that pakeha ask your advice and pay you
it may mean that Maori women who are intimidated by your
supposed
knowledge
bow and curtail
and perhaps even sleep with you and have your children

getting a tohu degree means something,
but it doesn't give you the right to make others feel
less-than-you.
less than you in your new-found opulence
pounamu-couloured opulence, apple-mac opulence
citing your "boil-up" past or your oppression.

you don't impress me
though I admire hard work and persistence, intelligence
and the ability to get things done.
it doesn't impress me if it tells lies about women,
if it ignores children, if it is so rigid

> that it forgets justice in the insecure worry
> that we will "lose everything." (Potiki 31)

> Colonial power structures lie just under the surface for some writers. For others, they are dominant . . . the colonialist Pakeha is set against the Maori . . . the language becomes the crucial issue over which integrity and survival are fought. (Dunsford 15)

> One of Grandmother's pet hates is having Roimata and me drop in unannounced, in case her old biddy friends are visiting for their afternoon soiree. Neat word that, eh! I read it in a book written by Gertrude Stein. I used to pronounce it 'soyree' until I heard one of my teachers say it properly. I love that word. You'd think that if I could learn to say a tauiwi word like 'soiree', Grandmother would learn to say my name properly.
> "Haareeartar Worryparpar"!'
> God, Grandmother! It's Hariata. Hariata Wharepapa. (Rika-Heke, "Grandmother" 159)

While the expressions of some Maori writers inevitably involve the condemnation of Pakeha colonization, we also look to the future and to world issues such as race, government policies and their impact on indigenous peoples, colonization, capitalism, environmental issues, and conservation.

Human Rights, a la Carte, With Salt

What's on the menu tonight, Sir?
There's poisson sans flesh
Delightful French cuisine.
Why no flesh, you ask, Sir?
The chef just told me that power
never belongs to the people.
And nuclear testing isn't convenient in Paris, Sir
The second dish is toheroa sukiyaki
A hint of the Orient and this country's foreign policies.
Oh, please don't blame the kitchen, Sir
Remember, promises written in a Treaty
have never been honoured.

Let me serve you human rights on the table, Sir
And how about a scoop of ice-cream of goodwill?
Good will to the people conquered
Beaming smiles to the barrel, to disease, to thieving legislation
Would you care for a salad of empty promises, Sir,
With a piquant little dressing of oppression on the side?

Let me serve you human rights on the table, Sir.
I can recommend the cocktail of poverty and despair
That should sharpen your appetite for more.
Perhaps you'd prefer hangi-ed pizza,
Fried noodles on a spit?

How about curried pancakes, with maple syrup,
That should please the cosmopolitans—
Oh dear, none of that to your fancy, Sir?

If you're faith-starving, Sir
We have some fruity little wines.
"Jesu of Mao' Desiring" is very popular
as is "Karl and Virgin Mary Marx",
Two cheeky reds.
We have a perky bubbly,
"Mohammed Messiah", tickles the nose.
What about a liquer for after dinner?
"Capitalism with Monopolies" is well sought after
Yes, we have all the spiritual idols of the world available here, Sir.

Let me serve you human rights on your table, Sir
Let me add driftnet, oil, chemical toxins for flavour and taste.
Let me prepare the detritus of our land as chickpea patties,
for the vegetarians, Sir.
Let me serve you hope that will never be realised
Until the world is ready to listen to the muzzled voice of humanity
And may I suggest, Sir, you add salt to the wound
Helps to whet the appetite. (Rika-Heke, "Human Rights" 86)

While it may be seen that contemporary Maori writing, which applies to a wide range of genres, is often based on the various styles of oral tradition, though not exclusively so, it must be acknowledged that many of the themes, the concerns, and the desires expressed by Maori writers reflect experiences and highlight commonalities which bring together and unite all peoples across cultural boundaries. It is, however, the Maori context—its concepts, imagery, metaphors and eloquence, as expressed by a number of Maori writers—that gives rise to the recognition of an emerging ethnic written literature and a continued oral tradition in Aotearoa.

Many stories blend a distinct usage of language with the English literary categories. Some of the sentence structures tend to follow Maori syntax. This appropriation of the colonizer's language has been adopted by the colonized, and used in a way quite distinct from "standard" usage. The enforced language allows access to some knowledge, but it is quite clear that, in the use of Maori-accented English, in the New Zealand situation, the language and culture of the colonizers have been adapted by the tangata whenua and used for our own purposes. This has resulted in a changed language which gives a cosmopolitan voice to the culture and language of indigenous Aotearoa.

Eeee! But they look stink!
Favouritism! Favouritism!
Favouritism my bum! You fullus are jealous we won!
The judges took more time over the men's teams. . . . Then he and the lady judge came

to us, frowning and shaking their heads. Suddenly, however, they saw Jerry, standing there in all his spotless glory. A hasty consultation took place. Then Nanny Kepa triumphantly pointed a finger at Jerry and announced that the Waituhi team would win the parade trophy.

The crowd clapped and cheered. The few derisive hoots were soon booed out of existence.

But that other team should have won! Jerry said.

Oh, they won last year, I answered. It wouldn't be fair for them to win the parade twice in a row. (Ihimaera, "Pounamu Pounamu" 10)

The works I have chosen to include in this essay share some underlying commonalities. Some speak of a sense of belonging to a particular place, to a special part of the world, together with a feeling of identification with a long line of ancestors who have also experienced that same belonging. Some of the writings convey a feeling of interconnectedness of people, of nature, of the individual, of a particular birthplace and kin group. However, most of the works, quite unmistakably, share the theme of loss of culture and language, but not the natural consequent loss of confidence and identity. In each work there is a real sense of, not only survival, but also a fighting back, despite the fact that the past 150 years has been an era of immense and sometimes tragic change for the tangata whenua of Aotearoa.

The world of Europe, particularly Britain, exploded onto my country. That explosion resulted in many Maori casualties, especially among women. Unable to defeat the Maori through military strength, Britain used political, economic and religious weapons to subdue the Maori. While my people prayed to the Pakeha god, with their eyes closed, the very ground they were kneeling on was stolen. However, the British also brought with them things that were desirable—new kinds of knowledge and technology, new medicines, new opportunities, easier access to the international community. As a result of negative and positive attributes, the European ways were soon colonizing, not only the land and the culture of the Maori, but also their minds and spirits. New governments, economies, trade dependencies, beliefs, and ways of perceiving and thinking were imposed or absorbed until the landscapes, populations and life-styles changed, some almost beyond recognition.

Although some of the writings express a discontent, an anger with the processes of colonization, there is also present a thread of hope for a more acceptable future—a future born out of rebellion, a rejecting of the new "old" order; of the generations of acquiescing Maori, tugging their forelocks, aspiring to be good brown Pakeha. And it is through and in the writings of Maori, severe casualties of an arrogant, defining colonial power, that the fight is being fought so eloquently, with control, with strength and beauty, and a sense of "there's nowhere to go but up" as well as the celebration and claiming of our "Otherness."

I'm part Maori, part English, half Irish. I don't know anything about the English bit but I *feel* Maori and I *feel* Irish and that feeling sings in me like the wind. (Bridger 37)

NOTES

1. See Sturm, *The Oxford History of New Zealand Literature.*
2. See Sturm.
3. See Wedde and MacQueen.
4. See Wolf.
5. See JanMohamed, "The Economy of the Manichean Allegory."
6. See Hilliard.
7. Thomas Bracken refers to the Maori as "a step beyond the brute." See "The March of Te Rauparaha." The Maori sense of belonging to a place is accordingly not a human choice but animal genetics. In contemporary fiction, the belonging animal, the indigene, is often used to emphasize the evil powers of the invading technohuman, the white man.
8. As Susan Woodhouse refers to the works of Patricia Grace in "A Family Affair."
9. See Pearson.
10. See Taylor, *Eyes of the Ruru.*
11. Te Ao Hou, Department of Maori Affairs publication, initially edited by Erik Schrimmer, designed to reach a Maori audience. Under the editorship of Margaret Orbell (1962–65) especially, an increased number of Maori writers were published.
12. The journal *Koru* set up by Haare Williams after the 1975 Maori Writers and Artists conference at Te Kaha gives evidence of this.
13. See, e.g., the poems by Bruce Stewart ("Broken Arse") and Bub Bridger ("The Girl in the River").
14. See Ihimaera, *Tangi* and *The Matriarch.* Also see Grace, *The Dream Sleepers* and *Cousins*; Hulme, *The Bone People* and *Te Kaihau/The Windeater*; Stewart, *Tama and Other Stories.*
15. See Maihi, *Pakake! Pakake! Whalesong.*
16. See Grace, *Electric City and Other Stories*; Ihimaera, *The New Net Goes Fishing.*
17. See Gadd, *Pacific Voices*; and Ihimaera, *Pounamu Pounamu*, and *The New Net Goes Fishing.*
18. See Blank, *Nga Kokako Huataratara—The Notched Plumes of the Kokako.*

WORKS CITED

Blank, Arapera Hineira Kaa. *Nga Kokako Huataratara: The Notched Plumes of the Kokako.* Auckland: Arapera Blank and the Waiata Koa Trust, 1986.

Bracken, Thomas. "The March of Te Rauparaha." In *Lays of the Land of the Maori and Moa.* London: Sampson Low, Marston, Searle and Rivington, 1884.

Bridger, Bub. *Up Here on the Hill.* Wellington: Mallinson Rendel, 1989.

———. "The Girl in the River." In *Into the World of Light.* Ed. Ihimaera and Long. Auckland: Heinemann, 1982.

Dunsford, Cathie, ed. *Subversive Acts.* Auckland: Penguin, 1991.

Frame, Janet. *A State of Siege.* Sydney: Angus and Robertson, 1982.

Gadd, Bernard, ed. *Pacific Voices: An Anthology of Maori and Pacific Writing.* Auckland: Macmillan, 1989.

Goldie, Terry. *Fear and Temptation.* Kingston, Canada: McGill-Queen's University Press, 1989.

Grace, Patricia. *Electric City and Other Stories.* Auckland: Penguin, 1987.

———. *The Dream Sleepers.* Auckland: Longman Paul, 1980.
———. *Cousins.* Auckland: Penguin, 1992.
Habib, Rowley. "Moment of Truth." In *Into the World of Light.* Ed. Ihimaera and Long. Auckland: Heinemann, 1982.
———. "Memorial Day." In *Into the World of Light.* Ed. Ihimaera and Long. Auckland: Heinemann, 1982.
Hilliard, Noel. *A Night at Green River.* London: Hale, 1969.
Hulme, Keri. *The Bone People.* Wellington: Spiral, 1983.
———. *Te Kaihau/The Windeater.* Wellington: Victoria University Press, 1986.
Ihimaera, Witi. "Brown Is Beautiful." *New Zealand Listener* (January 11, 1971).
———. *Pounamu Pounamu.* Auckland: Heinemann, 1972.
———. *Tangi.* Heinemann, 1973.
———. "Deep South." *Otago University Students' Association Review* (1975).
———. *The New Net Goes Fishing.* Auckland: Heinemann, 1977.
———. *The Matriarch.* Auckland: Heinemann, 1986.
Ihimaera, W. and Long, D. eds. *Into the World of Light.* Auckland: Heinemann, 1982.
JanMohamed, Abdul R. "The Economy of Manichean Allegory: The Function of Racial Difference in Colonial Literature." *Critical Inquiry* 12:1 (1985): 59–87.
Johns, Atihana. "He Pakete Kanara." In *Into the World of Light.* Ed. Ihimaera and Long. Auckland: Heinemann, 1982.
Kohu, Rosemary [Hinewirangi], and Robert de Roo. *Broken Chant: Poems.* Tauranga, Don Kale Printing, 1983.
Maihi, Toi Te Rito. *Pakake! Pakake! Whalesong.* Auckland: Iwa, 1992.
Orbell, Margaret, ed. *Contemporary Maori Writing.* Auckland: Heinemann Educational, 1970.
———. *Maori Poetry: An Introductory Anthology.* Auckland: Heinemann Educational, 1974.
Pearson, Bill. "Witi Ihimaera and Patricia Grace." *Critical Essays on the New Zealand Short Story.* Ed. Gerry Hankin. Auckland: Heinemann, 1982.
Potiki, Roma. *Stones in Her Mouth.* Auckland: Iwa, 1992.
Rika-Heke, Powhiri. "Grandmother." In *Subversive Acts.* Ed. Cathie Dunsford. Auckland: Penguin, 1991.
———. "Neighbours." *Spiral* 7. Ed. Spiral Collective. Wellington: Spiral, 1993.
———. "Human Rights, a la Carte, With Salt." *Gulliver* 33, Berlin/Bremen, 1993.
Said, Edward. *Orientalism.* London: Routledge and Kegan Paul, 1978.
Stewart, Bruce. "Broken Arse." In *Into the World of Light.* Ed. Ihimaera and Long. Auckland: Heinemann, 1982.
———. *Tama and Other stories.* Auckland: Penguin, 1989.
Sturm, Terry, ed. *The Oxford History of New Zealand Literature in English.* Auckland: Oxford University Press, 1991.
Taylor, Apirana. *Eyes of the Ruru.* Wellington: Voice Press, 1979.
Wedde, Ian, and Harvey McQueen, eds. *The Penguin Book of New Zealand Verse.* Auckland: Penguin, 1985.
Williams, Mark. *Leaving the Highway.* Auckland: Auckland University Press, 1992.
Wolf, Eric R. *Europe and the People without History.* Berkeley: University of California Press, 1982.
Woodhouse, Susan. "A Family Affair." *Thursday* (June 13, 1975).

On Women's Writing in Aotearoa/New Zealand: Patricia Grace, Keri Hulme, Cathie Dunsford

Sigrid Markmann

There are two cultural maps in New Zealand: Maori and Pakeha. The dominant one is drawn by the Pakeha culture and with it the influence and the supremacy of western-patriarchal modes of thought. In his satire *The Battle of the Books*, Jonathan Swift conjures up the image of a spider that has spun its web in a library corner, in which a bee has become entangled. While the spider spins the threads of its intricate web out of its own self, the bee—outside its own being—is dependent upon nature in order to be able to produce honey. In a figurative sense, the bee symbolizes the cultural map of traditional society with its lores and customs, its teachings on the universe and on creation; the spider, however, stands for the urbanity of contemporary, secularized, western civilization. Both spheres possess their own characteristic literature of "closed" and "open" texts. The rural land being synonymous with the oral tradition of so-called closed texts is passed on from generation to generation. Urban space, on the other hand, is affiliated more closely with open texts and is produced as a response to complex or polar realities. The tension between the rural and the urban becomes evident in the face of contrasting worldviews and a separate consciousness, each of which is founded on a distinct set of moral/cultural precepts. The essentials of Maori life are to be *tangatawhenua* (i.e., a "base"), and thus a right to speak on a *marae*. The *marae* is the key institution in Maori society, the center for ceremonies and gatherings. Throughout the past 150 years of colonial rule, the Pakeha spider has failed to devour the Maori bee, although at the beginning of this century, the Maori population had been threateningly decimated by an influenza epidemic. Since many Maori were looking for jobs in the towns, *marae* became dilapidated, their language repressed and Maori identity seemed almost completely destroyed. However, it is thanks to Maori leaders such as Apirana Ngata (1874–1950) and to a radical resistance that *Maoritanga* could survive. This survival was motivated by various circumstances: The *marae* saw a revival as the center of the *Te Wairua Maori* (Maori awareness/spirit); Maori land development cooperatives initiated the retreat to the land; even in the towns, *marae* were erected as a symbol of coexistence with the Pakeha.

Despite all diversity, the survival of the *marae* remains a miraculous fact. Their vitality and liveliness have created a cultural continuum which helps to establish and strengthen both cultural identity and self-confidence, as such being a focal point of reference for Maori writers, because they have *turangawaewae.*

There are two principal features that primarily define the development of written Maori literature. Its records are, above all, anchored in the Maori language and in the literature of an exclusively oral tradition—a fact that is most poignantly illustrated in the *waiata* (songs) and poems of Maori. From early on, some *waiata,* which were sung in the *marae,* have shown a connection between tradition and the present, with reference being made to a pre-European past, to the present situation and to a future with an autonomous and yet mutually permeating Maori and Pakeha culture. The underlying quest is that of recognition and acceptance, not of assimilation (Mitcalfe 157). In the writings of Maori authors, the process of cultural repossession and affirmation is manifest in their choice of themes from traditional Maori culture, its history and experiences.[1] Others, however—the majority of whom were brought up within the Pakeha system, leaving them almost victims of the spider—became aware of the loss of their language, traditions and values. They were primarily interested in the creation of a new self-awareness based upon an independent cultural tradition. Out of these efforts rose a kind of literature which, above all, highlighted the values of rural Maori society.[2] It was through the recapturing of the "base" that *Maoritanga* was brought out of the *marae* into the English-speaking literature and that a literature had been created which addressed Maori and Pakeha alike. For Maori writers in the 1970s, in particular, *Maoritanga* became an integral feature of this literature within an otherwise still dominant European-monocultural context. Maori literature of the 1980s defines itself essentially by reference to Maori philosophy and its system of values, with an intensity and self-confidence ultimately resulting in a change of perspective as in the cases of Keri Hulme, Patricia Grace and Witi Ihimaera, and in an increasing awareness of ethnocentrically biased documents and texts.

However, although the narrative focus is on the rural tradition and accordingly on the Maori part, the rediscovery of the land and of the Maori culture established the autonomy of written Maori literature within the medium of the English language and neglected for the moment the socioeconomic realities faced primarily by those Maori living in the towns or in suburban areas. They suffered a breakdown mainly of their social relations; they belonged to the lower classes of society; and they bore the social stereotype of idle, simple-minded children of nature and were discriminated against. Their children grew up within the Pakeha culture, knowing neither their own history nor their own language. Only a few were successful in the Pakeha system, and the percentage of Maori in prisons was disproportionately high.

The territory of the spider, in which many Maori lived, was to be the second characteristic feature of Maori literature. The reaction to the uprooting and alienation did not take the shape of blank/impotent anger/fury and desperation; nor did it suggest the retreat to a transfigured rural pre-European past. The prevailing mood was rather that of a conscious identification with one's own culture and a confidence in the as yet lingering power of the Maori heritage. It was through these channels that the recapturing/repossessing of the "base" could be made possible. Since the 1970s, the analysis of the urban situation of the Maori has become linked with a criticism directed toward Maori and Pakeha alike, urging them to see the need for a coexistence on equal terms. From the late 1960s onward, this reorientation has been confirmed by the Black Power movement from the United States as well as other civil rights movements. On the one hand, this has resulted in the call for a radical *Black Power* (as referred to in Stewart), yet on the other hand, there was an ultimate demand for human rights, with black awareness and Maori identity being juxtaposed to the Pakeha culture, so as to provide the perspective of the native population with a "base" and thus with the ability to assert oneself. Even though the "clenched fist," as described by Witi Ihimaera in *The New Net Goes Fishing*, symbolizes black identity (connected with the idea of worldwide black identity), Maori identity is essentially rooted in the strength and vitality of the Maori culture.

On the whole, Maori literature reflects a process which intends to negotiate between the spider and the bee, between Maori and Pakeha, the urban and the rural, as well as to overcome racism and fight for equality, for a coexistence: "There is still a need for . . . the best of both worlds" (Ihimaera, *The New Net Goes Fishing* 152).

PATRICIA GRACE AND RESISTANCE

Many Maori writers find themselves in a situation that Patricia Grace describes as follows:

> I am a person of mixed racial origins, being Maori and Pakeha by birth and by upbringing. So, although I have always identified myself to myself as Maori, my Maori experience has been limited. ("The Maori in Literature" 80)

Patricia Grace opts for her identity as an individual, being fully aware of the ethnocultural alternative, of her kinship relations, of her situation as a woman as well as of her affiliation to a social class. She defines herself as a woman of color, which means that she groups herself with those outside the structures: people to whom black is a symbol of resistance.[3] With her conscious choice, she transcends all those boundaries and attributes which the dominant culture of New Zealand has imposed, from the outside, on a social class, an ethnic minority. In emphasizing her bicultural background, she draws attention to the variety of her experiences in different areas of life as well as to the complexity of bicultural experiences reflected not least in the language itself. On the whole, she points to her cultural areas of reference, each with its own characteristic markings. She thus opposes a dominant Pakeha culture that is anxious to maintain its monocultural standards, having exerted an undiminished pressure for Maori to conform for the last 150 years. Just like other women authors, Grace sees her writing as a political act of solidarity and collective self-definition.

Fictional and nonfictional texts on Maori life have suffered greatly from ignorance of the basic problem on the one side and pedantic exactitude on the other. It is Grace's intention to counteract the stereotyping and the superficiality:

> I think it is important for me and other Maori writers to write about us in all our variousness, our feelings and aspirations and values; attitudes to life and death; affinity for land and land issues, about kinship and social orders and status; about the concept of aroha (embracing *awhina* and *manaaki*); attitudes towards learning and work, towards food—its growing and collecting and preparation. And most especially about the spiritual aspect of all these things. ("The Maori in Literature" 81)

The impulse to write is founded in her own life story and in her experience in the border land between the dominant Pakeha culture and the dominated Maori culture. As an urban Maori, she was not familiar with the Maori language and was unaware of many of the myths of the Maori ancestors. Through writing she wanted to discover and familiarize herself with her *Maoritanga*. Memories play a crucial role in her stories, not only because she connects a lost path with a confusing and confused present, but rather because memories of things gone by are an essential element of Maori tradition. Her (short) stories focus on childhood reminiscences, on memories of the ancient rural culture brought to life again through the reflecting minds of old and younger people, some of whom have difficulties in explaining the significance of their experiences to their children. Grace focuses on the thoughts of an old man who is leaving the country for the town so as "to make a ways for those who follow because I Love" (*Waiariki* 42); the thoughts of an older widower waiting for his death in order to be reunited with his wife; the thoughts of a Maori woman who lives in the town and, in her mind, reexperiences the whole anxiety and fulfillment of traditional hospitality, which a two-week visit from relatives demanded of her; the thoughts of a young Maori woman who is appalled at the voyeuristic behavior of Pakeha onlookers during a Maori parade through the streets of a small town and who is determined "to show others who we are" (*Waiariki* 88).

For their greater part, these stories are first-person narratives. Patricia Grace has developed a style in the English language which is based on the rhythms of Maori speech. These audible impressions are drawn from the author's own childhood, when she was listening to the old people's telling of stories and legends. More than anything, the language also reminds one of the Maori-English vernacular spoken in the country: "From the north he came, Toki, in his young day. Ah yes. A boaster this one, Toki, the fisherman" (*Waiariki* 7). In "Huria's Rock," the shift from a third- to a first-person narrative perspective mirrors how the old man perceives himself—just as if, at times, he were standing outside his own self:

> Old now these bones; and one leg with a stick to help it; old now: He sits, this old one with his stick, on the beach and the agar about him all spread to dry. It is good the stick, to turn the spread agar, and to poke the ashes round the big camp oven. . . . Many years now since last we came to camp and gather agar here, young days then I, and the leg without a stick to help it. Two good legs then, and a backstrong. Two good eyes, and the hands to pull the agar from the warm sea. (*Waiariki* 48)

The stories impart a feeling of what Norman Simms qualifies as "timelessness" (190), through which alone a continuity with the ancestors, the land, the seasons and the tides is established: the fisherman from the North could have lived today, yesterday or hundred years ago.

Although written in a more conventional style, the recollections of the younger protagonists convey a certain empathy and warmth, sadness and humor. The father, who recalls his own childhood and takes his children fishing down by the beach so as to let them share his memories, is unable to explain to them the meaning of an old custom:

> And there was regret in me too for the passing of innocence, for that which made me unable to say to my children, "Put your kits on the sand little ones. Mimi on your kits and then wash them in the sea. Then we will find plenty. There will be plenty of good kai moana in the sea and your kits will always be full." (*Waiariki* 42)

In "Beans," a boy—whether he is Maori or Pakeha remains unsaid—passes a big farm and takes deep breath: "a horrible great stink . . . a joyous big stink of pigs." After that he returns home and eats some lemons "because I don't want to miss a thing in all my life" (Grace, "Mirrors" 9).

Every single experience is important, has a distinct meaning. Also, a woman with Maori ancestors may share quite a few experiences with many other women in the town, as for instance in "Mirrors." Here, a mother gives up love and gets up instead to drink a cup of tea, before her family is awake at all; buys milk with her slippers on and in doing so is caught in a shower of rain and steps into dog's muck, whereupon she throws her already worn-out now filthy and wet slippers into the stove and washes her feet. Only then the family is awake. At first glance, these instances seem but trivial morning experiences; they are, however, recorded in a stream of consciousness dialogue, with observations of the early morning scenery, of the ocean waves on the shore and on the rocks of Mana Island being gently woven into it. She perceives numerous other small details like these. Reality is thereby not immediately given, but constitutes itself only through the conscious isolation and selection of single experiences and perception.

While the accent in this story rests on the mutual, in "Journey" it is on the differences. We hear the story of an old man who goes to Wellington in order to fight—thus acting contrary to his otherwise rather reserved bearing—for the land of his family, which is destined for government planning. Grace, whose protagonists are generally referred to as warm-hearted, cautious and nondemanding characters, makes them speak up for their rights and fight if the land is at stake and dispossession looming. In doing so, she points out the close relation between the Maori and their land: they are the land. The old man failed to assert himself; for him, the defeat implies destruction. On his journey into the town, he saw the worn-away hills, destroyed by the Pakeha:

> Funny people these pakehas, had to chop up everything. Couldn't talk to a hill or a tree these people, couldn't give the trees or the hills a name and make them special and leave them. Couldn't go round, only through. Couldn't give life only death. (Grace, "Journey" 57)

Fearing that one day, during some earthwork, his bones will be carelessly dug up by some bulldozers, he decides to have his corpse burned after his death. The young man in "And So I Go," who leaves the land of his ancestors to look for work in the town, does not distinguish between his love of his family and his love of the land. On parting, the land is the mother: "[I] [s]tretch out my arms on wide Earth Mother and lay my face on hers. Then call out my love" (*Waiariki* 47). And the old Maori woman in "Transition" attests that her progeny descends from both her and the land: "And from the two—the land, the woman—these ones have sprung. And by the land and the woman held and strengthened" (*Waiariki* 18).

Grace never once condemns the Pakeha for their disregard and disrespect of the Maori; the nearest she comes to an accusation is in "Journey," where her Pakeha protagonists respond to Maori values and sensibility with such bluntness and indifference that this discrimination quite obviously imparts a general idea of how the whites treat other ethnic groups who are virtually without power. She does not accuse directly, does not demand an account: yet she is aware of the wounds and the deprivation of rights that the Pakeha have inflicted on the Maori. She confines herself to a description, a clarification of the consequences, so as to alert the reader to them. She addresses both Maori and Pakeha alike, being anxious to revive the Maoriness for both groups: as a potential source of identification for the Maori and as an offer to the Pakeha to learn to respect an ethnocultural group through such virtues as knowledge and understanding. In a sensitive and convincing voice Grace's stories record the things that have a certain significance and tradition for the Maori, that mark their cultural heritage and give meaning to their existence: the faith in *aroha* (i.e., the love of the land and of the people as part of a branched family), the spiritual connection with the land, the affinity for the supernatural, for the cosmos, the attitude toward death. Furthermore she describes what it means to live as a Maori in a Pakeha society.

In her novel *Mutuwhenua*, the two ways of life and value systems of a young couple symbolize the coexistence of Maori and Pakeha: the spontaneous aroha of her Maori characters contrasts with the rather emotional coldness of her Pakeha protagonists. Although the respective parents and the grandmother serve to portray the two distinct ways of life, Linda and Graeme finally remain totally unaffected by it. Their problems, ultimately resulting from their divergent cultural backgrounds, are shifted to the outside. Whereas before the wedding, it was Linda's Maori grandmother, Ripeka, who feared that through this marriage Linda would lose her Maori identity, it is Linda's own cultural subconscious that, after the wedding, evokes problems: the house in which Linda and Graeme live was built on the ground of an old Maori burial place; Linda is haunted by dreams in which she is called by death. After she has told Graeme about it, they simply move into another house. Whereas Graeme shows empathy and understanding, Linda becomes "universalized: that is, she finally turns into something like a Pakeha woman and only sometimes shows signs of her Maori background. Within her Maori family, she maintains her individuality and personality. Outside, however, she seems shy and rather dull, always anxious to run the household properly and do the shopping—just like any conformist Pakeha woman. Grace's efforts to bring both cultures together turn, for their greater part, out to be at the expense of Linda, the Maori woman, who—thanks to her Maori family—retains her backing and identity and finally asserts: "I know it's possible to be close, and to love, and that even with differences you can be open to knowing" (152).

Grace is at her most convincing when she is not at pains to bring both cultures together, but when—as in *Potiki*—she explains *Maoritanga* in its own right as an autonomous entity and in its references to the Pakeha culture. She does so by reaching back to the imagery of the Maori past in order to strengthen the authenticity of the present in a Maori community that is steering toward an unknown future, yet showing faith in continuity, a continuity of Maori humanism which has managed tenaciously to articulate itself even within the dominant culture (and not least with their means). Not resignation, but an awareness is beginning to show here: the dignity in life, in the faces, in the utterances and ceremonies of the Maori are held up high; the knowledge of this dignity, the understanding of the ability to act accordingly and retain an identity. Grace's own transcultural experiences have made her particularly sensitive to the pressure of assimilation and have caused a turning to the preservation of traditions on the one hand and to a creative encounter with the threatening Pakeha culture on the other hand.

KERI HULME AND THE NEW VISION

Unlike Patricia Grace, Keri Hulme says of herself that she is neither a Maori nor a New Zealand Pakeha writer, but a bicultural one, which, for her, means "a Maori with qualifications" and with ancestors from Scotland and Lancashire. So what is a Maori after all?

In point of fact, we find this delicate issue reflected in *The Bone People*, in which the protagonist Kerewin Holmes, like the author, has multicultural origins and is surrounded by symbols, memories and artefacts from various different cultures. Yet, on the other hand, Hulme shows clearly that she strongly rejects any simplifying, binary division in favor of a variety that allows for a nonclassifying ambiguity. She discards the Maori-Pakeha dichotomy and with it an either-or identity and affinity. For her, these is just as little ground for assigning people in simplified terms to a certain sex and sexuality. In *The Bone People*, Hulme has drawn characters who do not live up to traditional attributes and ideas—neither in their outer appearance nor in their behavior. The novel is spun around three main characters: Kerewin Holmes, a painter with Maori and Pakeha ancestors; Simon, a mute boy with Irish origins; Joe, a Maori and Simon's foster-father. The gradually unfolding relationship among these three characters takes an almost fatal course, until a rebirth brings about resurrection. When Simon sees Kerewin for the first time, he is not sure whether she is a man or a woman. As for Kerewin, she loathes any stereotyping classification. Hulme's answer to stereotyped "femininity" is to be found in the description of her "heavy-shouldered, heavy-hammed, heavy-haired" (21) protagonist.

Simon, too, cannot be assigned unambiguously. On their way back from a holiday in Kerewin's Moerangi, they stop at an inn to get some refreshments. On seeing Simon, the innkeeper is wondering about the sexuality of the child. And Joe "waits resignedly for a crack about the length of the child's hair" (244). However, the characters are anything but mere reversals of historical stereotypes: Kerewin, Simon and Joe are individuals who combine passivity and activity, control and aggression, care and egotism, to rewrite racial stereotypes. In doing so, Hulme certainly leaves the conventional path of polarizing these characteristics. Joe is a caring person, much concerned about Simon, but is he violent, too. When Joe realized that Simon, whose foot he was bandaging at that very moment, had stolen one of Kerewin's rings, he hit him hard across the calf of his leg. The sound cracked around the room and Kerewin looked up sharply" (57). Kerewin is neither a hero nor intolerable. Her rejecting, almost hostile stance toward Simon, who intrudes into her tower, sometimes softens to some kind of unfriendliness and rough concern; and yet Simon senses her fundamentally ambivalent attitude toward him: "She got rings. She play the guitar for me. She liked you? NO" (80). Her passionate temper is of high complexity; when defeating Joe in a fight, she makes use of the techniques she has picked up in *aikido dojo* during a one-year stay in Japan. Describing aikido as "a way of material spiritual harmony" (99), Kerewin finally disarms herself:

> Since the techniques really concern spiritual development, I didn't pick up anything except enough physical knowledge to make me extremely dangerous in any fight with anyone who isn't an aikido expert. (200)

Through her passive stance she becomes implicated in the violence that Joe exerts on Simon. When she discovers weals on Simon's back, she decides to remain passive; she does not want to become "involved" (149) but prefers to keep out of the whole affair, rationalizing her behavior accordingly. She decides to "watch out for the brat" (151) until the time is ripe to give Joe a piece of her mind, preferably with her fists.

Not only are the sexes drawn in their ambiguity, but sexuality in *The Bone People* also defies the notions of social and literary heterosexual romanticizing standardization. Kerewin is not interested in explicating sexuality and therefore is sexually indifferent toward Joe:

> I've never been attracted to men. Or women: Or anything else. It's difficult to explain, and nobody has ever believed it when I have tried to explain, but while I have an apparently normal female body, I don't have any sexual urge or appetite. I think I am a neuter. (266)

Kerewin's sexual neutrality is pictured uncompromisingly and without assessment. This may show that human affection is not founded upon biological premises—neither for individuals nor for the relations between ethnocultural groups.

Kerewin lives separate and alienated from her family, showing no ambitions whatsoever to have her own family, to be a mother herself. Her behavior thus contradicts the myth of women's instinctive longing for motherhood. Even if Joe wants to include Kerewin in his life, his decision is not inspired by sexual motives. Although he considers marriage, his primary motive is the security of an "ideal" family—as he had experienced it with Hana, his deceased wife.

By taking out polarization as a source of constant movement Hulme mediated through the very act of writing: Poetry and prose, realism, dream and myth are gently woven into each other. What is more, although the novel as a whole is written as a third-person narration, the dominance/strength of Kerewin's consciousness leaves us with the impression of a first-person narrative. Her consciousness is winding its way through all sections of the novel, in almost every conceivable manner: in dialogues as well as in the reproduction of thoughts from individual characters, which stands out graphically. Though hardly noticeable, even the narrative text shifts in perspective from the third to the first person.

> She had begun a book of biorhythmic cycles for herself a long time ago, and when she first began to explore the little machines, she had been curious to find out whether they might reflect cycles too. The suneater's chart had been going for sixteen months: her set, for five years, six years o God this December. And I thought a year would be enough to discover the rhythms of my body and mind. . . . I'll finish it this year. The thing's become an obsession. (100)

Kerewin is also present in the third person (152) and pervades the consciousness of both Joe and Simon. Joe, for instance, borrows/assumes Kerewin's diction, when imagining her reaction to the fact that Simon is a bed-wetter (172). And Simon, being mute, draws on Kerewin's idiom, when he is thinking (177). Poetry and prose merge; Kerewin's style of speech is at times highly poetic. Her unspoken observations and thoughts vary from the almost trivial to the lyrical (273).

The use of both the English and the Maori language—with English being the dominant one—counts as an essential feature of the linguistic shaping of this novel. At first Hulme had intended to leave the Maori language without any translation aids for the monolingual English-speaking reader. As for the Maori language, such an undertaking would have implied an existence with equal rights, whereas for the monolingual reader, it would have meant an exclusion, so that, as a consequence, the alienation, the polarization would have been further emphasized. Through the selected glossary the Maori language is bedded into a firmly established context. In this way, the difference remains, and the still existent power gap is shown clearly. As long as the social power structures are not overcome, the mere lifting of the polarization within the individual characters will hardly be a solution. The emotional and physical wounds as caused by uprooting, alienation, oppression and stereotyping are inherent in the characters of *The Bone People.* These wounds are hidden behind Kerewin's fear of giving up her isolation, "getting involved"; they are hidden behind the bitter estrangement from her family; behind Joe's alienation from his Maori culture and his violent behavior toward Simon; behind Simon's painful past history and emotional wounds and scars. The changing of power structures, however, is only possible through the people, who, in fact, will need their own "base" so as to be able to create something new together. They will have to take the risk of new forms of life and of a new common ground. Thus, in the first part of *The Bone People,* titled "The End at the Beginning,"

> They were nothing more than people, by themselves. Even paired, any pairing, they would have been nothing more than people by themselves. But all together, they have become the heart and muscles and mind of something perilous and new, something strange and growling and great.
>
> Together, all together, they are the instruments of change. (4)

Early on in the novel, the symbol of the double spiral—conveyed through Kerewin—appears. As such the double spiral is a traditional Maori symbol, fundamental to the belief that change and renewal do not imply a total rejection of the past but spring from it. The title "Bone People" is derived from the Maori word *iwi,* which means both "bones" and "people." The "bone people" are, therefore, the ancestors—the old people—as well as those people who start moving things (Kerewin, Simon and Joe in the novel). The gradual evolution and change are reflected in the four sections of the novel, each of which is subdivided into three chapters.

Part I pictures the network of relations growing among Kerewin, Simon and Joe. In part II, Kerewin takes both of them with her to Moerangi, to her real home (Moerangi reminds her of Moeraki, the place where—according to legend—one of the boats of the Maori ancestors was stranded). In part III, the relationships among all three characters come to a violent and tragic end. The three chapters of part IV are dedicated to one character each. Staying in different parts of the country, all of them face death in one way or other, thereby undergoing various kinds of rebirth in preparation for the making of a new relationship and in order to create "something perilous and new." Kerewin and Joe manage to find their *Maoritanga* and, with it, their *turangawaewae*, or "base." Joe becomes the keeper of a *mauri*, one special philosophy of life that embraces the living, human and powerful spirit of the whole country; Kerewin rebuilds the *marae* in Moerangi and is reconciled with her family; Simon, the mute boy of Irish descent, through his most delicate sensory and perceptive faculties, is the first to realize that the three of them will "only make sense together." Crucial for this change is not *mamae* (isolation, alienation) but *aroha* (love of the land and its people). The circle closes with the rediscovery of the "base" through rebirth. The idea of time is a cyclic one, with the instance of rebirth as the crucial event. In this way Hulme points out that there is no conflict between the beginning and the end, between birth and death, but that time is a cyclic continuum, that the past is alive in the present and in the future.

Keri Hulme transcends boundaries and conventions; she retains differences as a constitutive element of the mutual. Kerewin, Joe and Simon represent a microcosm that serves as a perspective for social change. Hulme's bicultural background, her familiarity with Maori history and culture as well as with Pakeha reality, and her bilingualism allow for an extended perception that transcends the cultural, political and social boundaries and opens up new fields of identity. The spiritual perception of a different worldview of sacred places, moments and actions marks the transition to a magic realism that has a determining influence on both the philosophy of life and the ethics.

CATHIE DUNSFORD AND THE SYMBOL OF SOLIDARITY

Power lines do not run in a one-dimensional and straight line but cross one another and have differing impacts according to the individual cultures. Specific cultural forms of patriarchal, racist and sexist structures are woven into the social context of relation and meaning; making these transparent will help people to understand, change and resist, but not justify. Understanding without knowledge is, however, impossible, for knowledge demands the will to be able to learn from each other.

Cathie Dunsford in her recent collection of poems, *Survivors*, transcends the geographical and cultural sphere of Maori-Pakeha/Aotearoa/New Zealand to relate her experiences as a woman of color discovering and acknowledging her Maori *Whakapapa* (genealogy) to those of other women globally. The area of conflict between the things that unite and those that divide, between the mutual and the different, can be seen as the only truly productive force in this encounter, which may create something mutual through such devices as dialogue or discourse. Starting from here, Dunsford is anxious to relate the dividing principles to the uniting ones; in a poem dedicated to Paula Gunn Allen (a Laguna/Sioux woman) and recalling the fights for the tribal land now claimed by the government, it is the courage of the indigenous women that unites and urges the reader to cross the borders:

of real and imagined fences
tear them down in
the coal black night
like Katherine and the Old
Rainbow Warrior Women
at Big Mountain, Arizona
and sit with the Medicine People
to share our gifts from the
four corners of the earth. (Dunsford 32)

The diversity of their cultures and symbols is united: Hinewirangi, a Maori poet and medicine woman from Aotearoa, shares the fight for the land:

like Hinewirangi, who
with her medicine bundle containing
the dark moist, sacred earth
of Aotearoa,
placed it in the Navajo/Hopi border
created by the United States government
and sang her waiata of peace. (32)

The individual experience that Dunsford catches in her poems is not to be seen as an isolated moment but as a political process aiming at a form of social life where people change things together and inspire each other with strength, courage and faith. She wants to counteract the breakdown of relations, to strengthen awareness and see people going right up to each other and meeting as like-minded individuals on a mutual ground. Dunsford's poems are a record of the vision of a "universal sisterhood," founded upon the recognition of historically and traditionally motivated differences. And since the meaning of experience, actions and events can certainly not be defined universally but depends on the critical reflection of an active self, the historical and present social network of conditions can also be conveyed via the self. Dunsford's response to the poem by Michelle Cliff, "Claiming an Identity They Taught Me to Despise," (1980) reads,

It was "Claiming *an* Identity"
where you untangle the filaments
of your own colonial history
and unlock the secret in me. (Dunsford 60)

In all her poems, we find the connection between past and present and the search for creative self-realization. Dunsford's poems are to be regarded as narrative verse. They are founded upon a tradition within which the storytelling element unites music, dance, poetry, fiction and reality, history and myths into a coherent whole:

This poetry should be recited, sung, chanted alongside other stories, songs, poems of celebration, resistance, struggle and laughter.

Poetry that is performed, poetry that has the vibrancy and immediacy of one of the highest forms of art on the world: Oral story telling; an art often perfected by the women of the tribe. (100)

The performers function as the medium between their art and their audience. There is an immediate interaction, which Dunsford refers to in a poem dedicated to Audre Lorde:

I think of the womanly struggles
that have allowed us to sit together
in relative safety in this
subterranean cave, with food to eat
and poems and songs to share
and I believe
that this moment
is a miracle
of survival. (Dunsford 98)

Dunsford's poems speak out of the density of her identity as a woman of color and a lesbian author. If women are marginalized, if they are lesbian, if they are radical, if they are different from the stereotypes society has imposed on them, women will be able to cling to their identity of otherness. This is where the mutual connection comes in, which, however, can only be felt in the awareness of historically, ethnically and socially conditioned differences. As with Lorde, love between women is not regarded as something special or the "other," a taboo that needs to be broken, but rather as the natural integrity of female and male proportions in every human being. Dunsford's thinking is based on the idea of a holistic, universal principle, according to which the individual unites in herself the sum of an infinite number of various experiences and in which man and woman, myth and history, reality and imagination, the individual and nature, fight and reconcile from an integrated whole instead of polar opposites.

For all their differences, the three women writers show the following mutual ground: the category of sex is never considered as an isolated instance; the intersections of race, class and sex are neither presented in a hierarchy nor completely neglected. Differences and conflicts are not explored from their antagonistic content but as integral parts of an entity. In this way, it becomes clear that a change of awareness in terms of an overcoming of polarisation is essential for social change. Put concisely, the underlying idea is that of a connection between the political and the imaginary to eliminate existing power structures. This alliance is part of a utopia which says that the acceptance of differences and a holistic thinking without any hierarchical pattern will lead to an elimination of socioeconomic and ethnocultural discrimination. Such processes of change, however, would have to find their way first and foremost into Western European consciousness, so that intercultural boundaries of reception can be transcended and the intended effects of understanding be admitted appropriately.

NOTES

1. See Pat Baker, *Behind the Tattooed Face.*
2. See Witti Ihimaera, *Tangi*, and Margaret Orbell, *Contemporary Maori Poetry.*
3. See Marion Kraft and Audre Lorde 555.

WORKS CITED

Baker, Pat. *Behind the Tattooed Face.* Cape Cathley: Whatamongo Bay, 1975.

Beston, John B. "The Fiction of Patricia Grace." *ARIEL* 15 (1984): 41–53.

Dunsford, Cathie. *Überlebende—Survivors.* O.B.E.M.A. (Osnabrücker Bilinguale Editionen von Minoritäten AutorInnen). Münster: Wurf Verlag, 1990.

Grace, Patricia. *Waiariki.* Auckland: Longman Paul, 1975.

———. *Mutuwhenua: The Spoon Sleeps.* Auckland: Longman Paul, 1978.

———. *Potiki.* London: The Women's Press, 1987.

———. "Beans." *To Ao Hou* 74 (November 1973).

———. "Mirrors." *Islands* (Summer 1975a).

———. "Journey." *Islands* (October 1977).

———. "The Maori in Literature." *The Maori Ora.* Ed. Michael King. Wellington: Methuen, 1978. 80–83.

Hulme, Keri. *The Bone People.* Auckland: Sprial and Hodder & Stoughton, 1985. London: Picador edition, Pan Books, 1986.

Ihimaera, Witi. *Pounamu, Pounamu.* Auckland: Heinemann, 1972.

———. *Tangi.* Auckland: Heinemann, 1973.

———. *The New Net Goes Fishing.* Auckland: Heinemann, 1977.

———. "Maori Life and Literature: A Sensory Perception." *Turnbull Library Record* XV (1982): 49–53.

Ihimaera, Witi and R. A. Long, eds. *Into the World of Light.* Auckland: Heinemann, 1982.

James, Trevor. "Black Literature in the Pacific: The Spider and the Bee." In *Connections: Essays on Black Literature.* Ed. E. S. Nelson. Canberra: Aboriginal Studies Press, 1988. 61–74.

Kraft, Marion and Audre Lorde. "The Creative Use of Difference." *English-Amerikanische Studien* 3/4 (1986): 549–56.

Mitcalfe, B. *Maorie Poetry: The Singing Word.* Wellington: Victoria University Press, 1974.

Orbell, Margaret. *Contemporary Maori Poetry.* Wellington: A. M. and A. W. Reed, 1970.

Pearson, Bill. "Witi Ihimaera and Patricia Grace." *Critical Essays to the New Zealand Short Story.* Ed. Cherry Hankin. Auckland: Heinemann, 1983. 166–84.

Simms, Norman. "Maori Prose Writers: Patricia Grace." *Pacific Moana Quarterly* (April 1978).

Stewart, Bruce. "Broken Arse." In *Into the World of Light.* Ed. W. Ihimaera and R. A. Long. Auckland: Heinemann, 1982.

Nesting in the Ruins

Norma C. Wilson

The Pre-Columbian Gold and Currency Museum in San Jose contains over eighteen hundred pieces of indigenous gold articles, some over two thousand years old. Some of these objects take the shapes of frogs; others, the fantastic forms of visions and dreams. When the Spaniards first explored Costa Rica in the early 1500s, they found gold works of art hanging from trees. Europeans who sought to accumulate gold as a way of increasing their individual wealth must have assumed that this communal expression meant there were vast quantities of gold in the region. Failing to respect the Native impulse to decorate trees with gold as a way of honoring nonhuman nature as the source of their life, the Spaniards thought of gold and trees as commodities to be taken to increase their own individual wealth and property. The indigenous gold of Costa Rica is only one example of the various forms of art the native people of the Americas have created over thousands of years, expressing their dreams and visions of the meaning of life.

I have a beautiful pair of earrings intricately braided from brown and white horsetail hair. They were made and given me by Tony Long Wolf, Jr., an Oglala Lakota who learned the art from his father. My friend's great grandfather learned the art of braiding horsetail hair in prison at the turn of the century for being a "hostile." When I met Tony Long Wolf, Jr., almost fifteen years ago, he too was in prison, for a crime committed under the influence of alcohol, and he had started writing poetry. A few years ago he returned to the Pine Ridge Reservation where he grew up and began working as an alcohol and drug abuse counselor. In his poem, "The Electrical Historian That Will Replace The Old Folks And Their Stories By The Camp Fire And We Can Still Have Buffalo Soup And Crackers—Afterwards!!!!," Long Wolf imagines, with not much exaggeration, the absurdity of Native people looking to the computer age as a way out of poverty on the reservation. Inventing names for computers, like "Existent-1868," "Relocation Solution #1953," and "Warriors Reincarnation #1973," Long Wolf gives an overview of the history of his tribe, and the continued appropriation of his culture. The colonization process continues, Long Wolf implies, sometimes under benevolent guises. And as long as a people remain colonized, there are no long-term gains. This may be the computer age, the irony suggests, but the soup is still rationed as in prewar days. Portions are limited to "one cup" (21). Hunger is a fact of life in the poorest county in the United States, where Long Wolf lives. How ironic and also how horrible that the Lakota people of Pine Ridge have been reduced to this state of poverty when two hundred years ago their society thrived on the abundance of the Plains region and their sacred Black Hills that are now being strip mined for gold.

In writing about postcolonial Native American art, I engage in a sense in the colonization process all over again since my own ancestors were European, and I live on land that Europeans stole from the Yankton Sioux. My writing is unavoidably influenced by the fact that I have lived outside the cultures indigenous to this place, and though my highest aim is to recognize and affirm the indigenous right to justice and self-determination, my understanding of Native cultures and experiences is limited by the fact of my own origins. The Native people give and give and give. Their way teaches that creation and giving of oneself are the only way to live—a way of life totally antithetical to the life of the European colonizer, *wasichu*, taker of the fat of the land. It is time to give back. Winona LaDuke says, "The native struggle in North America today can only be properly understood as a pursuit of the recovery of land rights which are guaranteed through treaties. What Indians ask—what we really expect—from those who claim to be our friends and allies is respect and support for these treaty rights" (Churchill 4). In surveying art and literature by Native Americans which have been influenced by colonization, it is clear to artists as well as to Native environmentalists like LaDuke, that land is the central issue.

Underlying the art of Long Wolf and other Lakota artists is the violation of the Fort Laramie Treaty of 1868, which had guaranteed to the Lakota, Arapaho and Cheyenne the undisturbed use of the Black Hills and a large surrounding area. Following the Custer expedition of 1874, verifying that there was gold in the hills, miners began violating the treaty in droves. Custer's attack and defeat two years later at the Little Bighorn was just one more battle in the four hundred year colonial war to take the land. Some have called the Wounded Knee Massacre of 1890 the cavalry's revenge for Custer's defeat, but it was only the last of the armed conflicts occurring during what Helen Hunt Jackson termed the "century of dishonor." A Miniconjou band, under the leadership of Big Foot, had fled the Cheyenne River reservation, afraid that otherwise they would be killed or forcibly removed. When Big Foot and his band of Miniconjou and Hunkpapa headed southward toward Pine Ridge Agency on the evening of December 23, it was in the desperate hope that they would find protection there. By December 28, when Major Whitside of the Seventh Cavalry intercepted them, Big Foot was hemorrhaging from pneumonia. Whitside "demanded an unconditional surrender, which was at once given" (Mooney 867), and directed them to move on to

Wounded Knee creek and camp there that night. They were joined by a number of Oglala visitors. The following day, December 29, the Seventh Cavalry disarmed and slaughtered more than 250 of the Miniconjou and Hunkpapa and Oglala Sioux, the majority of whom were women and children. Approximately 470 cavalry fought against 106 unarmed warriors (Mooney 867).[1] According to most eyewitness accounts, the slaughter erupted after a single shot was fired from an Indian gun that two cavalry men were attempting to wrest from its owner. In this incident, even repeated re-telling will never provide catharsis for the colonized.

Perhaps the most powerful response to the massacre is a painting entitled *Wounded Knee Massacre* by the artist Oscar Howe, a Yanktonai Sioux. In his painting the soldiers stand in the shape of a rigid tombstone. Below them are the bodies of Dakota people, writhing in agony, "like human red flames" in the creek bed that "gives the impression of an open grave" (Howe no pagination). Comparing Howe's painting to a photograph of the burial trench, one can see the origin of Howe's design in the actual scene. Howe's painting was purchased by the television show "This Is Your Life" in 1960 and presented to President Dwight D. Eisenhower, and is now owned by the Eisenhower Center in Abilene, Kansas. How appropriately ironic and consistent with our colonial history that the painting was presented to a military man, a former general, whose presidential administration was responsible for the disastrous policies of termination of indigenous nations and the relocation of indigenous people to urban environments during the 1950s. *Wounded Knee Massacre* is America's Guernica!

Native American artists from many different nations have responded to "Wounded Knee." Combining her insights as a Native American with facts she learned in anthropological studies and using a modernized dramatic monologue poetic technique, Hopi-Miwok poet Wendy Rose imagined the words of a Dakota woman killed in the Wounded Knee Massacre in a poem published in her 1977 chapbook, *Academic Squaw.* The poem opens with the woman speaking of her suffering: and her brutalized body: "peeled, tasted, discarded" (n. page.) But the last lines of the woman's testimony rise above her suffering to a statement of power and spirituality because her "ghost" dances out of the range of the "bullets." Rose's voices are defiant, always showing their suffering yet proud of the pain. They rise from the ruins, in the manner of "Naawva Taawi," her modern Hopi fight song about the miraculous survival of the indigenous people, who have used the leavings of European culture to rebuild their own. This poem from her book, "The Halfbreed Chronicles," ends by mocking "Pahana" and by praising the indigenous people, who can "nest in your ruins." (35) Pahana, Rose explains in a footnote, means whiteman in the Hopi language, and refers to a "way of life, a set of institutions, rather than to male human beings of European ancestry." She states the belief that "all of us, including such men, are victims of the 'whiteman.' "

Reexamining American history, Frederick W. Turner III said in 1971, "there has been among whites a planned destruction of the past—or at any rate, all of it that did not illustrate the national mythology" (introduction xii). In *Beyond*

Geography (1980), Turner examined the roots of the artificial culture we live in, tracing them to the ancient Near East, "where humans began to enact the dream of mastering the natural world" (21). The closest Turner came to defining the national mythology was in calling it the "mythology of power" (30). In his recent book, *The Spirit of Place*, Turner goes on to explore the "Making of an American Literary Landscape," beginning with Thoreau and progressing somewhat chronologically through the work of nine writers, ending with a chapter on Laguna writer Leslie Silko's *Ceremony*. Turner believes that the creators of this literary landscape "remind us to remember and to care" (xi) about the places where we live.

In *The Conquest of Paradise*, a reexamination of Columbus and his legacy, Kirkpatrick Sale says of the European antipathy to nature:

> The roots of this attitude are essentially biblical, found in that creation myth which is central to any society. The Hebraic Yahweh, so little a part of nature that He actually spends most of His time using its elements to wreak vengeance on His flock, creates humans in his image and as His surrogate "to have dominion over" all the animals of the earth and to "replenish the earth, and subdue it." (80–81)

Whatever its roots, European colonization has been so violent that the presence of a wide-spread hysteria, particularly in the minority populace of the United States, is only natural. As Vine Deloria, Jr., so succinctly stated in *Custer Died for Your Sins*, "violence is America's sweetheart" (251).

Cherokee author Jimmie Durham places blame on the education system that has glorified "filthy murderers" (10), "liars and crooks" (11) like Columbus, Pizarro and Cortez, General Miles, Daniel Boone and General Eisenhower, in his poem, "Columbus Day." Instead, Durham writes, we should remember Many Deeds, Greenrock Woman and Laughing Otter, who were part of the resistance, solely to commemorate "Columbus' victims" (11). He goes on to suggest that children be named for these native heroes who resisted colonization.

Also reminding us to reject America's false history, Dakota author Elizabeth Cook-Lynn writes with a firm respect for the courage, traditions and culture of her people. Connections among money, history and the invasion of Dakota land are made in "My Grandmother's Burial Ground," from her chapbook, *Seek the House of Relatives*. Cook-Lynn refers to the buying of land as the "coins invaders played": a very interesting and ironic choice of words, as we see casinos dotting Indian country today. This is just one of the results of the earlier attempts to transform the landscape of Native Americans into a land speculator's casino. That the history we have inherited is as ephemeral and false as these gamblers' profits is suggested in the poem's final lines because "that counterfeit absurdity" can never match the horrific reality of Native American colonization.

In *Seeking the House of Relatives* Cook-Lynn searches amid the artificial culture she exposes for what is lasting and real. This is characteristic of Native American poets in general. "Warrior Artists of the Southern Plains" is Klallam poet Duane Niatum's narrative of the nineteenth century ledger artists. Describing the art of White Horse, Howling Wolf and other prisoners, who began drawing as their only means of escape from prisons at Fort Marion and St. Augustine, Niatum provides essential contexts for understanding the visions in this historical form of Native American art. The art work simulates a journey of the mind, which in turn creates a parallel reality where the metaphor of the free-roaming Native American spirit carries a poignant message.

Also grounded in history, but at the same time using his modernistic imagination, Osage poet Carter Revard satirizes the Columbus myth in his poem "Discovery of the New World," first published in 1975. His poem can be considered a predecessor to Gerald Vizenor's recent raucus novel on the quincentennial, *The Heirs of Columbus*. Revard exposes the mythology of power through the voice of a creature from another planet, who is giving an account of human beings to his higher up. By placing the reader in the position of victim, where we'd all be if colonized by those little green people from Mars, Revard makes his audience feel what it's like to be considered unequal and expendable. He argues that because the colonizer cannot "grasp" the fact that "they are our lawful food and prey and slaves" (43). Even more poignant is the history leaking out like "holographic rainbows" (43) from the "brain" of the colonized. Revard cleverly shows what it is like to be a "helpless creature" under the control of another group of creatures, superior in their technological capabilities, but certainly inferior in their humanity.

Perhaps influenced by Wendy Rose, who has written such poetry for more than a decade, Joy Harjo adopted the dramatic monologue technique for her recent poem, "Strange Fruit." By means of her title, that of a blues song written by Lewis Allen and recorded by Billie Holiday, Harjo blends the history of the lynching of African American men with the 1986 lynching in California of the National Association for the Advancement of Colored People (NAACP) organizer Jacqueline Peters. It is impossible to distinguish the voice of Harjo from that of Peters. They seem to be one and the same and both enunciate the ravages of colonization. And maybe that is her vantage point. Increasingly Native American writers are going beyond their own culturally specific backgrounds, to reveal not only the victimization of their own people, but that of others who have been oppressed. Harjo tells the bitter truth, with a spiritual strength that affirms the worth of a woman who was killed out of racial hatred. Harjo's vision in her recent poems constantly moves between historical and contemporary contexts and between her own experiences and those of many others. This broad vision, far from being contradictory to the worldview of Native Americans, is fully consistent with a philosophical understanding of reciprocity and the interrelatedness of the universe. Acoma poet Simon Ortiz is always reminding us, "I hope, finally we will all learn/something from each other. We must. We are all with and within each other" (Preface to *From Sand Creek*).

In *From Sand Creek* Ortiz considers the effects of colonization on both Indians and people of European heritage. Like Cook-Lynn, he describes his historical enemies as those who have lusted for profit; and he carries this a step further, showing how historically, the heroes of American history have used and discarded, not only land, but people, for their monetary gain: Andrew Jackson serves as the prototypical, mythical master who forced "his slave women [to] bear his children for profit" (84). He continues this profit and rape metaphor and presents these illegitimate sons as the reverse picture of the sons of the colonizers. The poem indicates the loss of humanity that accompanies such an obliteration of one's past, one's trails, when one lives only for the profits available from other peoples and from some new place. When Abenaki poet, Joseph Bruchac, asked him how history can be used in poems, Ortiz answered, "You have to use history. History is the experience we live. . . . We have to acknowledge that certain terrible things happened. If they don't want to say it, then we have to say it for them" (Bruchac 223). In the same interview, Ortiz went on to say, "we have to be revolutionary poets. Decolonization requires it" (227).

A singer of traditional songs, and well aware of the traditional respect for language among the Acoma, Ortiz says, "My poems are prayers as well" (Interview). In her essay, "Who Puts Together," Linda Hogan has written that "as energy, language contains the potential to restore us to a unity with the earth and the rest of the universe" (177). Emerging from cultures fragmented by colonization, Native Americans aim at restoring unity between humans and the rest of nature as they retell history. "I think of my work as part of the history of our tribe and as part of the history of colonization everywhere," says Hogan (Swann and Krupat 233), whose work is not merely a vehicle for Chickasaw history, but a maker of it as she consciously identifies with all colonized people. One finds in the works of Hogan and many other Native American artists what I term a visionary history that reconsiders, retells, and interfuses ancient with contemporary experience. These artists have viewed history with the creative vision they inherited from their ancestors through traditional oral literature and religion. The language and techniques they have used to write or paint this visionary history are a far cry from the dry and static recapitulation of past events that history has meant to most Americans.

Hogan finds deep, intuitive images to exert the power of language in shaping her poetic historical vision. In "To Light," she writes of "the trees with their rings," which record every criminal act (197). Native American artists like Hogan have learned to use the tools of Western civilization to dismantle it and to create their own distinctive and sophisticated works of art. Native American painting has developed from the hide paintings and ledger drawings of the nineteenth century to the formalized style of Dorothy Dunn's Santa Fe Studio, where Oscar Howe studied in the thirties, and on to explorations like Howe's blending of traditional Sioux geometrical designs with the Modernist techniques of cubism and abstract expressionism. The visual statements of paintings like Howe's *Wounded Knee Massacre* and *Big Foot at Wounded Knee* have helped those familiar with these paintings to understand the brutal impact of colonization on the Sioux and on Native peoples in general.[2]

Over his twenty-five-year career, Howe's student, Robert Penn, has progressed beyond his mentor in the creation of highly provocative works in a wide variety of styles, media and techniques—from pen and ink to oil, from abstract to representational and symbolic, three-dimensional art. In his recent *Urban Indian* series, Penn's four by five foot acrylics are portraits of modern Native Americans looking and walking out of the walls of the city. One in the series is a self-portrait, showing the artist as a young boy in the background, and also as an adult in the foreground, who is stepping out a broken door onto rocks at the edge of a clear pool of water. To his right is a buffalo skull, to his left, a hawk. It is a vision of hope. This Lakota-Omaha man is stepping out of an alienating artificial world, into the natural/utopian world of his vision.

Similar themes are found in the literature that has developed over the past century. Many writers, who began as poets, have later expressed their historical visions in fiction. This is true of N. Scott Momaday, often considered the initiator of the Native American literary renaissance with his novel, *House Made of Dawn*. Momaday has continued to write poetry, sometimes merging it with his fiction. This is also true of Leslie Marmon Silko. Many other Native American writers have demonstrated a capacity to write in a variety of established genres and, like Momaday and Silko, to invent new ones. For example, Linda Hogan, who began as a poet, has recently published an unconventional novel, *Mean Spirit*, based on the history of Osage people in Oklahoma who were murdered in the 1920s for their oil. Before that, Louise Erdrich followed her first book, *Jacklight Poems*, with an unconventional novel, *Love Medicine*. Erdrich uses an innovative technique of juxtaposing multiple voices in nonchronological historical sequence; the chapters range in time from the nineteen eighties to the thirties and back to the eighties.

One of America's most skilled and visionary novelists, Leslie Marmon Silko emphasizes in her novel *Ceremony* the fact that the United States economy is based on consumptive greed. Her protagonist, Tayo, a Laguna veteran of the Second World War, comes to see humanity as "one clan again, united by the fate the destroyers planned for all of them" (246). Carefully weaving the ancient stories of the Lagunas together with the experience of living at Laguna Pueblo in the late 1940s, Silko wrote the novel as a ceremony for healing. At the end, Tayo is healed and whole again. He has learned to accept and understand his experience and to live in harmony with the nature around him and with his Laguna culture.

It would be hard to find a work of contemporary art more grounded in the ruins of colonialism than Leslie Silko's recent novel, *Almanac of the Dead*, which foretells a huge influx of native people from the south who will join with the poor in North America to overthrow the "Destroyers," Silko's name for those who have exploited and destroyed the balance of nature. The terrain of this book ranges from Laguna Pueblo to Colombia, and Silko explicates the decadent context for revolution in great detail, prefacing her narrative with this statement adjacent to a map on the inside cover:

> Sixty million Native Americans died between 1500 and 1600. The defiance and resistance to things European continue unabated. The Indian wars have never ended in the Americas. Native Americans acknowledge no borders; they seek nothing less than the return of all tribal lands.

That it is only a matter of time until the end of colonial rule is the common belief and hope in the visionary history contained in contemporary Native American art. It is not a naively romantic hope, but one grounded in a full vision and appreciation of the past and the present meaning of life on the planet. This attitude is mirrored in Penn's painting *Waiting for You to Go Away* as the artist, facing his audience, is painting his canvas red.

NOTES

1. As a means of curbing Native resistance to the taking of land, the United States government had arrested and killed leaders of bands that had not entered one of the designated military forts in the Plains region. In mid-December orders had gone out for the arrest of Big Foot. A band of Hunkpapa Sioux had fled the Standing Rock Reservation after the assassination of their leader, Sitting Bull, on December 15, 1890. They needed food and clothing, and Big Foot and his people had taken them in.

2. More recently, William Truettner has edited an anthology called *The West As America: Reinterpreting Images of the Frontier, 1820–1920,* where art historians critically examine the meaning and nature of the brutal colonization of Native Americans.

WORKS CITED

Bruchac, Joseph. *Survival This Way: Interviews with American Indian Poets.* Tucson: Sun Tracks and University of Arizona Press, 1987.

Churchill, Ward. *Struggle for the Land.* Monroe: Common Courage Press, 1993.

Cook-Lynn, Elizabeth. *Seek the House of Relatives.* Marvin: Blue Cloud Abbey, 1983.

Deloria, Vine, Jr. *Custer Died for Your Sins.* New York: Macmillan, 1969.

Durham, Jimmie. *Columbus Day.* Minneapolis: West End Press, 1983.

Harjo, Joy. *In Mad Love and War.* Middletown, Conn.: Wesleyan University Press, 1990.

Hogan, Linda. "To Light." In *Harper's Anthology of 20th Century Native American Poetry.* Ed. Duane Niatum. San Francisco: Harper & Row, 1988.

———. "Who Puts Together." In *Studies in American Indian Literature.* Ed. Paula Gunn Allen. New York: MLA, 1983.

Howe, Oscar. *Oscar Howe: Artist.* Vermillion: University of South Dakota Press, 1974.

Long Wolf, Tony, Jr. "The Electrical Historian That Will Replace The Old Folks And Their Stories By The Camp Fire And We Can Still Have Buffalo Soup And Crackers—Afterwards!!!!" *Vermillion Literary Project* 8 (1990): 20–21.

Mooney, James. *The Ghost-Dance Religion and the Sioux Outbreak of 1890.* 14th Annual

Report of the Bureau of Ethnology. Washington, D.C.: Government Printing Office, 1896.

Niatum, Duane. "Warrior Artists of the Southern Plains." *Michigan Quarterly Review* 29 (1990): 406–409.

Ortiz, Simon J. *From Sand Creek.* New York: Thunder's Mouth Press, 1981.

———. Interview. *The Circle: Hocoka.* By Shirley Sneve. South Dakota Public Television. KUSD, Vermillion, South Dakota, 1985.

Revard, Carter. *Ponca War Dancers.* Norman, Okla.: Point Riders Press, 1980.

Rose, Wendy. "Academic Squaw." *Blue Cloud Quarterly* (1977).

———. *The Halfbreed Chronicles and Other Poems.* Albuquerque: West End Press, 1985.

Sale, Kirkpatrick. *The Conquest of Paradise.* New York: Alfred A. Knopf, 1990.

Silko, Leslie Marmon. *Almanac of the Dead.* New York: Simon & Schuster, 1991.

———. *Ceremony.* New York: Penguin, 1986.

Swann, Brian, and Arnold Krupat, eds. *I Tell You Now: Autobiographical Essays by Native American Writers.* Lincoln: University of Nebraska Press, 1987.

Truettner, William H., ed. *The West As America: Reinterpreting Images of the Frontier, 1820–1920.* Washington, D.C.: Smithsonian Institute Press, 1991.

Turner, Frederick. *Beyond Geography: The Western Spirit against the Wilderness.* New York: Viking, 1980.

———. "Introduction." In *I Have Spoken: American History through the Voices of the Indians.* Ed. Virginia Armstrong. Chicago: Swallow Press, 1971.

———. *Spirit of Place: The Making of an American Literary Landscape.* San Francisco: Sierra Club, 1989.

Aboriginal Writing: Twisting the Colonial Super-narrative

Hugh Webb

Cultures can be seen as permeable, Edward Said writes. How permeable is Australian culture? "Cultures may," Said claims, "be represented as zones of control or of abandonment, of recollection and of forgetting, of force or of dependence, of exclusiveness or of sharing."[1] The fluidity implied in this definition is certainly attractive, foregrounding (as it does) historical and cultural process at the expense of the monolithic nation-state model.[2] And who could doubt after the Bicentennial—a remarkably fraught and inconclusive "celebration of a nation"—that Australia is on edge about defining cultural identities and norms? Edginess, though, breaks both ways and "cultures" can also operate "on the whole (as) defensive boundaries between polities."[3]

The major defensive boundary being deployed now, as it has been from the start here, is marked by a willful forgetting and a consistent exclusion of indigenous culture, meanings of the land and the facts of colonial dispossession. Aboriginal art is on our walls and on our T-shirts. Yet another form of "defensive" cultural hegemony is in operation. It goes like this: respect the other; give the other respect for being Other. No need to contemplate common cause and shared situation on the land-mass. But there is a counterforce, too. With Prime Minister Keating supporting the push for a republic and speaking of the need to avoid making forgeries of Europe, with the High Court's decision in the Mabo land case recognizing the validity of native (indigenous) title and overruling the absurd "terra nullius" claim that facilitated invasion and dispossession,[4] the hegemonic Anglo-Celtic culture is moving into crisis mode. White Australian culture is now not so much permeable (in Said's sense) as cracking. And the defensive boundaries look increasingly shaky. Into the fissures moves an evidently more confident body of Aboriginal writings.

Implicitly this is a putative postcolonial situation (although there are problems with the term, as I will suggest later). Much of the contemporary writing does involve "the radical interrogation and fracturing of . . . imposed European perspectives, and their systematic replacement by an alternative vision, or the attack on or erosion of the very notion of system and hegemonic control itself," as Helen Tiffin has defined the postcolonial perspective.[5] While Aboriginal spokespeople question their role in any future Australian Republic (indeed, partly *because* they do), the old Eurocentric colonial story—named as History and Culture—is under major revision. In her provocative piece entitled "Beyond Orality," Kateryna Arthur asks, "Is there a way of rewriting the future as well as the past by twisting the thread of the colonial super-narrative?" (23–24). Yes, Aboriginal writing suggests that there is a way (several ways) of twisting, rewriting, even demolishing the self-fascinated and self-justifying stories of the invader culture. Aboriginal writers and speakers have, arguably, the most important stories to tell about both a continental past and future. When one of the Fitzroy River drovers can speak so confidently (in a cultural sense) of his experience on the whitefellas' cattle stations it is clear that indigenous culture is on the counterattack. This is the voice of Ivan Watson, a Nyikina man, in *Raparapa*:

> Once in the wet I was building a woolshed. They had a Russian, George a'Linsky looking after the place, he was the verandah boss. That's what I call 'em. We've had different ones like old Doug Mew, he used to be a manager over Kulakulaku, but to my eyes he had positions that he shouldn't have held, you know, because nowhere was he as good as that. He might have been pencil-wise, but that's about all that gave him his job, carried him. Ability he had bugger all, he had nothing, lose himself in the twilight that fella.
>
> I said to this Russian, "What about the boss doing a few days work?" We were building the wool shed. So he came out and I gave him a big hammer. I remember, he had three swipes at the standards, and he said, "Well bugger that—who's gonna do this? Nobody!" Put it down and away he went. George a'Linsky his name was, I wonder where they would have got him from? (138)

That final "they" (the odd people, the outsiders) work powerfully to reverse the colonial paradigm. Those who, as they say, "never had to arrive" now turn to view the Others. Those who, for over two hundred years, have had control of cultural definitioning are now seen as strangers who have lost their way while writing endless tales about their inability to live at peace in and with this land.

The Bicentennial celebrations of 1988—an iconic series of events marking two hundred years of white settlements—can now be seen in hindsight as being the historical pivot around which the indigenous counterattack gathered momentum. Three years before these events Colin Johnson (now Mudrooroo) circulated his powerful epic poem *Sunlight Spreadeagles Perth in Blackness: A Bicentennial Gift Poem*. It is, in many ways, an exemplary text, and a close scrutiny will demonstrate the discursive tactics involved. I will cite an extensive segment from the work to illustrate the rhetorical power deployed to interrogate white Australian assumptions.

The title page of this text carries the following inscriptions in addition to the title: "By Colin Johnson" (a marker of origins, of specific making) and, below,

"Perth, Western Australia 1985" (which, as I will show, is much more than a sign of location). Sunlight paradoxically brings Blackness to the "City of Light" in the "State of Excitement" with its spreadeagled body on view:

> In any passage of the sun or moon,
> Fragments flutter,
> The ancestors and children of this time.
>
> Unable to escape the lying hands of the cop outstretching, I flee into the nighttime dawning without hope of any but the thistle seeds of yesterdays fallings, dreaming of the outstretching body of a woman in those hands, letting them flutter me beyond the hills where the air turns away from the gasoline—still there are the straight roads dotted with landmines of sadness and the little mission a blot of snow upon the brown earth where once I dreamt to dream dreams away in Perth and its too many newspapers crying out distresses seldom heard though read as language not making it to line the squares of television images which really matter. Seeing is believing, yuh know!
>
> In any passage of the sun or moon away from the soft dawning of the dusk, the Nyoongars of this city add their wailing to the Njamadji, Nanga, Koori and Murri. This Australia, a wrecked black body swarming with white termites.
>
> Fragments flutter into Yagan's grave. He rises moving on the reincarnated ceremony north where the heat keeps them at bay and allows Pigeon and his band to survive the deluge of the grog echoing with more than the cry of a black swan floating in the airship skies and an emu weighing heavy as he puts his foot down and says no more!
>
> The ancestors and children of this time fight to find a strand of dream arcing over the sunlight and the senseless meetings of the parliament brought into being by a blackman singing I'm proud to be an Aussie through sucking bottle lips and a long suffering guitar playing German chords passed on from a German father, sounding out words long dead and alive in his hidden ear.
> Tali warruniwarruni
> ngabangaba nunda,
> ngamurkalba nunda, hou!
> Tabaleua kurna kurnaangpirri
> kurnaangpirri maguua kurna, hou!
> (Oh, handsome you with your black tongue;
> Oh, handsome you with your dark skin patterns.)
>
> In the middle sun-sinking, this city brought to bay by an overgreedy exposure to imaginations redfaced with gin and lime and endless sermons against the pornography of sky and earth, though the stubby grey penis on the rise mocks their antiseptic cries and the suburbs curl like pubic hair around the base waving a fertility in the shopping arcades airconditioned

into market boredom of material congealed into plastic wares.
Let the river flood away this abomination of a city;
Let the sand turn quick to eat away its bowels;
here the blacks huddle drinking life away in others profits;
Here even the trees are amputated to prevent their roots from contradicting the tar and cement of how many lives moving along roads towards goals of less than great intent.

In the sunsetting, the river lies on its back warming its belly; The last light stretches black shadows in an effort to recapture in an orgy of red and gold.

And this colonial outpost teetering on the world's edge;
And this metropolis of the Nyoongar people fills with a crowd lost in a haze of jet lag from Europe. Inert strangeness moving etness with meaning only known to those adding meaning in some frenzied seeking by the crowd rushing home to homes barricaded into solitudes by walls and fences etching the city into pools of lonelinesses in which a black man slinks his heaviness filled with a drunkenness better left hidden in some far suburb. The city centre falls victim to American sailors famished for a sight of home sweet home: the colonial outpost becomes San Diego, and even the women are white with English mouths gaping for the Yankee dollar.

And in this American city bereft of the old, in this camping ground grown into a faintness of what they used to know, the Nyoongar wander disowned and owning.
This crowd is tinted brown;
This crowd is islands in the stream of whiteness.
People moving without visible strains until the shrieks begin, wither away into ugliness as they cry: Don't let the blacks remain!

In this disowning city the owners are ownless except for the clothing picked out of the rubbish of the welfare agencies. They stink, they mutter strange words of long ago intent.

Yagan's land, Yagan's land! Here is his tree, scratch it and it bleeds his ancient blood, scratch it and it bleeds the blood of a Nyoongar spitting out his teeth in a police station, coughing up his lungs in a charity hospital, vomiting his blood from a shattered skull in Fremantle prison just a short gasp and a death away.

In this disowning city, suffering under the constant sun language of heat exhaustion, they cry as they erect a statue to their disembowelled leader, John Forrest, father of many a Nyoongar as its told, or lied. He smirks a black beard at the street marked step by step with bronze heroes on the sidewalk and even Yagan becomes a doormat for shoddy hooves of disrupt patriotism.

In any passage of the sun or moon lies this lying city, this pretty town, this arsehole of the universe.

> Piles break quickly into sores leaking pus over the nice clean lawns,
> Vengeance becomes heavy here! (1–3)

So what, discursively, is going on here? First, and most clearly, fragments fluttering: traces, a play of developing traces, a discursive operation of/on language (*on* discourse); an *operation* rather than a presented state, an active movement, a process of demotivating discursive connections[6] and therefore, in consequence, a process of demystifying. The poem is a structure of signifiers which *absorbs* and *reconstitutes* the signified—yes, precisely.[7] It has been claimed that "poetic discourse is the equivalence established between a word and a text, or a text and another text."[8] Hence the intertextual workings of discourse. This *Sunlight* text centrally speaks (and *means*) within the location of the intertextual. And what of the "equivalences" involved, the key discursive sets? A scheme founded on these connections: body/land, belief/expression of that belief, power (in a larger sense, Culture/writing).

The register of this poem is that of the epic; with epic (as a category) cutting across the current division of cultural genres, cutting up the colonial "canon" (cannon), reaching across standard forms, ordering a different map of the field of culture.[9] One powerful destination of this reaching out and reworking is that much-believed definitional category for identifying seminal elements in West Australian writing: a Sense of Place. Certainly there *is* a sense of place here, in fact an intricately worked-on sense that is developed via an ideological counterplay of signs. Yet that Sense is a major discursive target: "the Swan edged with the smudge of putrification termed Perth" (8). The central cultural icon—the Swan, the river—is presented as a "term," as a temporary naming askew from its canonical, hegemonic power reference.

There is an evident stream of semiotically rendered (and saturated) consciousness being foregrounded. Combined with a performative multiplicity of representations, the result is a mode of passionately deployed rhetoric. Yet the various discourses given voice in the text are *not* deployed in a fragmentary manner. The effect is quite the reverse: a type of hammered-out, confident cultural consciousness. So we have here fragments (bits and pieces of discourses) and, at the same time, a subversively reworked montage of dominant representational patterns. The method is one of *bricolage*, a proclaimed cultural matrix (intimately known and recognized) is precisely reordered, reclassified and rearranged into new structures. Skirting and subverting the frenzied, childish significations of bourgeois Perth—"a great place to live," "We love you Perth" and so on—a new road map, a different lyric (a new semiotic set of song lines) is produced for Perth and, by extension, for the continent.

Sunlight as bricolage, a quite different sort of dappling. The minutiae of the physical world are discursively reordered by a means of logic that is not normally (that is, not culturally) their overt pattern of organized signification.[10] The result, on first glance an ad hoc portrayal of the discursive environment, works to establish homologies, analogies between the ordering of nature and that of the social domain of official Reality and of official languages of representation. Put another way, the bricoleur *relocates* significant cultural objects into a different position within the semiotic ensemble while seemingly using the same overall repertoire of signs.[11] Or, with another twist, these cultural objects are placed within a different total ensemble (for example, that of the Aboriginal cultural field). Empty offices and building foundations are articulated alongside (together with) initiation rites, grains of sand and a silent screaming child. From the text:

> Fragments flutter as the screaming child forgets to scream his silence
> numbed into dumbness by the first initiation here performed as the north
> descends to bleed the south in holy ecstasy blocked with grains of sand
> pressed into backs cutting the foundations of empty office buildings
> rising vacant with the greed of ill intent and discontent fading away in that silent
> screaming child. (6)

A clearly oppositional discourse is constituted and the old nexus of connection is radicalized. The result is a difficult-to-read, explosive junction: poetry as "guerrilla warfare."

Bricolage (as a discursive strategy) can never work by accident. On the contrary, a highly precise semiotic pointing to lexical meanings is involved. Take the line "This Australia, a wrecked black body swarming with white termites." Two readings from Webster's Dictionary:

> *swarm*:—"a great number of honey bees emigrating together from a hive in company with a queen to start a new colony elsewhere."
>
> *termite*:—"any of the numerous pale-coloured, soft-bodies, social insects (order Isoptera) that live in colonies consisting of winged sexual forms, wingless sterile workers, and often soldiers, feed on wood, and include some which are very destructive to wooden structures and trees—called also white ant."[12]

It is evident that a very precise replay (play on) the dominant definitional inscriptions is involved here and this process is typical of the discursive tactics at work throughout the *Sunlight* text. By the same process, History—the increasingly problematized (Bicentennialized) platform legitimating the Commonwealth of Australia—becomes now an object *constituted within* knowledge.[13] And this text performs a quite different kind of knowledge: one of the temporary, of the artificial, of the imposed, of the sexual, of the oppressive, of a falsely conceived conquest.

Similar semiotic tactics are evident in the Glossary, "normally" a neutrally directed assemblage of informational details within the discourse of lists. Here, in the bricolage Glossary, there is nothing of the sort. Taking up the terms that have already been mentioned, there is:

Perth: Capital of the state of Western Australia and of the Nyoongar nation, rest and recreation centre for the United States Indian Ocean Fleet.

Fremantle: Port of Western Australia near Perth which is centred on the State Prison.

Tobruk: A town in North Africa fought over by the Europeans in the 1939–45 World War.

Boong: An insulting, cruel term used by Europeans for Aborigines. Origin uncertain, though there is a white joke definition that it is the sound an Aborigine makes bouncing off the hood of your car.

Yump (Nyoongar): revenge (46–48)

It is a necessary effect and consequence of these tactics that Yump—revenge—is, of course, the last textual word.

There is much more that could be said about this Gift text; about the deployment of Aboriginal language items within (and alongside) "official" linguistic structures; about the tendency toward the creation (though fragmentation of linguistic codes) of an anti-language,[14] about the juxtaposition of liquid Aboriginal discourse patterns with the harsher codes of English, rendered here problematically as both alien and normal; and about the movement toward a new rhetoric and a new social semiotic of Being. The thread of the colonial supernarrative is here being twisted beyond breaking point. As an Aboriginal cultural story, *Sunlight* works to put in crisis the set of paradigms that underpin the national enterprise called "Australia."[15]

In the face of a work such as the Bicentennial Gift Poem, clearly *anticolonial* in nature, it is tempting to see indigenous writing from this continent as postcolonial. But there are dangers in such a critical move. The terms of the debate need closer scrutiny. "Postcolonial writing": what is this term or, more precisely, *whose* term is it? Whose interests does it serve?

The "postcolonial" is a confused misnomer in an Australian context. As a framing discursive marker for Aboriginal culture it is also an oppressive misnomer. In a perverse logic drawn from colonial discourses, Aboriginal writing is now post- (i.e., after) the colonial period. The "colonial" in Australia has ended? I would not want to try to tell that to writers such as Robert Bropho, or to Ruby Langford, or to Oodgeroo Noonuccal, in particular. It might be said that the "postcolonial" is merely a term deployed within the discourses of literary criticism to describe a certain trend in contemporary writing. Maybe. Or that the "postcolonial" is an enabling term, allowing previously silenced voices to be heard; that it is a compliment, a recognition of liberated difference. But clearly it is necessary to ask, Who is still defining and controlling that difference?

Whose social and political needs are fulfilled by the claim that what was the "colonial" is of the past? And whose temporal scheme of past-present-future (pre-present-post) informs the category? Not that of Aboriginal culture. It is not Aboriginal cultural forms that have necessitated the creation of a postcolonial enterprise. In a sense it is an enterprise that answers to a developing Eurocentric recognition of (and need for) a cogent, sustainable schema of theoretical explanation that can relatively unproblematically position those texts of the former "natives" that otherwise would have a worryingly subversive *lack* of position. Unchallenged, the danger is clearly that of a new form of imperial hegemony that tends to stress a kind of neutralized similarity at the expense of necessary recognition of specific cultural histories. At best, this process would produce what Mishra and Hodge describe as "a celebration of specious unity rather than a critique" (403). At worst, a subtle form of canonical (colonial) incorporation. Within this process the "postcolonial" is constructed as an object of knowledge that (suitably enough for Eurocentric intellectual dispositions) can then be critiqued through a postmodern/novelistic critical discourse. The tendency, as they point out in discussing *The Empire Writes Back*, is to "remove the post-colonial as a radical political act of self-legitimation and self-respect locked into practices which ante-date the arrival of the colonizer" (407). And, at the same time, it can be seen that the "practices" of the colonizing group are almost invisibly subsumed within the fetishised concepts of "language" and "culture" that are deployed as realist summaries of the colonial-contact situation or, at least, as fractions of a truth-telling summary of social experience. The individual text becomes separated from the *indigenous-defined* realities of its origins and cultural meanings. The "postcolonial" becomes "a purely textual phenomenon, as if power is simply a matter of discourse and it is only through discourse that counter-claims might be made" (401).[16] The Aboriginal text becomes text-as-discourse to be scrutinized now like almost any other signifying artefact.

The lack of cultural specificity in the notion of "postcolonial" is a strikingly political feature, in terms of rhetorical effects, that seems to include all while particularly recognizing none. What cultural specificity (indeed, what cultural respect) can be acknowledged within a postcolonial category that is defined as covering what Ashcroft et al. state in *The Empire Writes Back* as "all the culture affected by the imperial process from the moment of colonization to the present day" (2)? Apart from the obvious problem of cultural "lumping" that such a definition suggests, how would one decide which parts of a culture are those "affected," and by *whose* definition of that culture is the impact assessed? Specifically, in the case of modern Aboriginal writing, the definition is that of the invader-culture's discourses of understanding. This leads to the quaint situation where the newcomers are defining an existing culture as a type of damaged cultural artefact while, in the process, ignoring the fact that it is Aboriginal culture which is the *senior* culture on this continent (and not only in a temporal sense). Interestingly, in *The Empire Writes Back*, these contradictions are tacitly acknowledged—albeit tentatively in the area of textual analysis. A listing of major authors is provided (144) but no discussion of specific texts. While this tentativeness does not prevent the authors from making the sweeping and unsupported claim that "Aboriginal writing provides an excellent example of a dominated literature" (32) (where the easy parallelism of *excellent* and *dominated* signifies more than is perhaps realized), overall the sense is one of a cautious hesitancy about the specifics of Aboriginal writing.

Yet the move to incorporate Aboriginal writing into the hegemonic discourse of the "postcolonial" is well under way in this country. The booklet issued for the 1991 Writers Festival in Fremantle is rather poetically entitled *Old Lands, New Writings: Literature and Post-Colonialism*[17] and lists the invited writers (the majority of whom are identified as "Aboriginal").[18] The Leavisite ring to the title—based on a superficial binary that suggests some form of fascinating dialectic between old/new, land/culture—evidences the colonial nature of the discursive fields involved and, within those fields, the writings of Aboriginal people are positioned as both symptomatic of this purported dialectic *and* representative of literature in a period of "postcolonialism." These are writings, the booklet makes clear, forged by the experience of postcolonialism. And what is the nature of that experience? It is defined as "growing up with a language formed in another place and for another culture" (2). Despite the almost ludicrous reductionism of this definition (where the "postcolonial" is situated like some incipient childhood nightmare of a linguistic kind), the decision to focus on the categories "language" and "culture" is a revealing one. The central move is to equate language with culture in a contextual domain where culture is seen to be present *because of* language, absent because—unlike in the "old days"—there is "English" (or "english") and not some putatively defined "real" Aboriginal language. This is, simultaneously, the voice of nostalgia and domination. We see here a fetishization of languages employed in texts as if "language" is the most valid marker of colonial (*and* postcolonial) experience. The result: a remarkably mechanistic, static, syntactical view of Aboriginal culture.

The whole question of "language and culture" in the defining process surely needs to be challenged. Is there any reason to accept, so unquestioningly, that (for instance) writing is "power," nonwriting—read "oral culture"—is "nonpower"? In any case, was/is Aboriginal culture dominated by language (words) or by the gun, the chain and racist sociopolitical power? There is a revisionist mystification of historical processes at the heart of this "language" fetish, one constructed from a superior stance of the technological. The booklet continues: "Before whites came to Australia Aboriginal narrative was entirely oral—told to each generation, rather than written down or processed on a keyboard" (2). This is, of course, a massive oversimplification of the dominant (multimedia) modes of Aboriginal culture that include drawing, body inscription, painting and the physical narrative of the land. And if the feeling is of something lost or displaced, is it the "keyboard" that is, in practice, the key metaphor? After all, what is so powerful, so defining, about a keyboard? In all these definitions of the "postcolonial," the sense given is of a people *struggling* to express themselves in an alien context. Even a cursory reading of, for example, Bill Neidjie's *Story about Feeling* leaves this sort of claim seeming very dubious indeed. The book, transcriptions of Neidjie's speaking, constitutes a powerfully central commentary on Australian continental culture.

What has occurred is that the "postcolonial" is no longer a term operating in the classificatory spaces of a literary history. It is now functioning something like a genre—a genre not only of texts but of peoples, of cultures. And we know (following Jameson) in *The Political Unconscious* that a genre operates as "a socio-symbolic message . . . immanently and intrinsically an ideology in its own right" (141). The cultural framing involved in this process becomes clearer when one considers the ratification function involved. Genres can be seen as "the socially-ratified text-types available within a community,[19] as Terry Threadgold has pointed out. So who is ratifying the ascription of the "postcolonial" to Aboriginal writing? Not the Aboriginal community.

Regardless of positions created for it, the sheer cultural confidence (the palpable narrative force of its cultural intervention) is the most striking feature of Bill Neidjie's *Story about Feeling.*[20] If *all* Aboriginal culture has been colonized, changed utterly, then how can this book (from the Magabala Press in Broome) appear? We read—or, more properly, listen to—a series of interlocking narratives that have the Aboriginal notion of *story* as not only their formal linkage but, more interestingly, as their thematic focus. Or, given the unity of functions in this *Story*, it is more accurate to say that formal/thematic elements coalesce. This is a story about a story (which is also feeling):

> Tree smooth
> What about you' n' me smooth skin?
> Might be sunburn you but you got white, no-matter me.
> But this the story. You can't split im,
> you can't change im, you can't do anything.
> This story you got to keep im . . . in your feeling.
> Tree for us, eagle . . . anything.
> Eagle, bird, animal, rock . . . this the story. (Neidjie 32)

A tight cluster of important cultural terms—"skin," feeling, tree, bird, animal, land—is deployed in a powerful rhetoric of unity directed against the splitting semiotics of non-Aboriginal ontologies. The notion of story provides the encompassing meaning structure (as it is enunciated). Subject/object, speaker/story dichotomies are thus radically challenged. In "Laying Down," story is again both the central organizing category and the means of cultural expression:

> Listen carefully, careful
> and this spirit e come in your feeling
> and you will feel it . . . anyone that.
> I feel it . . . my body same as you.
> I telling you this because the land for us,
> never change round, never change.
> Places for us, earth for us,
> star, moon, tree, animal,

no-matter what sort of a animal, bird or snake . . .
all that animal same like us. Our friend that.

This story e can listen careful
and how you want to feel on your feeling.
This story e coming through you body,
e go right down foot and head, fingernail and blood.
through the heart.
And e can feel it because e'll come right through.
And when you sleep you might dream something. (19)

Clearly there is a complex discursive event taking place (being performed) in/by these narratives. Patricia Baines—in her study of Nyungar stories from the fringe dwellers—describes some of them as being "a careful configuration of meaning and metacommentary woven into the waiting moment" (240). That can stand as an exact description of *Story about Feeling* too.

There is a positivity in the Neidjie text that makes nonsense of the "struggling, oppressed post-colonial" syndrome. It is a text that *initiates* (in a cultural sense) rather than simply reacting to an invader culture. This feature has been noted by Veronica Brady, who writes of "a kind of heuristic device" at work in *Story* that has the effect of (as she puts it) "leading us out from our own limited order into a more inclusive and insightful way of conceiving the world" (92). This more inclusive narrative "way" is very much a physical and an environmental way. *Story* is certainly part of a physical process:

Listen carefully this, you can hear me.
I'm telling you because earth just like mother
and father or brother of you.
That tree same thing.
Your body, my body I suppose,
I'm same as you . . . anyone.
Tree working when you sleeping and dream.
The story e can listen carefully, e can listen slow
If you in city well I suppose lot of houses,
you can't hardly look this star
but might be one night you look
Have a look star because that's the feeling.
String, blood . . . through your body. ("Laying Down," 3)

And while white Australia has the obnoxious Toyota advertising story—"Oh, what a feeling!"—complete with platoons of leaping humans, Neidjie's story is an ethical one, confident and eloquent. In "Earth" he raises and answers the question "What's wrong with Toyota?":

This ground, tree, water, anything . . . for us.
Body in your body.

> You cover, you sleep, you sleep with earth.
> Earth for us, lily, any sort of a thing, plum.
> This Toyota not for us but we learning something.
> But e don't want to forget.
> I don't forget.
>
> "What's wrong with Toyota?"
>
> I said . . .
> "Well something wrong!"
>
> I had a argue little bit but I hang on my culture. (161)

A reading of (listening to) *Story about Feeling* suggests this to be, if anything, a very modest claim and the plethora of published life stories by Aboriginal women—Ruby Langford's *Real Deadly*, Sally Morgan's *My Place* and Glenyse Ward's *Wandering Girl* can be cited to represent a widening cultural field—demonstrates that the process of indigenous decolonization of the subject is by no means purely a male-centered phenomenon.[21] "Hanging on to culture" is now a surging renaissance, working against a previously unthinking white Australian hegemony by not bowing to received conventions of representation or to the sham of official histories. When Allan Barker sings, "There's a change going moving down," that, too, is an understatement in the light of the gathering impact of Aboriginal writing in (and on) Australia.

NOTES

1. Edward W. Said, "Representing the Colonised: Anthropology's Interlocutors" 225.
2. See Homi K. Bhabha (ed.), *Nation and Narration*, on discourses of the "nation."
3. Said 225.
4. See M. A. Stephenson and Suri Ratnapala (eds.), *Mabo: A Judicial Revolution*.
5. See Tiffin, "Post-Colonialism, Post-Modernism and the Rehabilitation of Post-Colonial History" 172.
6. See Jacques Derrida, *De la grammatologie* 74, and Jonathan Culler, *Structuralist Poetics* 241–54.
7. See Culler on Jakobson, in Culler 163.
8. Michael Riffaterre, *Semiotics of Poetry* 19.
9. Johnson describes the "surviving fragments" of Aboriginal oral literature as "the *Iliad* and *Mahabharata* of Australia." See Colin Johnson, "A Literature of the Fringe: A Study of Modern Aboriginal Literature in Australia," honors dissertation, Perth: Murdoch University, 1986, and Mudrooroo Narogin, *Writing from the Fringe: A Study of Modern Aboriginal Literature*.
10. See T. Hawkes, *Structuralism and Semiotics*, and Dick Hebdige, *Subculture: The Meaning of Style*, 103–104.
11. See John Clarke, "Style" in *Resistance through Rituals*.
12. I am indebted to Lorraine O'Brien for bringing these definitions to my attention.
13. B. Hindess and P. Hirst, *Pre-Capitalist Modes of Production* 308–311.

14. A process strongly canvassed by Johnson in his "Guerrilla Poetry: Lionel Fogarty's Response to Language Genocide."

15. The Johnson dissertation (1986) ends with a call for Aboriginal works to be created "reflecting the Aboriginality of the land and the people" that will, in the process, "be helping towards establishing an Australian culture beyond the mishmash of multi-cultural imports which now mark the continent" (349).

16. See also Mishra and Hodge, *Dark Side of the Dream: Australian Literature and the Postcolonial Mind.*

17. *Old Lands, New Writings: Literature and Post-Colonialism*, 1991 Writers Festival booklet (Festival of Perth), Fremantle Arts Centre, March 1991.

18. Specifically: Jack Davis, Patsy Cohen, Sally Morgan, Bill Rosser, Daisy Utemorrah and Jock Shandley.

19. Terry Threadgold, "Talking about Genre: Ideologies and Incompatible Discourses," 109. Genres are seen here as providing "the possible formats for the construction, combination and transmission of the discourses and stories."

20. Neidjie, *Story about Feeling*, (ed.) Keith Taylor.

21. See Kateryna O. Longley, "Autobiographical Storytelling by Aboriginal Women."

WORKS CITED

Arthur, Kateryna. "Beyond Orality: Canada and Australia." *Ariel* 21, no. 3 (1990).

Ashcroft, Bill, Gareth Griffiths, and Helen Tiffin. *The Empire Writes Back: Theory and Practice in Post Colonial Literatures.* London: Routledge, 1989.

Baines, Patricia. "A Litany for Land." In *Being Black: Aboriginal Cultures in 'Settled' Australia.* Canberra: Aboriginal Studies Press, 1988.

Barker, Allan. "Landrights." *Fire Burnin.* Abmusic audiotape. Perth.

Bhabha, Homi, ed. *Nation and Narration.* London: Routledge, 1990.

Brady, Veronica. "Review of *Story about Feeling.*" *Westerly.* no. 1 (March 1990).

Clarke, John. "Style." In *Resistance through Rituals.* Ed. S. Hall, et al. London: Hutchinson, 1976.

Culler, Jonathan. *Structuralist Poetics.* London: Routledge and Kegan Paul, 1975.

Derrida, Jacques. *De la grammatologie.* Paris: Minuit, 1967.

Hawkes, T. *Structuralism and Semiotics.* London: Methuen, 1977.

Hebdige, Dick. *Subculture: The Meaning of Style.* London: Methuen, 1979.

Hindess, B., P. Hirst. *Pre-Capitalist Modes of Production.* London: Routledge and Kegan Paul, 1975.

Jameson, Fredric. *The Political Unconscious: Narrative as a Socially Symbolic Act.* London: Methuen, 1983.

Johnson, Colin, [Mudrooroo]. *Sunlight Spreadeagles Perth in Blackness.* Unpublished manuscript poem. Perth, 1985.

———. "A Literature of the Fringe: A Study of Modern Aboriginal Literature in Australia." Unpublished dissertation. Murdoch University, Perth.

———. "Guerrilla Poetry: Lionel Fogarty's Response to Language Genocide." *Westerly* (September 3, 1986).

Langford, Ruby [Ginibi]. *Real Deadly.* Sydney: Angus and Robertson, 1992.

Longley, Kateryna O. "Autobiographical Storytelling by Aboriginal Women." In *De/Colonizing the Subject: Politics and Gender in Women's Autobiographical Practice.* Ed. S. Smith, et al. Minneapolis: University of Minnesota Press, 1992.

Marshall, Paul, ed. *Raparapa Kularr Martuwarra: Stories from the Fitzroy River Drovers.* Broome: Magabala Books, 1988.

Mishra, Vijay, and Bob Hodge. "What is Post (-) Colonialism? Reading *The Empire Writes Back.*" *Textual Practice* 5 no. 3 (1991).

Mishra, Vijay and Bob Hodge. *Dark Side of the Dream: Australian Literature and the Postcolonial Mind.* Sydney: Allen and Unwin, 1991.

Morgan, Sally. *My Place.* Fremantle: Fremantle Arts Centre Press 1987.

Narogin, Mudrooroo. *Writing from the Fringe: A Study of Modern Aboriginal Literature.* Melbourne: Hyland House, 1990.

Neidjie, Bill. *Story about Feeling.* Ed. K. Taylor. Broome: Magabala Books, 1989.

Old Lands, New Writings: Literature and Post-Colonialism. Writers Festival booklet, Festival of Perth, March 1991.

Riffaterre, Michael. *Semiotics of Poetry.* London: Methuen, 1980.

Said, Edward W. "Representing the Colonised: Anthropology's Interlocutors." *Critical Inquiry.* 15 no. 2 (1989).

Stephenson, M. A. and Sumi Ratnapala, eds. *Mabo: A Judicial Revolution.* Brisbane: University of Queensland Press, 1993.

Threadgold, Terry. "Talking about Genre: Ideologies and Incompatible Discourses." *Cultural Studies* 3 no. 1 (January 1989).

Tiffin, Helen. "Post-Colonialism, Post-Modernism and the Rehabilitation of Post-Colonial History." *Journal of Commonwealth Literature.* xxii no. 1 (1988).

Ward, Glenyse. *Wandering Girl.* Broome: Magabala Books, 1987.

Bibliography of Further Reading

Achebe, Chinua. *Morning Yet on Creation Day.* New York: Anchor Press/Doubleday, 1975.

Adam, Ian, and Helen Tiffin eds. *Past the Last Post.* Hemel Hempstead, England: Harvester Wheatsheaf, 1991.

Ahmad, Aijaz. *In Theory: Classes, Nations, Literatures.* London: Verso, 1992.

Amuta, Chidi. *Theory of African Literature: Implications for Practical Criticism.* London: Zed Press, 1989.

Anderson, Benedict. *Imagined Communities: Reflections on the Origin and Spread of Nationalism.* London: Verso, 1983.

Appiah, Anthony. *In My Father's House.* New York: Methuen, 1992.

———. "Is the post-in postmodernism the post-in post-colonial?" *Critical Inquiry* 17 (1991): 153–78.

———. "Out of Africa: Topologies of Nativism." *Yale Journal of Criticism* 1, no. 2 (1988): 153–78.

Ashcroft, Bill, Gareth Griffiths, and Helen Tiffin. *The Empire Writes Back: Theory and Practice in Post-Colonial Literatures.* London: Routledge, 1989.

Balibar, Etienne, and Immanuel Wallerstein. *Race, Nation, Class: Ambiguous Identities.* London: Verso, 1991.

Barker, Francis, Peter Hulme, Margaret Iversen, and Diane Loxley, eds. *Europe and Its Others,* 2 vols. Proceedings of the Essex Sociology of Literature Conference. Colchester: University of Essex, 1985.

Bhabha, Homi. "Of Mimicry and Man: The Ambivalence of Colonial Discourse." *October* 28 (1984): 125–33.

———. "The Other Question—the Stereotype and Colonial Discourse." *Screen* 24, no. 6 (1983): 18–36.

———. "Representation and the Colonial Text: A Critical Exploration of Some Forms of Mimeticism." In *Theory of Reading.* Ed. Gloversmith, Frank. Brighton, England: Harvester, 1984.

———. "Signs Taken for Wonders: Questions of Ambivalence and Authority under a

Tree outside Delhi, May 1817." In *'Race' Writing and Difference.* Ed. Gates, Jr., Henry Louis. Chicago: University of Chicago Press, 1986.

———, ed. *Nation and Narration.* London: Routledge, 1990.

Boehmer, Elleke, Laura Chrisman, and Kenneth Parkers, eds. *Altered State? Writing and South Africa.* Aarhaus, Australia: Dungaroo Press, 1993.

Brewer, Anthony. *Marxist Theories of Imperialism: A Critical Survey.* London: Routledge, 1980.

Brydon, Diana. "Commonwealth or Common Property? The New Literatures in English and the New Discourse of Marginality." *Kunapipi* XI no. 1 (1989): 1–16.

Chrisman, Laura. "The Imperial Unconscious? Representations of Imperial Discourse." *Critical Quarterly* 32 no. 3 (1990): 78–90.

———. "Theorizing 'Race,' Racism and Culture: Some Pitfalls in Idealist Critiques." *Paragraph* 16, 1 (1993): 78–90.

Coetzee, J. M. *White Writing: On the Culture of Letters in South Africa.* Berkeley: University of California Press, 1986.

Dash, Michael. "In Search of the Lost Body: Redefining the Subject in Caribbean Literature." *Kunapipi* XI no. 1 (1989): 17–26.

Davies, Carole Boyce, and Elaine Savory Fido, eds. *Out of the Kumbla: Caribbean Women and Literature.* Trenton, N.J.: Africa World Press, 1990.

During, Simon. "Postmodernism or Postcolonialism." *Textual Practice* 1 no. 1 (1987): 32–47.

Eagleton, Terry, Frederic Jameson, and Edward Said. *Nationalism, Colonialism and Literature.* Minneapolis: University of Minnesota Press, 1990.

Emberley, Julia. " 'Gift for Languages': Native Women and the Textual Economy of the Colonial Archive." *Cultural Critique* 17 (1990–91): 21–50.

Fanon, Frantz. *Black Skin, White Masks.* London: Pluto Press, 1986.

———. *The Wretched of the Earth.* Trans. Farrington, Constance. Harmondsworth, England: Penguin, 1967.

Giddings, Robert, ed. *Literature and Imperialism.* London: Macmillan, 1991.

Gilroy, Paul. "Cultural Studies and Ethnic Absolutism." In *Cultural Studies.* Eds. Grossberg, L., Cary Nelson, and Paula Treichler. London: Routledge, 1992.

———. "It Ain't Where You Are From, It's Where You're at. . . . Dialectics of Diasporic Identification." *Third Text* 13 (1990–91): 3–16.

Gugelberger, Georg. "Decolonizing the Canon: Considerations of Third World Literature." *NLH* 22 (1991): 505–24.

Hall, Stuart. "Cultural Identity and Diaspora." In *Identity: Community, Culture, Difference.* Ed. Rutherford, J. London: Lawrence and Wishart, 1990.

———. "Minimal Selves." In *Identity: The Real Me.* London: ICA Documents, 1987.

Harlow, Barbara. *Resistance Literature.* New York and London: Methuen, 1987.

Hobsbawm, E. J. *The Age of Empire.* London: Weidenfeld & Nicholson, 1987.

hooks, bell. *Yearning: Race, Gender, and Cultural Politics.* Boston: Southend Press, 1991.

Jameson, Fredric. "Third World Literature in the Era of Multinationalism Capitalism." *Social Text* 15 (1986): 65–88.

JanMohammed, Abdul. *Manichean Aesthetics: The Politics of Literature in Colonial Africa.* Amherst: University of Massachusetts Press, 1983.

Katrak, Ketu. "Decolonizing Culture: Towards a Theory for Postcolonial Women's Texts." *MFS* 35 no. 1 (1989): 157–79.

Loomba, Ania. "Overworlding the 'Third World.' " *OLR* 13 (1991): 164–91.

Mbembe, Achille. "The Banality of Power and the Aesthetics of Vulgarity in the Postcolony." *Public Culture* 4 no. 2 (1992): 1–30.

Mishra, Vijay, and Bob Hodge. "What is Post(-)Colonialism?" *Textual Practice* 5 no. 3 (1991): 399–414.

Mohanty, Chandra Talpade. "Under Western Eyes: Feminist Scholarship and Colonial Discourses." *Feminist Review* 30 (1988): 61–88.

Ndebele, Njabulo. *Rediscovery of the Ordinary: Essays on South African Literature and Culture.* Johannesburg: Congress of South African Writers, 1991.

Ngugi wa Thiong'o. *Decolonizing the Mind: The Politics of Language in African Literature.* London: James Currey, 1986.

———. *Homecoming: Essays on Africa and Caribbean Literature, Culture and Politics.* London: Heinemann, 1972.

Noyes, J. K. *Colonial Space.* Chur: Harwood Academic, 1992.

Parry, Benita. "Problems in Current Theories of Colonial Discourse." *OLR* 9 No. 1–2 (1987): 27–58.

———. "Resistance/Theorizing Resistance or Two Cheers for Nativism." *Postcolonial Theory and Colonial Discourse.* Ed. Peter Hulme. Manchester: Manchester University Press, 1993.

Said, Edward. "Representing the Colonized: Anthropology's Interlocutors." *Critical Inquiry* 15 (1989): 205–25.

———. *Culture and Imperialism.* London: Chatto and Windus, 1993.

———. *Orientalism.* London: Routledge and Kegan Paul, 1978.

———. "Third World Intellectuals and Metropolitan Culture." *Raritan* IX no. 3 (1990): 27–50.

Sandoval, Chela. "US Third World Feminism: The Theory and Method of Oppositional Consciousness in the Postmodern World." *Genders* 10 (1991): 1–23.

Sangari, Kumkum. "The Politics of the Possible." *Cultural Critique* (Fall 1987): 157–86.

Spivak, Gayatri Chakravorty. "Can the Subaltern Speak?" *Marxism and the Interpretation of Culture.* Eds. C. Nelson, and L. Grossberg. Evanston: University of Illinois Press, 1988.

———. "Feminism in Decolonization." *Differences* 3 no. 3 (1991): 139–70.

———. "Imperialism and Sexual Difference." *OLR* 8 no. 1–2 (1986): 225–40.

———. *In Other Worlds: Essays in Cultural Politics.* London: Methuen, 1987.

———. "Neocolonialism and the Secret Agent of Knowledge." *OLR* 13 no. 1–2 (1991): 220–51.

———. *The Post-Colonial Critic: Interviews, Strategies, Dialogues.* Ed. Sarah Harasym. London: Routledge, 1991.

———. "Three Women's Texts and a Critique of Imperialism." *Critical Inquiry* 12 no. 1 (1985): 262–80.

Suleri, Sara. *The Rhetoric of English India.* Chicago: University of Chicago Press, 1992.

———. "Woman Skin Deep: Feminism and the Postcolonial Condition." *Critical Inquiry* 18 (1992): 756–69.

Tiffin, Helen. "Post-Colonialism, Post-Modernism and the Rehabilitation of Post-Colonial History. *Journal of Commonwealth Literature* 23 no. 1 (1988): 169–81.

———. Post-Colonial Literatures and Counter Discourse." *Kunapipi* 9 no. 3 (1987): 17–34.

Trump, Martin, ed. *Rendering Things Visible: Essays on South African Literary Culture.* Johannesburg: Raven Press, 1990.

Viswanathan, Gauri. *Masks of Conquest: Literary Study and British Rule in India.* London: Faber and Faber, 1990.

Williams, Patrick. "Problems of Post-Colonialism." *Paragraph* 16 no. 1 (1993): 91–102.

Young, Robert. *White Mythologies: Writing History and the West.* London: Routledge, 1990.

Yuval-Davis, Nira, and Floya Antheas, eds. *Woman-Nation-State.* London: Macmillan, 1989.

Index

About the Editors and Contributors

CORA AGATUCCI teaches writing, literature, and Women's Studies at Central Oregon Community College in Bend, Oregon. She earned her doctorate in English-American literature at the University of California, San Diego, and taught in multicultural classrooms in the San Diego area universities and community colleges for ten years before coming to Central Oregon Community College in 1988. Her research interests integrate personal and professional commitment to include feminism, multicultural diversity, and collaborative teaching and learning. She has published on Doris Lessing, gendered theories of writing, and student autobiography. She is currently writing an article applying postcolonial literary theory to a feminist reading of fiction by Jamaica Kincaid and Doris Lessing.

P. S. CHAUHAN, professor and chair of the department of English, Beaver College, Glenside, Pennsylvania, has been writing and publishing on nineteenth-century American literature and postcolonial writing.

RALPH J. CRANE was born in England; has degrees from universities in Wales, Canada, and Australia; and is now a lecturer in the English Department at the University of Waikato, New Zealand, where he teaches postcolonial literatures. His research interests lie primarily in the field of Indian literature in English. He is the editor of *Passages to Ruth Prawer Jhabvala* (1991), and the author of *Inventing India: A History of India in English Language Fiction* (1992) and *Ruth Prawer Jhabvala* (1992). He currently coedits, with Radhika Mohanram, *SPAN* and the *Journal of the South Pacific Association for Commonwealth Literature and Language Studies.*

IAN CRUMP teaches Humanities at Shimer College. He has written on James Joyce, Flann O'Brien, Neil Jordan, Hanif Kureishi, and J. M. Coetzee. Currently he is at work on a book on "Authorization" in modern literature.

JEANNINE DeLOMBARD is a doctoral student in the University of Pennsylvania's Department of English and a graduate fellow at Penn's Center for the Study of Black Literature and Culture. Her research interests include testimonial literature, African-American slave narratives, and African prison memoirs in particular.

APARNA DHARWADKER and VINAY DHARWADKER teach at the University of Oklahoma. Aparna Dharwadker works in late-seventeenth- and eighteenth-century British drama, and postcolonial literatures in English. Her articles and translations have appeared in *Vagartha, The Humanities Review, The New England Review and Bread Loaf Quarterly*, and *The Chicago Review*. She has published an essay on the postcolonial uses of history in *PMLA*, and an essay on the politics of intertextuality in contemporary Indian theater in an anthology from the University of Pennsylvania Press. She is working on a book-length study of comedic and historical genres of satire in late-seventeenth-century drama and theater.

JOY HARJO is professor of English at the University of New Mexico, an editor, songwriter and a player of tenor saxophone. She was born in Tulsa, Oklahoma, and is a member of the Creek (Muscogee) tribe. She has published a number of books of poems: *In Mad Love and War*, which won the Poetry Society of America's William Carlos Williams Award; *She Had Some Horses*; *What Moon Drove Me To This*; and *Secrets from the Center of the World*. She has received an Arizona Commission of the Arts Creative Writing Fellowship as well as a National Endowment for the Arts Fellowship.

ALAMGIR HASHMI is a professor of English and Comparative Literature, editor, translator, and broadcaster in Pakistan, the United States, and Switzerland. He is the author of numerous books of criticism and poetry; the most recent are *The Commonwealth, Comparative Literature and the World* (1988), *The Poems of Alamgir Hashmi* (1992), and *Sun and Moon and Other Poems* (1992). Both his scholarly and his creative works are widely published throughout the English-speaking world and in 1985 he won the Patras Bokhari Award of the Pakistani Academy of Letters. He is the founder of the Townsend Poetry Prize (1986), is chairman of the Standing International Conference Committee on English in South Asia, and was a juror for the Commonwealth Writers Prize in 1990.

JOHN C. HAWLEY, a University of Pennsylvania graduate, is associate professor of English at Santa Clara University. He writes on postcolonial literature and on religious aestheticism in the nineteenth century. He has edited *Reform and Counter-Reform: Dialectics of the Word in Western Christianity since Luther* (1994) and *Cross-Addressing: Discourse in the Border* (forthcoming). His articles have appeared in *Ariel*, *Research in African Literatures*, and *Review of Contemporary*

Fiction. He has served on the Modern Literature Association's Executive Committee on Religious Approaches to Literature.

ANTHONIA KALU has her Ph.D from the University of Wisconsin-Madison and is associate professor and coordinator of the Black Studies Program at the University of North Colorado. She has held Ford and Rockefeller Foundation Fellowships and has published in the areas of multiculturalism and Africa/African-American relationships. She is currently working on *Re-Inventing the African Woman*.

LEON LITVACK, a lecturer in the School of English at Queen's University of Belfast in Northern Ireland, was born and raised in Toronto and graduated from the University of Edinburgh. He has worked extensively on ethnicity and multiculturalism in Canada, in both literary and sociological contexts; has lectured on these subjects in Europe and the Far East; and has published in these areas in the United Kingdom and North America. From 1987 to 1990 he served as the visiting professor of Canadian Studies at Kwansei Gakuin University in Nishinomiya, Japan, and as the coordinator of Canadian Studies for Western Japan. Currently a member of the British Association of Canadian Studies Council and editor of the association's newsletter, he is also the vice-director of the Centre of Canadian Studies at Queen's University. He is the author of *John Mason Neale and the Quest for Sobornost* and *Dombey and Son: An Annotated Bibliography*.

SIGRID MARKMANN teaches New Literatures in English and Feminist Cultural Studies. She has just relinquished her position as chair of the Department of English and American Studies at the Universitat Osnabruck, Germany, so that she can enjoy her students once more and has time to remember to smell the flowers growing.

RADHIKA MOHANRAM is a lecturer in the Department of Women's Studies at the University of Waikato in Hamilton, New Zealand, where she teaches gender and postcolonial theory. She has published widely in the areas of postcolonial theory and literature and is currently finishing a book on Edith Wharton and Diasporic subjectivity. Together with Ralph Crane she is the coeditor of *SPAN* and the *Journal of the South Pacific Association for Commonwealth Literature and Language Studies*.

GITA RAJAN, currently working on a project that examines the pleasure of play in the aesthetic traditions of India, was an Andrew Mellon Fellow in the Humanities at the University of Pennsylvania and had a fellowship from the Yale Center for British Art. She is the coeditor of *A Cultural Studies Reader: History, Theory, Practice* (1996). She has edited *Postcolonial Discourse and Changing Cultural Contexts* with Radhika Mohanram (Greenwood, 1995). She has published in the areas of postcolonial theory and fiction, Victorian studies, and film studies. She teaches Victorian literature, cultural studies, and postcolonial discourse at Fairfield University.

POWHIRI WHAREMARAMA RIKA-HEKE is proudly of Ngatihine, Ngapuhi, Te Rarawa, and Te Aupouri descent. Though she also has Irish and English ancestry, it is of lesser significance to her in Aotearoa, the land of her birth. Raised on a dairy farm in New Zealand's back-blocks she has since journeyed far. She is currently working on her doctoral thesis at Universitat Osnabruck, Germany, while on leave from her position as lecturer at the University of Waikato, New Zealand. Her doctoral thesis examines the emerging postcolonial themes in oral and written Maori women's literature in English.

HUGH WEBB is lecturer in English and Comparative Literature in the School of Humanities, Murdoch University, Perth, Western Australia. He has published *Passionate Spaces: African Literature and the Post-Colonial Context* (1991) as well as numerous articles on Aboriginal writing. He is currently teaching in the area of Aboriginal Culture and researching indigenous cultural constructions of land and country.

NORMA C. WILSON was born and grew up in Clarksville, Tennessee. She completed a Ph.D in English at the University of Oklahoma in 1978 and is currently teaching Native American Literature at the University of South Dakota. She has published a book of poetry, *Wild Iris*, and articles on the works of a number of American writers, including Walt Whitman, Eudora Welty, Meridel Le Sueur, N. Scott Momaday, and Leslie Marmon Silko. She serves on the South Dakota Humanities Council.

CHRISTOPHER WISE teaches third world and postcolonial literatures at West Georgia College in Carrollton, Georgia. He recently earned his Ph.D in Comparative Literature at the University of California, Riverside. Wise has published articles in *M.E.L.U.S, Rethinking Marxism, Philosophy and Literature*, and *Arena Journal*. He is the author of *The Marxian Hermeneutics of Fredric Jameson* (1995).

CPSIA information can be obtained
at www.ICGtesting.com
Printed in the USA
BVHW04*1248191018
529949BV00027B/84/P